GOOD NEWS STUDIES

Consulting Editor: Robert J. Karris, O.F.M.

Volume 32

Paul's Vision of Church

by
Helen Doohan

Michael Glazier
Wilmington, Delaware

About the Author

Helen Doohan is Assistant Professor of Religious Studies and Director of the CREDO Program at Gonzaga University. Her articles have been published in Biblical Theology Bulletin, Review for Religious and Journal of Religion and Health. She travels extensively, lecturing and offering workshops throughout the U.S., Canada, Australia and New Zealand. Her publications include *Leadership in Paul* and *Minister of God: Effective and Fulfilled.*

First published in 1989 by Michael Glazier, Inc., 1935 West Fourth Street, Wilmington, Delaware 19805.

Copyright ©1989 by Michael Glazier, Inc. All rights reserved.

Library of Congress Cataloging-in-Publication Data

Doohan, Helen.
  Paul's vision of Church/ Helen Doohan.
     p.   cm.—(Good news studies : 32)
  Bibliography: p.
  Includes index.
  ISBN 0-89453-746-6 : $12.95
  1. Church—Biblical teaching. 2. Bible. N.T. Epistles of Paul—Theology. I. Title. II. Series: Good news studies : v. 32.
BS2655.C5D66   1989
262'.0092'4-dc19   88-27234
                                        CIP

Typography by Angela Meades.
Printed in the United States of America.

*To my daughter, Eve-Anne
-a joy and delight-
with all my love.*

Contents

Introduction 1

1. Paul and the Early Church   11

    Historical Development of the Early Church   13
        Salvation history 13
        A missionary consciousness 14
        Christian groups 14
        The spread of the church 15
    Paul's Conversion to the Church 17
        The accounts of the conversion 18
        Paul's experience of Christ 19
        Paul's commissioning by Christ 20
        Paul's mission to the Gentiles 21
        Paul's understanding of the conversion 22
    Paul's Initial Vision of Church 23
        The role of Christ 23
        Ties with Judaism 24
        Incorporation of the Gentiles 25
        Relationships in the community 25
    Paul's Journeys to Develop the Church 26
        Paul's work in the churches 27
        Paul's travels to establish the churches 29
        Paul's encounters on the journeys 33
    Paul's Contributions to Early Church Development ... 35
        His focus on urban areas 35
        His understanding of equality in the churches 36
        His mission as an apostle 37
        His understanding of Christ 37

2. The Church in the First Century 39

Roots in Judaism 40
   Groups within the Jewish community 42
   Theological continuity with Israel 43
Influences of the Hellenistic world 46
   Judaism and Hellenism 46
   Social structures 47
   Religious influences 48
Pluralistic Interpretations of the Church 52
   The effects of continuity and change 52
   The effects of diverse communal responses 54
   The effects of eschatological hopes 56
Paul in the Letters and Paul in Acts 58
   Similarities in the letters and Acts 58
   Differences in the letters and Acts 59
   Perspectives on theological approaches 61
   Perspectives on ecclesial life 61
Unique Contributions of Paul to the Early Church 62
   Paul's personal approach 63
   Paul's understanding of the gospel 64
   Paul's theological reflections 65

3. Paul's Ministry to the Churches:
His Experience of Local Church 70

Aspects of Paul's Ministry in the Local Churches 71
Paul's Ministry in 1 Thessalonians 73
Paul's Ministry in Galatians 76
Paul's Ministry in 1 and 2 Corinthians 81
Paul's Ministry in Romans 88
Paul's Ministry in Philippians 93
Paul's Ministry in Philemon 96

4. Essential Components of the Church in Paul — 101

- The Sources of Church Life — 102
  - Called by God — 103
  - Baptized in the name of Jesus — 103
  - Sanctified and missioned by the Spirit — 105
- The Foundations of Church Life — 107
  - A common faith — 107
  - Justified by faith — 107
  - Responses to faith — 108
  - The central mystery of Christian faith — 109
  - Consequences of faith — 111
- The Experiences of Church Life — 112
  - The Christian assembly — 113
  - Baptism — 114
  - The Lord's supper — 115
  - Prayer — 116
- The Structures of Church Life — 117
  - Paul's authority — 119
  - Collaboration — 121
  - The Co-workers — 124
  - Functions of leadership — 125
  - Orthodoxy — 126
  - Discernment of Spirits — 127
  - Discipline — 128
- The Relational Aspects of Church Life — 129
  - Relationships with society — 130
  - Relationships within the community — 130
  - Relationships between the Jerusalem church and the Gentile communities — 131
  - Relationships between the churches — 133
  - Relationship with Peter — 135

5. Pauline Models of Church — 137

Descriptions of the Church in Paul 139
  The building 139
  The Ekklesia 141
  The household 142
  The family 143
Models of the Church in Paul 144
  The people of God 145
  The new creation 149
  The body of Christ 155
  The mystical person 161
The Dynamic Use of Models in Paul 165
  The underlying meaning of the models in Paul 166
  The application of these models by Paul 167
  The message for the contemporary church in Paul ... 168

6. Paul's Spirituality of Ecclesial Dedication — 170

Characteristics of Spirituality in Paul 171
  Key aspects of spirituality in the letters 172
Components of Paul's Spirituality of Ecclesial Living ... 175
  A constant dialogue with God 175
  The centrality of Christ 176
  A common vision of community 177
  The place of prayer 178
  Ethical principles 179
  Union with the dying and rising of Christ 184
  A common service of others 188
  Evangelism and the empowering
    of church life in others 190

7. The Interpreters of Paul — 194

2 Thessalonians 195
Colossians and Ephesians 197
  Letter to the Colossians 198
  Letter to the Ephesians 202

The Pastoral Letters	207
1 Timothy	211
2 Timothy	214
Titus	216
New Trends in the Pauline Interpreters	217
New directions	218
Evaluative comments on the interpreters of Paul	222

8. Paul's Vision of Church and His Challenge for Ecclesial Life   226

The Grounding of Paul's Vision in Theology and Experience	227
His theological perspective	227
His personal experience	227
The Expansion of Paul's Vision through Ministry and Models	228
His sense of mission	229
His use of models	229
The Challenge of Paul's Vision for Ecclesial Living	229
His emphasis on community	230
His sense of ecclesial dedication	230
The Interpretation of Paul's Vision by Others	231
His biblical interpreters	231
His contemporary challenge	231
Bibliography	233
Appendix A: Tentative Pauline Chronology	243
Appendix B: Maps	244
a) Palestine in Hellenistic and Roman Times	
b) Jewish Diaspora in the Roman Empire	
c) Paul's First and Second Journeys	
d) Paul's Third Journey	
Indices	
Subject	248
Biblical	254

Introduction

The letters of Paul offer an experience and understanding of the early church through the eyes of the apostle as he writes to the various Christian communities. The correspondence confronts the reader with powerful images, conflicting ideas, a developing theology, and the living witness of believers in the Lord Jesus. While there is no fixed doctrine of church, the dynamic portrayal of the life, commitment, and zeal of Paul, the co-workers, and the communities, is by far a more vital testimony to the reality of church.

It is never wise or appropriate to underestimate the importance of beginnings in any quest for significance. As the Christian churches approach the twenty-first century, the collective mind turns to the origins of the church with the hope that a new understanding of its beginnings will spark the creative insight necessary for its continued impact in a changing, and often religiously insensitive, world. It is appropriate to glance back, for our personal and communal life is a passage from beginnings, to beginnings, through beginnings, as Gregory of Nyssa perceptively noted. As church, we are at the beginning of a new era. While our recent past is extremely important, only a historical perspective will free us sufficiently for the challenges of the future.

Jesus preached the good news of the kingdom of God, called others to follow him, commissioned these disciples to preach to the ends of the earth, and promised to be with them always. While Jesus' own mission of renewal was primarily to those in rural Palestine, to the house of Israel, and to the outcast and sinner, his followers, Paul being a prime example, travelled to the cities, to the Gentiles, and to those of every social and economic class. A new community emerged, the community called church. This activity of apostles and disciples is an extension of the mission of Christ, a mission directed towards a qualitative change in life and attitudes. "Mission does not come from the church; it is from mission and in the light of mission that the church is to be understood."[1]

Paul, the apostle to the Gentiles, becomes involved in a very energetic and often controversial mission within the early Christian movement. He is rightly identified as a person of three worlds: the world of Judaism, of Hellenism, and of a distinctive Christianity.[2] He lives in conversation with the main currents, ideas, and aspirations of his time. His understanding of church develops from the tradition, through controversy, in his missionary experience and world involvement, and always, under the guidance of the Spirit. Paul is visibly in touch with the practicalities of life as well as with the movement of history. He interprets both in light of the faith he has received, demonstrating that he is a person of his times and also astonishingly ahead of them.[3] The apostle is an original thinker, allowing the message of Jesus to penetrate the social realities of his day. His vision transforms early Christianity from an apocalyptic sect within Judaism to a missionary movement in the Hellenistic world, and his influence stretches beyond his own time as Christianity becomes a world religion.

The letters of Paul, shed light on the later gospels, particularly in their understanding of the message of Jesus and experience of church, for they specify what the historian might otherwise only surmise about this earliest period. Likewise, the process of theological clarification in critical and developing situations offers insight to the reader. We need to observe how Paul spent his time and to discover the source of his zeal and energy. The autobiographical statements throughout the letters suggest a single purpose and focused direction, namely, his total dedication to Christ as the centerpoint of his commitment to the churches. Paul utilizes all the opportunities, structures, people, and ideas available to him for the sake of

---

[1] Moltmann, p. 10.
[2] See Perrin, p. 107.
[3] See Banks, p. 7.

the gospel. Rather than define the church, he draws on many images and metaphors to express this new reality in Christ. The church is not an end in itself, but the community in which Christians live out the new reality of their life in Christ. Since Paul's understanding of community is a dynamic and changing one, then equally so is his understanding of church. However, the early church also sees itself in terms of its roots in Israel, its call by the Lord, its relationship to others, its mission, and its faith. Recent developments in biblical studies, including biblical hermeneutics and sociological studies, open new directions for us and enable us to examine the text in different ways.[4] Within the New Testament are possibilities for continued transformation and creative development, rather than simply an original unchanging model or pattern of church life unadaptable to new times.[5]

This book is an attempt to go back to the beginning of the church by examining both the authentic letters of Paul: 1 Thessalonians, Galatians, 1 and 2 Corinthians, Romans, Philippians and Philemon, and the later Pauline letters. Paul himself joins the Christian community/church because of a profound conversion experience. His journeys to develop the church, a direct result of his commission by the Lord, must be seen within the context of the historical development of the community. Paul contributes to a church that already formulated a theological perspective and handed on traditions. While the roots of the first century church are in Judaism and in the Hellenistic world, many believers, including Paul, interpret the message of Jesus for new times and new situations, giving rise to the rich diversity and pluralism in the letters and in other New Testament writings.[6] Paul draws from his back-

---

[4] See D.J. Harrington, "Biblical Hermeneutics," pp. 7-10; and "Sociological Concepts," pp. 181-190.

[5] Fiorenza, *Bread*, p. 61, quotes R. DuPlessis, who distinguishes between archetype and prototype. While both refer to original models, archetype is usually understood as an ideal form that establishes an unchanging pattern, while prototype is critically open to the possibility of its own transformation.

[6] See Leonard Doohan's series on *Matthew, Mark, Luke,* particularly his assessment of differing perspectives on church in each gospel and how each writer interprets the tradition for new situations in the church, in chapters 5, 6, and 5 in the respective books.

ground and makes a unique contribution to the developing Christian community.

However, the apostle's understanding of church comes primarily from his experience of local church, the communities he establishes, sustains, and challenges. Paul's vision, etched out of his contact with these communities, reflects his concern for their life and growth, his clarification of issues problematic for them, and his tireless working for unity. From this rich and diverse experience, as well as from his religious insight, Paul formulates a vision of universal church, inclusive of Jew and Gentile. The components of Paul's ecclesiology are surprisingly integrated, soundly theological, and delightfully practical. He expresses this vision in the variety of images and models of church reflected on the pages of scripture. The models portray a community characterized by unity and diversity, freedom and responsibility, because of their identity in Christ. For Paul, however, ecclesiology is the basis for an enriching spirituality that ensures personal and communal growth.

It is remarkable how this apostle is prepared for his mission, lives according to his vision, and through his letters inspires a host of followers even beyond his death. Just as Paul interpreted the gospel for his time and situation, so others interpret Paul for another generation. Thus, Colossians, Ephesians, and the Pastorals represent later developments of Pauline ecclesiology. In the correspondence, a vision of Christian life emerges: Christian life is ecclesial living, living as church. Toward this end, the apostle will carry the burdens of the churches, wrestle with God on behalf of the community, and strive always to finish the course. The importance of the church is not so much in what it is at any point in time, but in its call and its vision. This insight impels Paul and those who follow him, to always be open to an ongoing assessment of their life in Christ. They commit themselves to the continual growth of the church, growth in numbers, but more importantly, growth in significance.

Going back to our beginnings as church is an enriching and hope-filled experience. Jesus was not only remembered, but his message creatively interpreted by his earliest followers. Paul too was not only remembered, but his message was reinterpreted by others. As a Christian people and as a church approaching a new age, we too must remember our beginnings and continue the process of reinterpretation. Understanding Paul's ecclesiology is a first step to another new beginning as church.

Paul of Tarsus

The extraordinary ministry of Paul to the churches often conceals the human attributes of the person in his ability to work, his need for friendship, and his search for appropriate responses to the developing communities. Paul of Tarsus is more than the typical first century Hellenistic Jew, but he is that as well. Born in the cosmopolitan city of Tarsus in Cilicia, the education of Saul included the local opportunities afforded any young man of his age, as well as contact with the rabbis in Jerusalem. His insertion into the Hellenistic and Jewish world, his fluency in Greek, Aramaic, and Hebrew, and his training as a Pharisee prepared him for his life experience. This zealous and religious Jew did not personally know Jesus of Nazareth, but claimed a profound contact with Christ, the Risen Lord. His conversion marked the change from zealous Pharisee to believer in Jesus, although his religious understanding takes into account the continuum of his experience.

From this transitional point in his life, Paul utilizes his background and experience for the sake of the gospel. The persecutor of Christians proclaims the gospel message throughout much of the world of his day. His proclamation integrates the religious concepts familiar to him and his understanding of the Jewish scriptures.

Likewise, Paul inserted himself into the world of his day and moved with the flow of its history. In the Acts of Apostles written by Luke, Paul has contacts with leaders in Jerusalem and with the civil authorities of his day. Proconsuls and other local magistrates become part of the events of Paul's life as he journeys from place to place, encounters opposition and imprisonment, affirmation and support. His own accounts in the letters testify to his awareness of the issues of his time and the aspirations of his people. Paul was a controversial figure because of his radical interpretation of the law, his departure from the rabbis' understanding of justification, and his ability to bring all members of the community into the missionary spirit of the early church.

The chart in Appendix A identifies significant events in Paul's life and the events of his contemporary history. Dating for the period is approximate and the biblical references give an indication of the sources of information.

Communication in Paul's World

Proclamation of the gospel message occured in two ways in the time of Paul. Missionaries proclaimed the word in synagogues, forums, workplaces, and homes of early believers. In those gatherings clarification of the message and its meaning occurred as a by-product of the dialogue and adaptation of the gospel to different audiences. The second form of communication was the written word, and for Paul the letter was the usual vehicle for his ongoing contact with the churches. After proclaiming the word to various communities, the apostle Paul writes back to a number of the communities, responding to questions, developing his teaching, and encouraging them in their Christian life.

The letter form used by Paul was typical of the Hellenistic world. Simple yet complete, it consisted of introductory greetings, body, and concluding comments. The introduction identified the sender and recipients, and included salutations and blessings. The thanksgiving followed the introduction in all the letters of Paul except Galatians, and it generally spoke of the community's faith and Christian life. Paul readily used exaggeration here to make a point, and the positive tone of this section of the letter also gave an indication of the theme of the rest of the correspondence. The body of the letter consisted of a theological or dogmatic part and exhortations on Christian life. Here Paul is the teacher providing the basis for Christian belief in the main section of his writing and following it with examples of how to live the Christian message in daily life. The conclusion of the letter offers interesting information regarding the people in the churches and Paul's missionary plans. The apostle and his co-workers extend greetings, making their final points in a friendly way. The form of the letter thus expanded, includes the introduction, thanksgiving, body with theology and exhortations, and conclusion. However, in the New Testament letters Paul uses these components with flexibility and creativity, often overlapping the sections or eliminating one of them as in Galatians.

Paul writes letters rather than epistles. The letter presumes a relationship between sender and recipient, the tone is informal, and the content determined by mutual concerns and interests of sender and recipient. The epistle is more like a treatise, stating general principles in a formal way, with little personal connection between sender and recipient. Ephesians comes closest to this description in the Pauline correspondence.

Another designation regarding the letters is authentic or genuine and inauthentic or deutero-Pauline. Authenticity refers to whether a letter actually comes from Paul himself while taking into consideration the concept of authorship that allows for secretarial assistance, as in Romans 16:22, or the supplying of the ideas for another to compile or edit. Deutero-Pauline indicates consistency with the Pauline tradition as in 2 Thessalonians, or a letter written in the name of Paul for another time after the death of the apostle. These later letters take Paul's ideas to a new level, as in Colossians and Ephesians, or adapt them to new situations as in the Pastorals. The situation of the letters, theology, church development, language, and style are indicators of the letter's authenticity.

Integrity of the correspondence refers to whether the letter as we have it in the New Testament is the original form or whether modifications, insertions, or rearrangement of the material occurred. The integrity of authentic letters can be questioned, such as the integrity of 2 Corinthians which appears to be a composite of two letters of Paul to the Corinthian church, possibly with other additions.

Of the thirteen letters attributed to Paul, only seven come unquestionably from the apostle himself: 1 Thessalonians, Galatians, 1 and 2 Corinthians, Romans, Philippians, and Philemon. Some commentators question Paul's authorship of 2 Thessalonians; Colossians and Ephesians contain a theological perspective in the Pauline tradition; 1 and 2 Timothy and Titus consider pastoral concerns at the turn of the century and

8 *Introduction*

present a church different from the Pauline communities. In the following diagram, only the inner circle represents the authentic letters of Paul.

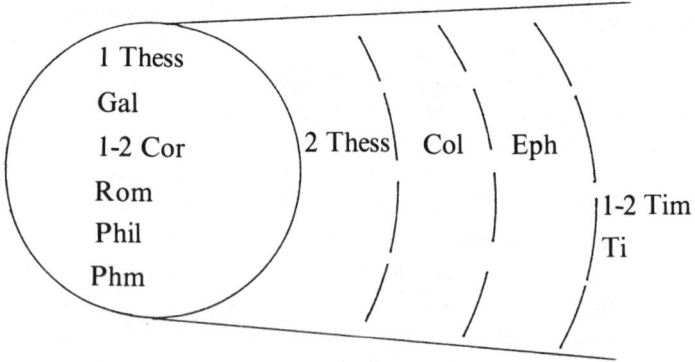

Paul communicated the gospel message through his preaching of the word and his written correspondence. Both forms of communication occurred during the apostle's activity as a missionary and while he journeyed from place to place establishing new communities. His most prolific period as a writer was the third missionary journey, with the major letters coming from this period. The maps in Appendix B indicate the world of Paul and the areas of his missionary work.

Paul wrote his letters to communities he established with the exception of Romans, written prior to his visit to an existing Christian community, and Philemon, written to a head of the house-church rather than to the church itself. Thus, occasional or situational letters describe the written communication of Paul. Understanding the community, its background, and the issues of interest, enlightens the meaning of the correspondence for the twentieth-century reader.

Paul's world affects his communication to the churches and Paul's own choice of language and concepts. Some of the points he develops, such as the meaning of the law and the relationship between biblical promises and their fulfillment in Christ, are particularly significant for the first century Christian. However, a number of points in the letters impinge on the task of ecclesial life in today's world. These include Christ's relationship to believers, the urbanization of Christianity, the approach to the socially prominent, the pluralism of early Christianity, the priesthood of all the faithful, the link between accepting the gospel and joining the community, the distinction between equality and uniformity, the insistence on prayer, and a theology of gifts that balances talents with needs. These aspects of Paul's ecclesiology emerge in the pages of this book.

The letters of Paul insert us into the church and the world of his day. The importance of these beginnings and an understanding of Paul's ecclesiology are essential to the next phase of our life as church. This book examines the formative elements in Paul's ecclesiology and the gradual development in his understanding of church that emerges from his ministry to the churches. The models of church and the spirituality implied in them challenge Christians today as they did in the time of Paul himself.

1

Paul and the Early Church

"It is God who establishes us with you in Christ, and has commissioned us;..." (2 Cor 1:21)

Paul's relationship to the early church and his understanding of church life begin prior to his conversion experience. In effect, he is born into an already existing church at the time of his call by the Lord. The early church provides a context for Paul's missionary journeys, and his contributions extend the initial perimeters of the church both geographically and theologically. The New Testament the church develops through various stages, originating with the eschatological preaching of John the Baptist and followed by Jesus' own proclamation of the kingdom. The activity of the twelve, the identification of the Jerusalem church as a sect within Judaism, and the missionary expansion into a Gentile world, precede Paul and provide the framework for his apostolic activity. Following Paul and before the turn of the century, the church breaks with Judaism and a new Christian synthesis emerges.

Scripture itself provides valuable information about this early period of the church. However, discovering the original meaning of the text requires sophisticated tools. The task of biblical interpretation is to probe the text on various levels in order to understand its religious meaning within the social context of the author, who uses literary forms from a vastly different and distinct cultural horizon. The skilled exegete frequently identifies a dialectical tension underlying the text, which affects our knowledge of the situation of the community.

The language of scripture is an area of examination since words both reveal and conceal the reality they attempt to express. For example, the androcentric language of scripture and the patriarchal structures of society tend to marginalize women and make them invisible, unless we critically analyze the text and apply a new hermeneutic.[1]

The very nature of the biblical texts requires an acquaintance with the literary forms used by the authors and the overall structure of the letters or other documents. Extensive work on the Pauline letters identifies the use of apologetic speech and rhetoric (Gal 3:1-4:11), refutation (Gal 1:1.8.11-12.15), chiasm (2 Cor 10-13), allegory (Gal 4:22-31), analogy (1 Cor 1:12-27), typology (1 Cor 15:45-49), and metaphor (1 Cor 3:6-9).[2] Understanding these forms enables us to unearth the fuller meaning of the biblical text. Furthermore, the letters of Paul are occasional literature, often written in response to questions or opposition, with beliefs expressed in typical first-century thought patterns. Their theology and ecclesiology emerge as the reader identifies and pieces together the various components of the picture. In addition, the apostle himself uses great freedom in reshaping the tradition, rereading the Jewish scripture in light of his Christian faith, and utilizing the interpretive techniques of the rabbis of his day.[3] He also presents autobiographical material within the text, indicating his personal and apostolic interests. An understanding of Paul in his world makes the contemporary reader sensitive to the nuances of the correspondence and offers a deeper appreciation of the early church.

This chapter focuses on the early church that Paul embraces in his conversion experience. The historical development of the early church provides the backdrop for Paul's conversion and his initial vision of church. The apostle then begins his own missionary activity, journeying to new places and estab-

---

[1] See Fiorenza, "Emerging Issues in Feminist Biblical Interpretations," pp. 47 and 49, and L. Russell, "Women and Ministry," p. 91.

[2] See Brinsmead, pp. 54 and 83, for the genre of apologetic speech and its relation to the overall structure of Galatians; Betz, p. 24, for the use of rhetoric; Gale's work for a thorough study of the topic.

[3] See A.T. Hanson, *Technique,* for Paul's approach as an exegete.

lishing communities of believers. His contributions result from his ability to integrate his own experience with that of others, while keeping a firm eye on the future. The context and contours of the early church affect Paul's experience as an apostle.

The Historical Development of the Early Church

The historical development of the primitive church provides the context for Paul's mission. The church already has a history and a perspective before Paul becomes a Christian and before he actually engages in his own missionary work. The early church grows initially as a Jewish sect, gradually spreading into the Hellenistic world. The perspective of both these worlds impacts the believers as they pursue their own communal identity. Various groups emerge and differences in approach begin to surface very early in the church's history. This section presents the understanding of salvation history, the mission of the church, the emergence of different groups and views, and the spread of the primitive church.

SALVATION HISTORY

Biblical history is not simply a record of events, but history with a goal and purpose in mind, written for a group of people who believe that within the historical events is the revelation of God's action on behalf of humankind. Christians and Jews speak of salvation history, since both groups believe God acts in and through people and events. Likewise, when believers view history from the perspective of faith, they discern God's plan of salvation. It is significant that the early church assesses its history in this way, and transmits it with this perspective in mind. Even within the so-called historical accounts of scripture, the primary goal of the author is to reveal God's unfolding purpose. In the early church believers consistently interpret their history through the eyes of faith. They chronicle God's action in their oral tradition and eventually in the written word. When Paul views the early church, he sees events that will become salvific events for him only after his conversion.

A MISSIONARY CONSCIOUSNESS

The early church is a missionary church and an awareness of mission affects its reflection and theology.[4] While Jesus is the primal missionary, Christians acknowledge their indebtedness in this area to the Jewish community. The strength of the Jewish mission in the diaspora prepares the soil for the Christian movement throughout the Roman empire. The Jews form religious communities in the towns and these people find in the scriptures sources of their catechetical and liturgical life, and come together regularly for worship. The Jewish community is known for its defense of monotheism, its historical theology, and its ethics. They also share a conviction that the spread of their faith is a firm responsibility.[5] In the beginning, the Christian mission is a continuation of the Jewish effort, capitalizing on their strengths.

Like Judaism, the Christians spread their message by means of travelling missionaries, utilizing trade routes and business people and maximizing their effectiveness. The Christian apocalyptic sect moves into the Gentile world, building on the foundation of the Hellenistic Jewish experience, and spreading into the larger Gentile world from Jerusalem, not Galilee. Syrian Antioch, where believers are first called Christians (Ac 11:26), becomes a vital center for the movement. Antioch is a missionary-minded church, strategically located for this purpose. Paul would eventually be among the lively group of active and potential missionaries in this city. The movement spreads to Rome fairly early, so that by 49 CE the Jewish Christians in the capital city of the empire suffer expulsion with the Jews under the emperor Claudius.

CHRISTIAN GROUPS

The Acts of Apostles (6:1-6) identifies different groups within this early period of church life. The Hellenists are Greek-speaking Christians of Jewish descent living in diaspora. The

---

[4]See Hengel, *Between*, p. 64, and Ben F. Meyer, *The Early Christians: Their World Mission and Self-Discovery*.

[5]Harnack, p. 15, identifies the six areas of indebtedness in his interesting work.

Hebrews are Christians of Jewish descent living in Palestine, using the Aramaic language. These two groups articulate differing views of the church, as do the major centers of Jerusalem and Antioch (Gal 2:11-21). Further evidence of the diversity of the early missionary movement is the variations of the Jewish Christians and their Gentile converts in terms of their relationship to the tenets of Judaism. Four groups emerge, the first group consisting of Jewish Christians and their Gentile converts, who insist on the full observance of the Mosaic Law, including circumcision. The second group does not insist on circumcision but does require the Gentile Christians to keep some of the Jewish observances. A third group eliminates the requirement of circumcision and also the observance of the Jewish food laws. The fourth group of Jewish Christians and their Gentile converts do not insist on circumcision, or food laws, and see no abiding significance in the Jewish cult and feasts.[6] Within a few decades of Jesus' death the community not only spreads geographically, it develops theologically. The Jesus movement in Palestine becomes the Christian missionary movement in the Greco-Roman world, adapting itself to a new environment and appreciating diversity in its self-understanding.

THE SPREAD OF THE CHURCH

Within Palestine, the so-called Jesus movement provides an alternative approach within the Jewish community and attempts to renew it through the prophetic challenge of Jesus' message. It is a response to the problems in Jewish society and presents a radical understanding of equality, freedom, sharing, and service. The Christian missionary movement within the Greco-Roman environment also suggests an alternative vision and a countercultural lifestyle for its followers.[7] Such diverse movements affect the local churches and enrich this period with very different approaches to community life. Believers could accept the poverty of life rooted in the Jesus tradition or

---

[6]Brown and Meier, pp. 2-6.

[7]See Fiorenza, *Memory,* pp. 100-101.

they could transcend the social and economic distinctions in a communal spirit of mutual love and respect.[8] Paul would choose the latter approach of love-patriarchalism, effectively utilizing the richness of the social differences and other resources in the community. He would also challenge the institution of patriarchy by recognizing the importance of women to the Christian mission.

The house-church, so significant for the spread of Christianity, provides an alternative environment with its equal opportunities for women. The homes were not only places to meet, but they also offer support and actual leadership for the community. Women have a significant role in the development of the house-church and in this sphere, they are often at the center of the Christian effort. Furthermore, women could spread their influence far beyond the base of their house community, as many of the co-workers attest.[9]

An appreciation of the house-church furthers our appreciation of the apostolic church. In this setting, a distinctly Christian worship is possible from the beginning of the apostolic age. The great attention to family in the early literature is intelligible in this setting, as well as the tendency to party strife among several house-churches in one city and the effects of social stratification in the experience of the community. The house-church is also a vital training ground for church leaders.[10] We will continually see that Christianity uses the structures that are in place for the spread of its message: patriarchy, the household, the synagogue, voluntary associations, schools of philosophy and of rhetoric. In its initial phase of development, the church reflects society, but it also challenges it in extremely significant ways.

Within a short period of twenty years, the believers in Jesus are an identifiable group within Judaism and spread to several areas outside of Palestine. While the Christians utilize the mission network of diaspora Judaism, the groups of believers are largely independent of the synagogue and linked primarily

---

[8]See Theissen, p. 11, for distinctions between "itinerant charismatic beggar" and "love patriarchalism."

[9]See Fiorenza, *Memory,* pp. 175-177, and Lohfink, p. 97.

[10]See Filson, pp. 109-112.

to one another. While the early followers could be described by some as the "community of the disinherited,"[11] they are also the community of the wealthy, the educated, and the mobile, as they move into the Hellenistic world. Paul becomes a part of this church in his conversion, interacts with its leaders in Jerusalem and Antioch, and expands its frontiers through his missionary journeys.

Paul's Conversion to the Church

Paul's conversion experience, a powerfully significant event for him, is a dramatic and disruptive event in the life of a zealous religious person, but not an initial religious experience. Paul tells us in Gal 1:13 that he persecuted the church of God, trying to destroy it, a fact which Acts also confirms (8:1-3; 9:1-2, 13-14; 22:4-5; 26:9-11). Paul goes on to say: I "advanced in Judaism beyond many of my own age among my people, so extremely zealous was I for the traditions of my fathers" (Gal 1:14). He was "circumcised on the eighth day, of the people of Israel, of the tribe of Benjamin, a Hebrew born of Hebrews; as to the law a Pharisee,... as to righteousness under the law blameless" (Phil 3:5-6). The early church knows this well documented background of Paul.

As a Jew, he had little reason to change his convictions or his mission, proving his righteousness and orthodoxy by his zeal against the church in the Hellenistic diaspora. However, his conversion results in a radical reversal of values. On the road to Damascus, "The Pharisee became a Christian; the devoted upholder of the Jewish Law became its severest critic; the zealous persecutor of the Christian 'way' became its most passionate advocate; the man trained for the Jewish mission in the Hellenistic world became the archetypal Christian missionary."[12]

---

[11]Gager, p. 23.
[12]Perrin, p. 91.

THE ACCOUNTS OF THE CONVERSION

The conversion is a transformational experience for Paul, an event so central for him and for the church, that Paul not only refers to it in his letters (Gal 1:11-17; 1 Cor 9:1; 15:8-10; Phil 3:4-11; Rom 1:5; 2 Cor 4:1-6; 5:16), but Luke uses a single tradition with little variation in his three distinct accounts in Acts (9:1-19; 22:4-16; 26:12-18).[13] In all the accounts, God takes the initiative in the choice of Paul as apostle to the Gentiles. The strength of this call affects Paul's religious convictions and his ministry. As Paul reflects on the event that so effectively changed him, he uses prophetic language to describe his purposeful election (Gal 1:15). In Acts too, Luke parallels aspects of Paul's vocation with the call and commissioning of the prophets, notably Isaiah and Jeremiah. The apostle will present himself in his ministry as both prophet and servant of the Lord, and he will appeal to this revelatory experience in his work with the churches.

While authors and commentators have given different interpretations of the conversion, Paul himself "never speaks of the inner event of his conversion but only of its theological content: his commission to preach the gospel to the Gentiles."[14] Paul's apostolic call and commissioning move him into a service of the church on an equal basis with Peter and in conjunction with other missionaries of the period. For Paul, the essence of the event is his experience of Christ as Risen Lord. In this encounter, his understanding of salvation gradually changes and his theological emphasis shifts. Paul would challenge the tenets of Judaism in terms of justification and the law, emphasizing the universality of God's gift of salvation and working tirelessly to bring the gospel to the Gentiles. Paul's theology, dominated by this encounter with Christ, would prove incompatible with the convictions of the Jews whose mission he served so well. His conversion to another movement within Judaism would eventually be interpreted as a deviation from his religious heritage.

---

[13] See Kim, p. 30; Hendrick, p. 417, while acknowledging similar motifs, identifies 3 different literary modes: Acts 9:1-19, a miracle story; Acts 22:4-16, a healing narrative redacted into a commissioning narrative; Acts 26:12-18, a commissioning narrative.

[14] Conzelmann, *Theology,* p. 163; Kim, p. 56; Rigaux, pp. 50-57 for an overview.

PAUL'S EXPERIENCE OF CHRIST

On the road to Damascus, "as to one untimely born, he appeared also to me" (1 Cor 15:8). In fact, Paul says that God "was pleased to reveal his Son to me" (Gal 1:16). Although Paul as a Pharisee would have known of Jesus, it is only in this primordial experience that he comes to a faith knowledge of the Lord. The crucified and Risen Lord dominates the conversion episodes in Acts and constitutes the essence of Paul's christology, a functional christology with its prime interest in Christ's activity on behalf of the community. His own encounter with Christ accounts for this orientation. For Paul, Christ is not only Messiah but God in Christ acts on behalf of humankind, and reveals himself in Jesus, the Lord.

However, Paul sees even more in this event, for the conversion account in Acts reveals a significant insight in the dialogue. "Saul, Saul, why do you persecute me?... Who are you Lord?... I am Jesus, whom you are persecuting" (Ac 9:4-5). The repetition in the conversation brings out the force of its impact on Paul, for he is made aware of the mystery of the relationship that exists between Christ and Christians, Christ and his church.[15] This identification of Christ with believers permeates not only the accounts of Luke, but also the letters of Paul. The apostle speaks about Christians being in Christ and Christ in them. He continually draws out the implications of this reality as he develops a clearly intertwined christology and ecclesiology. The revelation of the union of Christ with believers, constitutes the essence of Paul's Christian consciousness. God intervenes in history through Christ and continues to be present through the spirit of Christ in the community of believers. Paul sees the Risen Lord, not as an individual, but identified with the Christian community, a formative insight for him. The church, from this moment on, is a reality for Paul, and he commits himself to its expansion and development.

---

[15] See Stanley, *Apostolic Church*, p. 296.

PAUL'S COMMISSIONING BY CHRIST

Paul considers the christophany on the road to Damascus comparable to the resurrection appearances to the apostles in their commissioning by Jesus (Mt 28:16-20; Mk 16:14-18; Lk 24:36-43; Jn 20:19-23; 21:15-19; 2 Cor 11:5), for the appearances produce a similar result. God's revelation of Christ to Paul is for a purpose comparable to that of the earlier apostles, "in order that I might preach him among the Gentiles" (Gal 1:16). Paul does not distinguish between his visionary revelation of Jesus Christ and his call to be an apostle (1 Cor 15:8-9). The manifestation of Christ is integral to the commissioning account in Acts and certainly in Paul's own mind (Gal 1:11-12). Beker states it well: "Paul's conversion experience is absorbed by the greater reality of his apostolic calling. He does not celebrate his 'conversion experience' to mark his own spiritual grandeur, because he understands it as the commission to proclaim the gospel, that is, to serve Christ among the Gentiles."[16]

This call to be an apostle is a distinctive one in the early church. It is not equated with baptism but is a special gift to the infant church that sends out missionary witnesses to the ends of the earth. The call comes from the exalted Lord, and apostleship has an itinerant quality about it, for these persons are not associated with any one place. Their authority comes from the one who issues the commission, and while there is no office connected with this responsibility, Paul will claim his authority to function as a missionary in the church and to proclaim the gospel he has received. He equates the call to be an apostle with the message received,[17] and frequently reminds the churches that his call authenticates both his gospel and his mission.

Paul's dependence on God for his message and his mission, gives him an independence from others. He makes this point to the Galatian community when he clearly identifies the kind of relationship he has with the Jerusalem church (Gal 1:11-12,17; 2:2). He initially presents what he did not do; he did not

---

[16]Beker, p. 6.

[17]See Schmithals, p. 30; also see Pierce, pp. 72-76; Peterson, p. 123; Meeks, p. 131.

go up to Jerusalem after his conversion. There is no need for this contact since the gospel does not originate with the Jerusalem authorities. Paul will frequently remind communities of the divine origin of his message, even though he also acknowledges handing on the traditions he has received from those who were apostles before him (1 Cor 15:3-7). Each claim is valid and used appropriately by Paul in his ministry. The situation in the individual church usually dictates the particular emphasis Paul uses regarding the origin of his message.

PAUL'S MISSION TO THE GENTILES

Paul speaks in Christ's name because of his commissioning, and because of it, he also claims an extraordinary mission to the Gentiles. This mission gives the pagans the possibility of gaining salvation before his own people, the Jews. Because of his distinct mandate, Paul not only establishes Christian communities throughout the vast area of the Roman empire, but he also sustains these communities in their struggles as they grow towards a new maturity in Christ. Part of this growth is their relationship to Judaism, a key issue in the development of Paul's apostolic ministry. The pillars of the Jerusalem church, James, Cephas, and John, recognize this strong relationship between Paul's call and his mission (Gal 2:7-9). However, more than a missionary strategy is at stake in the issue. Paul's concept of salvation is salvation for all humankind, for God's action in Christ has universal implications. The Gentiles who believe in Jesus, will even bypass a relationship with Israel. Paul develops these ideas on salvation, justification, and the new people of God, as he ministers to the churches, a ministry that results directly from his conversion.

As we have seen, the conversion is not an initial religious experience for Paul, since he was a distinguished Pharisee, clearly committed to upholding the law, and involved in the mission of his people. Likewise, the conversion is not Paul's initial contact with the church, since his persecution of the believers in Jesus was the result of his religious zeal as a Jew. Rather, the conversion is the occasion for a reversal of values in regard to his understanding of Judaism and a radical change in his conviction about Christ and believers. It leads to a shift in his own role in relation to the Christian movement, the persecutor of the church becomes its missionary to the Gentiles. The significance of this experience will be seen throughout Paul's apostolic career, but its initial meaning is worthy of examination.

PAUL'S UNDERSTANDING OF THE CONVERSION

Paul's call describes his conversion to the church, for in the call, Paul receives the transformational insight so central to his ecclesiology, Christ's relationship to believers. The event itself, initiated by God, is a religious experience and its meaning is primarily, but not exclusively, seen on the level of faith. Paul understands faith as a free and gratuitous gift from God, a gift of faith that removes the scales from his eyes, allowing him to see Jesus differently. He is able to move from Judaism to another belief that reflects the true meaning and fulfillment of God's promises to Israel. Only a revelation could effect this kind of transformation.

The experience has other practical consequences as well, for Paul responds not only in faith but in mission. He is an ambassador for Christ, involved in the ministry of reconciliation (2 Cor 5:18-20). He speaks the word of God to the nations, like the prophets of old, and suffers in the service of the Lord as the prophets before him. Like the prophetic figures, he will reinterpret the scriptures and its message of justification, but with Christ in mind. He will pursue the broad implications of God's call, salvation for all humanity and the gathering of a new people in his name. Of all the practical consequences of his conversion, Paul's activity on behalf of the churches is the most visible. His religious encounter with Christ occurs while involved in ministry, not in prayer, in the temple, or in the synagogue. Ministry will not keep him from an intimate and abiding relationship with the Lord.

The conversion is a watershed for Paul personally and a building block for his theology. He will draw on the kerygma of the early church, the religious traditions of his day, and his own experience of ministry in the churches. But the essence of his understanding of church is in this encounter with Christ and its profound revelation. Paul responds in faith with the totality of his being and begins a new life in Christ that includes mission and ministry.

Paul's Initial Vision of Church

The apostle's vision of church rests solidly on the fundamental event of his conversion. In his call and commission, Paul moves from the level of ideas about the church, to the far more significant realm of convictions. These new convictions about Christ and the gospel motivate, direct, and orient his way of thinking, speaking, and acting,[18] and drive Paul to accomplish great things for the sake of the gospel (1 Cor 9:23). To understand Paul's commitment to the church, we must appreciate the strength of his faith convictions for these focus his purpose and redirect his boundless energy. Bornkamm notes this progression of events: "One of the most marked features of his character is that the insights granted him by faith mapped out the path he was to follow, and that he himself pondered very deeply—independently, sometimes indeed in a self-opinionated way—on his life's experiences."[19] His initial Christian convictions are a powerful motivating force for the apostle, and as he lives out his vocation, he will call into play all the personal qualities that shine through his letters.

THE ROLE OF CHRIST

Some do say that Paul's christology, the core of his convictions regarding the church, was complete before he set off on his great missionary journeys.[20] For Paul, Jesus is the Lord who has authority over him. This term implies a relationship that affects both his personal life and his understanding of church. Being in Christ is a transformational insight that deter-

---

[18]Patte, p. 13, contrasts ideas and convictions.
[19]Bornkamm, p. xxviii.
[20]See Hengel, *Between*, p. 39.

mines every aspect of the believer's life. Once called into this personal relationship, the believer and the community respond totally. Paul's vision of church and its connection with Christ, the Risen Lord, condition his challenge to the communities in terms of the quality of their life. For Paul, "Christ is not only the founder of the community of believers, but in a real sense *he is the community* (1 Cor 6:5; 12:12) because it is through the community that the saving reality of Christ is made effective in the world."[21] Faith in Christ, lived out in the community and through its service of others, is the cornerstone of the church and this early insight regarding Christ directs Paul's further theological reflections.

TIES WITH JUDAISM

Paul's Christian faith forces him to reconsider those central issues in Judaism that are implicitly or explicitly challenged by Jesus. He finds himself differing with other Pharisees who believe the Torah is the complete and final revelation and for whom sacred history is closed.[22] Paul proclaims a new revelation in Christ, and sees a dynamic type of faith which is open to the possibility of further intervention by God. While the law is holy, just, and good (Rom 7:12), Paul's current understanding is in tension with the Pharisees' formulation, for his understanding of justification is by faith, with God justifying all those who believe in Christ. The apostle will ask, "what advantage has the Jew? Or what is the value of circumcision?" (Rom 3:1). Paul answers these difficult questions arising out of his initial vision of church with respect for his Jewish heritage, even though his theological insights develop in a different direction. The Jews have a special place in salvation history and God continues to be faithful to them (Rom 3:2-3). Paul affirms his appreciation of his past and of God's action through his people. "To the Jew I became as a Jew, in order to win the Jews; to those under the law I became as one under the law—

---

[21] Murphy-O'Connor, "Eucharist," p. 57.
[22] See Patte, p. 118.

though not being myself under the law—that I might win those under the law" (1 Cor 9:20).

INCORPORATION OF THE GENTILES

Paul's vision of church and his mission are not limited to the Jews, for "To those outside the law I became as one outside the law—not being without the law toward God but under the law of Christ" (1 Cor 9:21). His apostleship gives Paul freedom in regard to the Jewish law, which he understands in a new light. This perspective on his Jewish heritage is fundamental to his understanding of church and Paul will gradually grow away from his early ties and with conviction say, "neither circumcision counts for anything, nor uncircumcision, but a new creation" (Gal 6:15). This is "not merely exaggerated imagery"[23] but a development of his earliest conversion convictions. Paul filters his Jewish theology through the Damascus experience, allowing a new synthesis to emerge.

Paul's inaugural vision of church includes mission, a universal mission to the Gentile world. The breadth of his mission does not startle Paul for it has a precedent in Israel: Abraham was a Gentile, justified by faith; the prophetic mission was to the nations; the Pharisees and diaspora Judaism are at home in the non-Jewish mission and Hellenistic environment. Paul directs his energy to all potential believers, although he does not directly challenge the social and political problems of the Roman empire. Salvation, no longer by works of the law, is not limited to the house of Israel. While Paul cannot see the full implications of his mission, and we have only sketchy summaries of his earliest efforts after the conversion, he seems to be quite convinced of its scope and direction.

RELATIONSHIPS IN THE COMMUNITY

Paul's vision also includes an understanding of the importance of the Jerusalem church and of the role of its leaders, for his own mission relates to their apostolic activity. While

---

[23]Betz, p. 319.

Paul speaks of his independence of Jerusalem, he is also keenly aware of his indebtedness to them. Constitutive of Paul's ecclesiology is a personal and communal relationship in the church and between the churches. Frequently, opposition and conflict will bring home the difficulty of maintaining a good community spirit, but the actual experience of Paul affirms this integral aspect of church life. He works with others effectively and consistently as he proclaims the gospel (1 Cor 3:10). His co-workers include women and men, local leaders and other missionaries like himself. New patterns of relationship develop in the Christian communities, underscoring the importance of community, a significant ecclesiological insight for Paul. In some ways, Paul's vision of church transcends the social order and the religious world of his time, while in other ways, it emerges out of the context of his social and religious experience.

Because of his convictions and his vision, Paul dedicates himself to an extensive and expansive missionary endeavor. "No man in his right senses would have chosen the kind of life Paul lived, exposed not only to physical danger and hardship but to insult, abuse, loneliness, anxiety, conflict, and fear, of his own free will."[24] His journeys confirm this assessment as the apostle lives according to the vision and mission he has received.

Paul's Journeys to Develop the Church

The conversion of Paul is only the beginning of his Christian life journey. While it is a profound experience, its full impact is seen in his missionary activity and in his subsequent theological reflections. The authenticity of his call is likewise confirmed by the fruitful perseverance of Paul's life. The missionary journeys are the most practical consequences of the apostle's call to preach the gospel to the Gentiles. Acts documents these travels well: the first missionary journey in Acts 13:1-14:28; the second in 15:30; the third in 18:23-21:17;

---

[24]Barrett, pp. 53-54.

and the last journey in Acts 27:1-28:16. Although Luke does alter and revise his sources, the journeys are not imaginative constructions. The general picture is correct, although the itinerary is probably not as neatly defined in Paul's actual experience.[25] Acts tends to give select episodes and incidents; the letters confirm or modify the accounts. The letters, for example, testify to three visits to Jerusalem by Paul: in order to meet Cephas (Gal 1:18-19), for the conference (Gal 2:1), and to deliver the collection (Rom 15:25). By contrast, the Acts report four visits (9:26-30; 11:27-30; 15:1-4; 21:15-23:11).[26]

The major journeys cover a span of approximately sixteen years, from 46-62 CE. A detailed chronology presents numerous problems, although the most certain date is that of the proconsulship of Gallio in 52 CE (Ac 18:12-17).[27] This date becomes pivotal for a chronology of Paul's life and work. The procuratorship of Felix, possibly in 52-59 CE (Ac 24:1-10, 22-27), and that of Festus around 60–62 (Ac 24:27; 25:1. 9-12), are other important but less reliable dates. The letters, of course, allow another kind of assessment of the chronological framework of Paul's life and mission. However, chronological details are not as significant for understanding Paul's work in the church as his approach to his missionary activity, his encounters on the journeys, and the development of his ideas regarding church.

PAUL'S WORK IN THE CHURCHES

Paul as an apostle and missionary has seemingly little to recommend him. He must apologize for his past persecution of the church (1 Cor 15:9; Gal 1:13; Phil 3:6), his appearance does little to establish a sense of presence, and his preaching ability is open to question (2 Cor 10:10). However, his motivation is strong and his strategy focused. Paul at this time, like

---

[25] See Perrin, p. 92; Jewett, p. 12.

[26] See Ludemann, p. 147; Doohan, L. *Luke,* pp. 29-32, for use of sources, and pp. 54-55, for outline of Acts according to ministry in the Church.

[27] See Ludemann, p. 8; see Wedderburn, pp. 103-108, for recent studies in chronology.

others in the early period, believes that the Lord will soon return in glory. This eschatological expectation creates a sense of urgency to proclaim the word and to establish living communities of faith. There is dynamism in the Christian movement and appeal in the message. Paul capitalizes on the momentum and perhaps creates his own.

Paul utilizes his background for the sake of the gospel. As a diaspora Jew, he is aware of the five to six million Jews living outside of Palestine in the first century and of the proportion of Jews in any given city, usually ten to fifteen percent of the total population.[28] He preaches to the Jews during his travels, knowing that the synagogue network is an excellent starting point for his missionary endeavor (1 Cor 9:20; 2 Cor 11:24; Ac 13:46; 17:17; 18:6-7). This strategy facilitates the development of the early Christian movement from a Palestinian sect into the larger Gentile world.

The apostle Paul is also a city person, at home in the urban environment. The population density in any city of the period provides a unique opportunity for him. The shared language, customs, clubs, and workplaces, facilitate his contacts. The larger homes of the wealthy are the potential house-churches that could accommodate other Christians for meetings and meals. The church in Paul's experience, encompasses a cross section of society. His background as a Roman citizen, implied in the letters, enables him to appreciate the ranking and stratification within society and creates opportunities for him. His faith convinces him to direct the benefits of social structures for the growth of the community.

Although Paul is at home with the prosperous people in society, he also engages in leather work, using the workshop, as well as the synagogue and house, as a setting for preaching the word of God.[29] Workshop conversations make converts, for in this important social environment, intellectual discourse, preaching, and tent-making could occur simultaneously. We should note that "Paul was essentially a part-time, not a full-time, missionary, carrying on his evangelistic and pastoral

---

[28] See Meeks, p. 34.

[29] See Hock, p. 450.

activities alongside the practice of his trade. This makes his achievements all the more extraordinary."[30] While Paul expects compensation from his preaching of the gospel, he also establishes a level of independence by maintaining his own ability to earn a different kind of living. The usual means of spreading the faith in the early period is clearly the preaching of the gospel. By using the synagogue and the household, Paul and other travelling missionaries form a network of information and actually contribute to the unity of the church. Paul also writes letters, primarily to the churches he founded, as a substitute for his apostolic presence. The letters come from the peak period of his missionary activity and reflect his experience in preaching and teaching. Surprisingly, the content of the correspondence ranges from "the utterly secular—menus and shopping for food—through the way to treat company, the permissibility of settling law suits in heathen courts, the regulation of social distinctions in the church, the correct mode of living in view of the morals and conventions of paganism, down to the real problems of the Christian community, its worship, faith, and hope."[31] Paul remains a part of his world while challenging the communities to live differently and his letters testify to this integrated approach to his mission.

PAUL'S TRAVELS TO ESTABLISH CHURCHES

The spread of the faith in the early period is due in large measure to the mobility of the early church. Ronald Hock notes that Paul travelled nearly ten thousand miles during his reported career. He was on the roads with "government officials, traders, pilgrims, the sick, letter carriers, sightseers, runaway slaves, fugitives, prisoners, athletes, artisans, teachers, and students."[32] His journeys and his encounters with people

---

[30]Banks, p. 153.

[31]Bornkamm, p. 72; my own book, *Leadership in Paul,* for the range of issues in each of the authentic letters.

[32]Quoted in Meeks, p. 16.

provide fascinating perspectives on the life of the apostle and on the early church itself.

On his *missionary journeys,* Paul preaches the gospel and establishes churches. Although we know little of his early period in Arabia (Gal 1:17), he does extensive work during his first two missionary journeys. Before the Jerusalem conference, Paul undertakes missions in Galatia, Macedonia, and Achaia. He probably travels from Jerusalem to Syrian Antioch, Cilicia, Derbe, Lystra, Phrygia, Galatia, Troas, Neapolis, Philippi, Thessalonica, Beroea, Athens, and Corinth.[33] On the second journey Paul writes his first letter to the Thessalonians. During the third missionary journey Paul sends his major letters to the communities he founded in Galatia, Corinth, and Philippi, and to a community he intends to visit, Rome. The last journey brings Paul to Rome, a long anticipated destination. It is appropriate to examine the significance of some of the places Paul visits, before dealing with his actual ministry to the churches and his developing ecclesiology.

The apostle's prime interest is not in the conversion of individuals but in the founding of churches (1 Cor 3:6.10; 9:1; 2 Cor 8:23; 12:13; Rom 15:20). Some of the churches, like those in Asia Minor, may be small, but there are strong links between the centers through the travelling merchants and missionaries. Some cities, like Sardis and Apameia, know of no Pauline mission, although they have strong Jewish communities and are easily accessible to Paul and his associates. Apameia, for example, is midway between Pisidian Antioch and Ephesus.[34] Places like Alexandria and Egypt, are not on his itinerary. In addition to cost and delays, travel does have its demands, with Paul identifying "afflictions, hardships, calamities, beatings, imprisonments, tumults, labors, watching, hunger" (2 Cor 6:4-5). However, if the "Sitz im Leben of Pauline theology is the apostle's mission,"[35] the places and his travel provide an entry into his understanding of church.

---

[33]See Murphy-O'Connor, "Pauline Mission," pp. 71-79, who identifies parallels in Paul's letters with the second missionary journey in Acts. Luke transposes the earlier journey to after the conference.

[34]See Meeks, p. 45.

[35]Hengel, *Between,* p. 50.

The arrival of Paul in *Antioch* marks the beginning of an important period for him. Antioch is the usual place for missionaries to embark on their travels, and it is probably in this Syrian city that Paul consolidates his own mission to the Gentiles. In this place Peter and Paul clash over the relationship of Jewish and Gentile Christians (Gal 2:11-14). Although not mentioned in the letters after the Galatian incident, Antioch is an important and exciting city in the early church.

A bodily ailment provides the opportunity for Paul to first preach the gospel in *Galatia* (Gal 4:13-14). In southern Galatia, Paul founds churches in Antioch, Iconium, Derbe, and Lystra, cities influenced by the power of the Jewish settlers. Whether Paul works with the more remote and strongly ethnic northern Galatians is open to question.[36] His converts, however, are enthusiastic until opposition develops in the community. Eventually, they turn away from the gospel of Paul, and he writes them a strong and convincing letter from Ephesus, or perhaps Corinth or Macedonia.

Paul's journeys take him through clusters of cities like those in the Lycus valley, Colossae, Laodicea, and Hieropolis. However, a prime area for his apostolic activity is the Roman province of *Macedonia*. It is a less populated area, mostly Greek in influence, and generally poor (2 Cor 8:1-2). His major work is in the cities of Philippi, Thessalonica, and Beroea. Paul visits the agricultural center of Philippi at least twice (2 Cor 2:13; 1 Thess 2:2), being shamefully treated during one of the visits. While difficulties persist (Phil 3:2; 4:2-3), this community is generous to Paul and his work (Phil 4:10-16). A strong bond exists between them, perhaps in part, because Philippi is his first congregation on European soil. Women are active in the churches in Macedonia, with Lydia and her household converted by Paul (Ac 16:14-16). The apostle will write to this community from prison, revealing his warmth and tenderness, despite the difficulties they both encounter. Paul goes on to the important trading center and harbor of Thessalonica, a visibly Greek city, after his expulsion from Philippi. His mission progresses to Athens and Corinth and Paul frequently

---

[36]See Meeks, p. 43.

expresses his desire to revisit his congregations in his letters (1 Thess 3:1-7; 2:17).

Corinth is an exciting and flourishing city, recently rebuilt, and a center of Greek life and culture in Paul's time. The relationship between the apostle and this church is a long and arduous one. Paul's initial preaching in Corinth keeps him in the city eighteen months, followed by two visits, a painful one (2 Cor 2:1-2), and another to receive the collection for the Jerusalem church (2 Cor 9:5; 12:14; 13:1). Despite his long sojourn among these Christians, the community constantly misunderstands Paul. "They were the most exasperating community that he had to deal with, for they displayed a positive genius for misunderstanding him."[37] His four letters to the Corinthians (1 Cor 5:9; 2 Cor 2:3.9; 7:8),[38] are attempts to further the gospel and rebuild a spirit of mutual love and respect. Because of their penchant for misunderstanding, the apostle refuses to accept personal financial support from the community, alienating them further. In Corinth, Paul must not only proclaim his gospel in a Hellenistic environment, but also deal with a diverse and socially stratified community. The apostle steers his way through myriad issues and situations which his letters reflect. He probably writes to the Roman community from this city during a shorter three-month visit.

In 1 Cor 16:8-9, Paul mentions his work in *Ephesus,* the presence of adversaries in the community, and the proposed length of his stay. His imprisonment in this city gives rise to letters to the churches. Paul writes letters to the Galatians and Corinthians during his three years in Ephesus, and possibly to the Philippians and Philemon. Romans 16 may originally be sent to this church.

Paul goes, of course, to *Jerusalem,* a significant journey, bringing aid for the saints, just prior to his journey to Rome (Rom 15:25). In his earlier visits to Cephas (Gal 1:18) he discusses the circumcision question (Gal 2:1-10), thus gaining acceptance for his own apostolic mission. Now, in addition to the collection and its symbolic significance of unity between

---

[37] Murphy-O'Connor, *1 Corinthians*, p. ix.
[38] See Roetzel, pp. 53-63.

the churches, Paul probably has with him the letter to the Romans, with its carefully articulated theology. Jerusalem is the holy city and its leaders challenge Paul to understand his Gentile mission in relation to his Jewish roots.

Paul goes on to *Rome* because of the fullness and success of his previous apostolic activity. He completes his missionary task in the eastern part of the Roman empire. "I no longer have any room for work in these regions" (Rom 15:23). He seems to lay the foundations of the church and then move on. The flourishing city of Rome has been the focus of his attention many times. Its Gentile community commands his interest (Rom 1:13), and their present situation of integrating Jewish Christians previously expelled under Claudius, would benefit from a renewed appreciation of Christianity's Jewish origins. However, Paul also sees Rome as a steppingstone to further missionary activity in Spain (Rom 15:24.28).

During his missionary journeys Paul is "afflicted in every way, but not crushed; perplexed, but not driven to despair" (2 Cor 4:8). He often faces mortal danger and imprisonment (2 Cor 1:8-11; 7:5; Phil 1:12-26; 1 Thess 2:2). He experiences opposition and finds himself in the midst of controversy. Treated as an impostor (2 Cor 6:8-10) and having to deal with veiled hostility, he labors with his own hands, blesses when reviled, endures when persecuted, conciliates when slandered (1 Cor 4:11-13). Despite difficulties, he has the support of the churches, and particularly of his co-workers.

PAUL'S ENCOUNTERS ON THE JOURNEYS

While the purpose of the journeys is to establish churches, Paul also concerns himself about their life and development. In each place he visits, he meets extraordinary people and enlists their help as full or part-time workers to facilitate the growth of the communities. The co-workers embody many gifts for the church and represent the various strata of society. Crispus and possibly Sosthenes are rulers of the synagogue (1 Cor 1:1; Ac 18:17-18); Erastus is a city treasurer (Rom 16:23; Ac 19:22). Priscilla and Aquila, a married couple and friends of Paul, who risked their lives for him, are tentmakers (Rom

16:3; 1 Cor 16:19; Ac 18:18-20); Phoebe serves the community as a deaconess (Rom 16:1-2). Among the Corinthians, Paul himself baptizes Crispus, Gaius, and Stephanus (Rom 16:23; 1 Cor 1:14-16).

There are forty co-workers mentioned in the letters, eight others in Acts, and an additional ten in the Pastorals. A number come from the upper class, for Paul appeals to his social equals, particularly to those with Roman citizenship, since this enhances their respectability and visibility.[39] He works with effective missionaries like Apollos, and with other apostles like the woman Junia. Paul sends some, like Timothy and Titus, to visit the churches when he himself cannot. A connection exists between his own work and the work of others. Roles change as Paul initially assists Barnabas, while Silas, the prophet from Jerusalem, becomes Paul's responsible colleague. The journeys enable Paul to continually meet dedicated Christians and to build on their early work, as in Ephesus, evangelized by Priscilla and Aquila, and only later by Paul himself.

Many co-workers identify with communities and households and are responsible for the major developments within these local churches. Collaboration, so evident among Paul, his associates, and the leaders of house-churches, contributes to the development of these churches. Paul has contacts with the entire community in a given region but also with its leaders. He will enlist others in his mission and they will travel with him, providing leadership in the churches according to their gifts, and bringing a Christian presence to their work and their world. Paul's mission includes preaching the gospel and establishing churches, followed by making provisions for the community's growth towards maturity in faith. The co-workers are essential to each phase of the mission.

The mission of Paul in the early period of the church is unique. He does not have a geographical base but is constantly on the move. He travels from missionary center to missionary center, establishing communities, providing for their growth, and ultimately allowing them to exist on their own. Each

---

[39]See Theissen, p. 105.

community, in each area, is quite distinctive, a fact that will continually challenge Paul in his ministry to the churches. Understanding Paul's mission, the places, people, and strategy, is essential to understanding his theology and ecclesiology. Even the conflicts, hardships, and imprisonments, refine his insights into the mystery of Christ (Phil 1:19-26). What emerges from these journeys, and from the letters he writes during them, is a vital contribution to the early church and a significant challenge to our own.

Paul's Contribution to Early Church Development

The conversion of Paul is a call to be a part of an already existing church, yet he brings insight and energy to further its development. Not limited by its present vision, models, or leadership, Paul preaches the gospel in new places and to new people, pushing forward the frontiers of the church. He works with others while maintaining a strong sense of his own gospel and his own leadership as an apostle. He acknowledges the mission of others and coordinates his own plans with the strategy of others, including that of the Jerusalem church. To the Romans he speaks of his ambition to preach the gospel, but not where Christ has already been named or on another person's foundation (Rom 15:20), a guideline Paul usually follows. In his travels and through his writing, Paul lives out the call and commission he received from the Lord, and in purposeful ways, uses his background and his experience for the promotion of the gospel. While Paul is not the first or only missionary to the Gentiles, he makes a commendable contribution to the early church, both geographically and theologically.

HIS FOCUS ON URBAN AREAS

Originally from the cosmopolitan city of Tarsus in Cilicia, Paul is responsible for the urbanization of Christianity. He takes his mission, as we have seen, to the small towns and sprawling cities, appreciating the urban atmosphere and capitalizing on its assets. His greatest impact is in this urban setting. Indeed, he preaches Christ to a considerable portion of the empire because he utilizes the structures and institutions available to him. Paul thinks in terms of travel, roads, centers, trade, commerce, households, synagogues, and forums. With delicate balance, he proclaims God's new acts and revelation to his own people, appreciating all the while that the values they hold are also the ones that motivated him as a zealous Pharisee. However, his prime emphasis is to the Gentile mission, and the churches he establishes witness to his effectiveness. In his work with various Jewish groups and with Gentile Christians, Paul seeks both continuity with the past and unity within and among the churches, a major contribution in this early and expansive period. We certainly associate urban Christianity with Paul and his mission.

HIS UNDERSTANDING OF EQUALITY IN THE CHURCHES

Paul is a "goal-oriented community organizer, breaking new ground and establishing independent groups apart from Judaism rather than 'grazing' among the existing groups of sympathizers."[40] He is a self-sufficient figure and certainly does not subordinate himself to, or become an emissary of, the Jerusalem church.[41] He proclaims equality of Jew and Gentile, slave and free, male and female (Gal 3:28), a radical egalitarianism that results directly from his faith in Christ. However, this does not cause him to bypass enthusiastic people, of social stature and means, and engage them for the sake of the gospel. Paul challenges the Jesus movement by his approach to the socially prominent, and undermines the prevailing hierarchy by his perspective on community. The early church appreciates diversity more than structure. His co-workers include well positioned, gifted, dedicated, and decisive people, often leaders in their own communities. Paul works with women, an emerging group in the Christian movement, and in so doing affirms

---

[40] Theissen, p. 40.

[41] See Holmberg, p. 56.

them and significantly contributes to the development of their role in the churches.

HIS MISSION AS AN APOSTLE

Paul's faith convictions determine his theological perspective. The Damascus event, so integral to his gospel, is a source of his strength and a guide for his focus. He begins to adapt his gospel to a Gentile world, clarifying in this process, the relationship of Christian belief to Judaism. As an apostle, he dedicates himself to the lifetime service of continuing the mission of Jesus. Paul's claim to apostleship and his understanding of apostolic authority, expand and clarify the meaning of these terms in the early Christian period.[42] As an apostle, Paul is not above the congregation but rather, continually works for, and with, the community. Paul's mission is to preach Christ, and his apostolic call confirms the message.

HIS UNDERSTANDING OF CHRIST

Paul's experience of the Risen Lord and his understanding of Christ are fundamental contributions to the early church, for they give him a unique insight into the connection between Christ and Christians. This relationship is the essence of church. Paul's christology and ecclesiology are the only reflections we have from as early as twenty to thirty years after the death and resurrection of Jesus. His letters, filled with the passion of his convictions regarding Christ and the community, present Paul and the community in this very important time of transition from one understanding of belief and mission to another.

Of all the figures in the early Christian movement, Paul is the one who grows as an apostolic figure before our very eyes, since he alone leaves us with his own writings. We see his stamina and resiliency, his commitment and his mission. He tells us that "In Christ Jesus,... I have reason to be proud of

---

[42]See Schmithals, pp. 21, 40.

my work for God" (Rom 15:17). The letters are eloquent testimony to his contribution to the church. However, before we examine his actual ministry to the communities from his own correspondence, we will look at the first-century church in regard to its formative influences, Judaism and Hellenism and the pluralistic interpretations of the heritage in the community of believers. By identifying the richness and diversity in the primitive church, we can better assess the unique theological contribution of the apostle Paul.

2

The Church in the First Century

"For I am not ashamed of the gospel: it is the power of God for salvation to everyone who has faith, to the Jew first and also to the Greek." (Rom 1:16)

The New Testament documents witness to the faith of the early Christians and to the church as a diverse community of believers. As we saw in the first chapter, underlying the testimony of scripture is also an appreciation of the social and historical environment that gives birth to the Christian movement. Its structures facilitate the spread of the gospel and contribute to the development of the church. This cultural milieu influences and shapes Paul's missionary journeys, the visible manifestation of his conversion experience. But to understand Paul, we need more than a historical or sociological sense. We must also identify the theological climate and formative religious influences that contribute to the development of this early community of believers.

Paul ministers in a church that has its origins in Judaism. Its religious language, concepts, and beliefs come from these roots. However, the broader Hellenistic influences of the period affect Judaism, as well as the Christian movement. Both groups respond to the needs of this Hellenistic world in their own missionary activity. This complex historical, sociological and theological framework provides the substance for the varied interpretations of church that we discover in the scriptures. Because formative influence, religious heritage, and cultural experience differ, pluralism becomes a part of our earliest heritage, as does conflict and change. Christian views on eschatology and salvation evolve from this background and atmosphere. Christianity's roots thus affect its theological interpretation. Paul ministers in this exciting and developing church and contributes to its ecclesiological self-understanding.

Scripture presents Paul himself from different perspectives, depending on whether the portrayal emerges from his own letters, the Acts of Apostles, or later Pauline interpreters. Integral to each portrayal is a distinctive understanding of church. A theological richness and diversity permeate the formative stages of church life, and Paul makes a unique contribution to the church by integrating many of these influences into a cohesive pattern of ecclesial life.

In order to better understand Paul's contribution, this chapter examines the Jewish roots and Hellenistic influences on the first century church. It then identifies some of the pluralistic interpretations of church, including Paul of the letters and Paul of the Acts, and finally, presents the uniquely Pauline contributions to an understanding of church. Thus, chapters 1 and 2 provide the background for Paul's ministry in the local church and for his resulting ecclesiology.

Roots in Judaism

The initial link between Christianity and Judaism is Jesus, the Jewish rabbi believed to be the Messiah by his followers. Jesus concentrated his mission in Israel, frequenting the synagogue, and preaching the good news of the kingdom of heaven throughout Galilee and Judea. As a Jew, Jesus was aware of the traditions of his people and used local language and imagery in his teaching. First century Judaism provides the background for the ministry of Jesus and for the development of the early church. Its rich theological diversity and self-understanding find a home in Christians' view of themselves. Continuity is evident, as is the adaptation and reinterpretation of Israel's hopes and expectations by the new community of believers.

Throughout its long history, Judaism reveals a vital dynamism, surviving oppression, and growing as an influential force by the Hellenistic-Roman period. To be a Jew implies a religious commitment with political implications. Israel is the chosen people of God, but its people also have a strong national consciousness, particularly in Palestine. The scriptures reflect the historical and theological heritage of the community. However, Judaism does not have a solidified understanding of the scripture, since certain traditions can be interpreted with specific cultural situations in mind.[1]

Although Hebrew is in use in Palestine in the first century, Aramaic is the common spoken language. Greek is the language of the empire, and the existence of the Septuagint, the Greek translation of the Hebrew bible, reflects the expansion of Judaism in the three centuries before Christ. This dispersion of the Jews necessitates the use of the synagogue, a major place of instruction for the Jewish community. Greek-speaking synagogues exist in Jerusalem in the apostolic period, while the synagogues, particularly outside of Palestine, welcome Gentiles.[2] The temple in Jerusalem, with its ritual and worship, remains a focal point for the Jews and for early Christians until its destruction in 70 CE. However, Judaism reflects a growing dissatisfaction with the priestly group of Sadducees in this period, because of their ties to the Roman authorities.

Some of the distinctive features of Judaism, like ritual holiness and the ritual commands of the Torah, serve to segregate the Jews from their environment. However, not even Jewish Palestine is "a hermetically sealed island in the sea of Hellenistic oriental syncretism."[3] While boundaries exist, Hellenistic Judaism attracts Gentiles in great numbers and the emphasis on Gentile mission facilitates the integration of Jews into the world of their day. While Israel has a strong sense of itself, it is also a diverse and developing community in the Christian period. Probably, theological diversity emerges as the most exciting aspect of Judaism, with Christian theology discovering its antecedents in the religious ideas and language of the Jewish community.

---

[1] See Patte, pp. 111-112.

[2] See Hengel, *Acts and History*, pp. 82-83; and Collins, p. 163.

[3] Hengel, *Judaism and Hellenism*, Vol 1 p. 312; also Davies, p. 66.

GROUPS WITHIN THE JEWISH COMMUNITY

An indicator of the various approaches to a Jewish self-understanding is the existence of distinctive groups within the community of Israel. Of the sects, the Pharisees, Sadducees, and Essenes reflect the theological currents of the period. While all three groups have a patriarchal bias, they differ in their theological orientation, understanding of the Torah, and eschatological perspective.

The *Pharisees,* usually described as the lay teachers of the law, have their primary influence in the synagogue and home. They strongly adhere to the Torah and attempt to preserve its centrality by focusing on its strict observance. However, the Pharisees are more than rigid legalists, for they respect not only the written Torah but the oral Torah as well. This reliance on the oral tradition gives them a flexibility in interpreting the word of God for new times and places, making them the liberalizing influence in first-century Judaism. Likewise, the Pharisees believe that God's revelation is not only in the Torah, but also in the prophetic books and in the later biblical writings. Because of their acceptance of the wisdom and apocalyptic literature, Pharisaic theology encompasses an eschatological perspective, with an interest in afterlife and resurrection.

Paul reflects his indebtedness to his own Pharisaic background in his basic understanding of the law, his eschatological emphasis, and his commitment to Gentile mission. While the Pharisees remain convinced of God's choice of Israel as his people and his revelation to them, they continuously adapt to new situations, a factor that insures their existence after the destruction of the temple in 70 CE.

The *Sadducees* represent a different orientation and focus in the Jewish community. As priests, they center their interests on the temple and its worship. As an aristocratic and wealthy group, their following and appeal differ from that of the Pharisees. The Sadducees are politically conservative, advocating peaceful coexistence with Rome. They limit their theological perspective to ritual and to the sacrificial prescriptions in the Torah, giving little importance to the prophetic and wisdom writings. The eschatological and apocalyptic expectations of many of the Jews have little appeal for them. Because of their narrow focus, they lose their reason for existence with the destruction of the temple.

The community of the end times is an apt description for the *Essenes*. This sect separates itself from the mainstream of Jewish life, developing a distinctive religious identity and lifestyle in the region near Qumran. Their apocalyptic orientation emerges in their dualistic approach to life, pessimism regarding the world and humankind, and varied messianic interpretations. They adhere strictly to the mandates of the Torah, while expecting the radical intervention of God and the end of this age. Rites of initiation and a ritual meal find counterparts in the Christian experience, and their radical lifestyle with its emphasis on celibacy, poverty, and silence, testifies to their intense religious commitment and eschatological hopes. The Essenes have a real and direct influence on Christianity, but it is probably less formative than that of the Pharisees and affects the church later.[4] The Roman armies destroy the community after the destruction of Jerusalem but our knowledge of the group expands with the ongoing analysis of the Dead Sea Scrolls.[5]

These three groups, the Pharisees, the Sadducees, and the Essenes, represent different theologies and different interpretations of the Jewish traditions. The groups of believers and Paul will present yet another understanding of the Torah and view of the end times, as they explore their own identity in relation to their Jewish heritage. Many of the methods of biblical interpretation, apocalyptic ideas, views on resurrection and afterlife in the early church originate in the Jewish tradition.

THEOLOGICAL CONTINUITY WITH ISRAEL

Judaism and Christianity are interconnected realities, not only in their mutual reliance on the scriptures, the synagogue, and the temple, but also in important formative theological influences. Continuity exists between the Christian community

---

[4]See Murphy-O'Connor, *Paul and Qumran*, p. 6.

[5]See Leaney, for a study of the period and its literature, and pp. 171-183 for the Qumran writings.

and the community of Israel, but like other sects of the day, Christians also reinterpret the tradition. This reinterpretation is the main task of Paul and the early church, as they examine the theological core of Judaism that is the basis of their Christian belief. The prime areas of theological continuity are the understanding of call, salvation, faith, eschatology, and mission, which Paul then modifies in light of his understanding of Christ and the church.

Israel's awareness of its *call* by Yahweh centers on the abiding covenant relationship. This election by God originates with Abraham (Gen 12:1.7), and continues in the covenant made with Moses (Ex 6:2-8), and David (2 Sam 7). In the Septuagint, the *ekklesia* of God describes the assembly or gathering of those chosen by him, a community aware of God's promises, and their identity as children of the promise (Gal 4:28). Promises engender hope for fulfillment and so implicit in the very call of Israel is an expectation that Yahweh will continually be with his people. Also associated with their call is the commitment of this people to the one God of Israel and their responsibility to live according to that relationship in worship and righteousness.

Throughout the Hebrew Bible, the Spirit as the creating and renewing power of God and the gift of the New Covenant becomes the life principle of the community of the future, and the possession of the Messiah.[6] God not only calls Israel to be a people, but Yahweh's Spirit sustains them. As the early church reflects on this call, it understands its own identity in terms of its deep connections with Israel.

Israel's understanding of *salvation* provides a basis for the theological reflection of the early church. Israel grounds its conviction of God's saving action in its historical experience, particularly in the Exodus event (Ex 14:13-20:18), and in its deliverance from adversaries (2 K 18:30-35; 19:34; 20:6). God acts on behalf of this community through people and events, instilling in Israel a confidence in his continued presence. Salvation is a gracious gift Yahweh offers to his people, an unearned gift accepted in faith by the community. The under-

---

[6]See Ridderbos, p. 215.

standing of salvation develops in the Jewish community, so that it becomes closely associated with eschatological expectation (Ps 14:7; 80:3-7) and renewal of life (Ps 106:47). God indeed saves his people, but his saving action is a sign to the nations, indicating that the Hebrew Scriptures contain the roots of universal salvation. Although Christians assess God's continuous action differently than the Jews, they build on Israel's basic understanding of salvation.

Underlying the call of Israel and its understanding of salvation is the *faith* of the people of God. God justifies Abraham because of his faith (Gen 15:6; Gal 3:6; Rom 4:3), and God continues to act on behalf of Israel because it calls upon his name. Faith, while a free gift, elicits a response, and so Israel receives the guidelines of the law. However, works of the law do not justify, for the history of Israel affirms the centrality of faith. While first-century Judaism shifts its emphasis to the works of the law, Paul returns to the more traditional understanding of justification by faith for his theological development.

From Isaiah to Daniel, and in the later apocalyptic writings, Israel expects the coming of the kingdom of heaven. This expectation of the end sharpens Israel's sense of its call and its response, for the dawn of the final age implies judgment. The *eschatological hopes* of Israel remain strong in the time of the primitive church. The apocalyptic writings, particularly important to certain groups in Judaism, disclose heavenly truths and other revelations. The dualistic language of these writers focuses on the contrast between this world and the next, and the old and the new. While the apocalyptic thinkers tend to be more dramatic in their presentations than others, their perspective becomes a prime consideration for Paul and the early church. The hope of Israel and the hope of the Christian community have the same basic foundation.

The roots of the church's understanding of *mission* is in Judaism, since the Pharisees and the diaspora Jews are particulary cognizant of their responsibility to the nations. They understand the universal call to holiness within their tradition and attempt to relate Judaism to the surrounding cultures. While Israel appreciates the distinctive aspects of religion, it also plays down some of these elements in an attempt to discover a common ground with Greek philosophy.[7] This commitment to universal mission, so central to Paul's understanding of himself and the community, rests on its foundation in Jewish theology.

In addition to these main theological perspectives, Paul's letters testify that Christianity draws on prophetic language and imagery, the apocryphal works in the Septuagint, the prayers and ritual celebrations of the Jewish community, and the great figures of Israel's past. Many of the religious titles and concepts applied to Jesus and to the church come from Judaism, as does the basic understanding of the human person and community. Although fuller and possibly different meanings gradually emerge, Christianity is rooted deeply within the Jewish tradition.

Influences of the Hellenistic World

If the Jewish community exhibits a variety of theological approaches, the Hellenistic world is one of contrast. Greek civilization embraces every sphere of life, political, social, economic, cultural, and religious. Its influence penetrates both the Jewish community and the Christian experience, and its social framework, literary techniques, religious concepts, and philosophic approaches, affect the early church and its first missionaries. New Testament writings reflect the complexity of Hellenistic life and culture, and an accurate interpretation of our biblical heritage requires an understanding of its particular view of reality.

JUDAISM AND HELLENISM

The initial Hellenistic influence on Christianity comes through Judaism. Beginning in the fourth century BCE with Alexander, Greek life and culture affect both Palestinian and diaspora Judaism. Struggles ensue as groups interpret the Torah in terms of this major secular influence, giving rise to

---

[7]See Collins, p. 195.

distinct Jewish sects during this period. Their willingness or unwillingness to integrate Hellenistic influences into their religious approach to life characterizes these groups, and it is appropriate to say that "In the Hellenistic age the Jews had a new reason to retell the story of their past."[8] Hellenistic influence persists in the Roman empire, affecting the ministry of Jesus and his teaching. "Even the milieu of the parables of Jesus, with its great landowners, tax farmers, administrators, moneylenders, day-laborers and custom officials, with speculation in grain, slavery for debt, and the leasing of land, can only be understood on the basis of the economic conditions brought about by Hellenism in Palestine."[9] These influences continue in the early church, affecting the Pauline communities. However, the influence is mutual since Judaism, and later Christianity, affect the Hellenistic world.

SOCIAL STRUCTURES

The social structures of the Hellenistic world affect the formation and development of the church. A characteristic of this period is the proliferation of small groups for political and social purposes, usually voluntary associations, that bind together people of different backgrounds.[10] The political association directs its attention to public life in the city or nation and the Greek word *ekklesia* refers to the regular assembly of citizens deciding matters of concern.[11] Other voluntary groups come together for specific purposes but more important for the Christian churches is the household, that binds people together because of birth or affiliation. The household provides practical services, including spacious rooms for gathering and local leadership. A spirit of community, partnership, and support, develops within the household. While the patriarchal structures dominate the household in the Greco-Roman world, the Pauline communities challenge and modify them. Another

---
[8]Collins, p. 25.
[9]Hengel, *Judaism and Hellenism*, Vol 1, pp. 56-57.
[10]See Banks, pp. 15-16; also Meeks, up 75-84, on the various groups.
[11]See Banks, p. 34.

group, the school, fosters philosophic discussions between disciples and teachers. These groups, the voluntary associations, households, and schools, are potential models for the Christian community, and as such, influence the development of the early church.

Within the Greco-Roman world is a keen awareness of status and social class, with the household structure typifying this social reality. Indicators of status include wealth, occupation, family, education, and citizenship. Many dimensions contribute to the development of a socially stratified community, as the studies on Corinth indicate,[12] and women have a variety of opportunities for accumulating wealth, thereby exerting considerable influence in Asia Minor, even under Roman rule.[13] Women belonging to the upper class assume different responsibilities in the community and slaves could differ in status depending on the variations in their background. The socially stratified world of Hellenism represents varied interests and customs, and the early church reflects this phenomenon in many of its communities.

This society appreciates ceremonies and festivals, celebrations that provide marvelous language and imagery for the apostle Paul. The arrival of the emperor, with its attendant preparation and expectancy, establishes a framework for the description of the parousia in the early Thessalonian correspondence, and the games and athletic images reflect the course and culmination of Christian life in later writings. Hellenistic groups, social structures, and language, provide a variety of resources for the Pauline communities.

RELIGIOUS INFLUENCES

In an age of intense religious and popular philosophic rivalry, we would expect to see these influences affecting the Christian community. The Gentile churches of Paul appreciate aspects of paganism, and this challenges the early missionaries to constantly clarify their beliefs in relation to other religious

---

[12]See Theissen, p. 232; Holmberg, p. 103; Murphy-O'Connor, *Corinth*, pp. 153-172.
[13]See Fiorenza, *Memory*, p. 249.

views. The Hellenistic philosophies "were not just systems of abstract thought for the few, but rather propagated for the many a way of life and a set of attitudes based on a particular understanding of the universe that each had developed."[14] Their pervasive impact affects not only their understanding of the transcendent, but also their lifestyle, making the religious world of Hellenism, a fascinating backdrop for the Christian experience.

Religious syncretism underlies the various systems of thought in the Hellenistic environment. Monotheism prevails with a principal deity absorbing secondary gods. An interesting confession of Sophocles demonstrates this progression: "One, truly, God is one, who created the heavens and the vast earth. We mortals, with our wandering hearts, have set up, to soothe our own sufferings, statues of gods of stone."[15] Emperor worship is also a reality, and an interest in immortality, future rewards and punishments, and angelic and demonic powers, prevails. Greek mysticism describes the kind of relationship between creature and creator envisioned by the Hellenistic community, which aims at union with God, being deified, and being filled with the infinity of God.[16] Likewise, a lofty wisdom constitutes the language of an appropriate statement about God, with the Corinthian church embracing a number of these perspectives (1 Cor 1:20-22; 10:20; 2 Cor 4:4).

A strong individualism prevails in most segments of Greek society alongside of a search for community. Devaluation of the world and of the body accompanies the general disenchantment with the age. However, another core-value emerges, a sense of limitlessness, that directs the community and the individual to "discover ways to overcome human finitude, human limitations, by means of virtual or actual deification, infinity."[17] Contrasts and aspirations seem to specify human existence, as the dualistic understandings of the person and world exemplify.

The Greek world provides a challenge for the early church

---

[14]Freyne, p. 28; also for overview of Jewish, Greek and Roman influences.

[15]Cerfaux, p. 45.

[16]See Davies, p. 14, for a comparison between Hellenistic and Jewish mysticism; Malina, p. 1309.

[17]Malina, p. 1309.

in terms of its use of religious concepts and language. It is also replete with dangers for Christian believers, such as idolatry and immorality. The appeal of various philosophies and religious approaches to life supports this assessment.

The *mystery religions* emphasize personal salvation, solidarity with the deity, mystical, and relational elements. They appreciate the cycles of nature, life after death, dying and rising, use rituals to entice the gods, and rites of initiation, including baptism. The cult of Mithras is particularly interesting in its development of stages of perfection and its focus on moral values.[18] The mysteries offer striking parallels to the Christian experiences (Rom 6:2-4; 1 Cor 11:26), but also great differences.

Stoicism emphasizes the purposefulness in the universe, a personal detachment, basic inner equality, and freedom. Paul reflects the Stoic ideal (Phil 4:12) and the churches build on its concept of freedom. The divine principle or logos that governs and pervades the universe leads to a pantheism for the Stoics but to a different perspective in the churches. Paul is familiar with this particular philosophy since Tarsus had a Stoic school.

The *Epicurean* approach to life, with its emphasis on individual happiness and the disinterest of the gods, leads to a passive attitude regarding the world. While not particularly popular, the Thessalonian attitude towards work may reflect its perspective (1 Thess 4:9-11).

Neo-Pythagoreanism cultivates a sensitivity to the divine element within the self. It has a strong mystical current and a belief in the immortality of the soul. The devaluation of the body leads to a repression or sublimation of sex, a life of celibacy, and sometimes a vow of silence. The interesting biographical account of Apollonius of Tyana reflects the first-century outlook, although written later.[19] This philosophic approach very likely influences the early communities.

The influence of gnosis, if not *Gnosticism,* probably affects the early New Testament communities.[20] Gnosticism's radical

---

[18] See Freyne, pp. 38-39.
[19] See Roetzel, pp. 24-25.
[20] See Wilson, p. 74.

dualism, its view of the world, and its negative assessment of the body, form a serious challenge to Christianity. The gnostic redeemer myth demonstrates its understanding of the need for redemption and view of the person, while ideas of pre-existence, heavenly man, the Son of Man, the logos, and savior, though differing from the Christian perspective, raise interesting questions regarding its early influence.[21] Paul may be encountering gnostic tendencies in Galatia and Corinth and gnostic background may affect the church's developing understanding of the role of the apostle.[22]

Certainly the religious influences of the Hellenistic world challenge the Pauline communities by their theological understanding, well formed rituals, and use of language. Many of the ideas, while appealing to the churches, lead to opposition and conflict, but the church integrates or adapts other perspectives into its Christian vision of life.

The Hellenistic culture influences the Jewish community, the Roman empire, and the Christian community in the first century. However, it is quite difficult to determine its precise influence on Paul, since the lines between Jew and Gentile are not clearly defined. "A major reason why it is so difficult to identify precise examples of the impact of Hellenism on Paul is that Judaism itself had already felt the same impact, even in Palestine. Consequently it is frequently impossible to determine whether a given piece of his theological equipment has come from one source rather than the other."[23] However, various sociological and literary influences are visible in the Pauline communities and in the apostle.

While many of the religious influences have counterparts in Judaism, particularly in the later apocalyptic literature and in groups like the Essenes, Hellenistic contributions do persist. The early Christian hymns probably originate in this environment, presenting a unique christological perspective (Phil 2:6-11; Col 1:15-20; Eph 2:14-16; 1 Pet 3:18-19; Heb 1:3). Each Pauline community has large numbers of Gentile converts bringing with them their views of a complex social and relig-

---

[21] See Perkins, pp. 595-598.
[22] See Schmithals, p. 204; also comparisons with the Cynic sage, pp. 111-114.
[23] Ziesler, p. 17.

ious world. The early church traces its beginning and its roots to Judaism, but the Christian church also acknowledges its indebtedness to the Hellenistic world. Whether direct or indirect, this influence creates the need for Christian interpretation, adaptation, and integration, and the churches have the ongoing challenge to meet the hopes and aspirations of these people. The Pauline communities create an atmosphere where their search can come to fruition.

Pluralistic Interpretations of the Church

The first-century church emerges from its roots in Judaism and from its integration of the influences of the Hellenistic world. However, in its attempts to be faithful to the tradition while meeting changing needs, the church manifests many different emphases before finding its true identity. These perspectives result as its leaders, and the communities themselves, interpret their Christian beliefs in different ways. Sometimes the understanding of the church reflects an emphasis on continuity with the earlier traditions; at other times the focal point is change. Community life takes on the characteristics of this complex development as the early Christians encounter their environment in new ways. The anticipation of the end times also affects the image of church, but an emerging vision, clearly centered on Christ, begins to direct the followers. While our emphasis is on the Pauline communities, these initial interpretations will affect later biblical writers who will adapt and modify them, resulting in the diversity of the first-century church.

THE EFFECTS OF CONTINUITY AND CHANGE

While continuity and change sound like competing or contradictory realities, quite the opposite is actually true. "The concepts of continuity and mutability are commonly seen as incompatible. According to the vision here proposed, the opposite should be said. The Church's abiding essence actually requires adaptive change; and such change, if it is healthy, serves to actuate and express more vividly the true and permanent nature of the Church itself."[24] This creative fidelity that Dulles speaks about, is the heart of our earliest attempts to be church. Continuity is the real issue in many of the experiences of the early church, the Roman Christian community being a prime example.[25] The convictions of Pharisaic faith often emerge in the letters of Paul, although he modifies them in terms of his conversional insights. Christians live in a characteristically mobile, changing, and questioning world, and fidelity to the tradition therefore takes into account the multiple factors affecting it. The church today lives with the practical consequences of these early decisions regarding continuity and change.

A core experience of the first three decades of the church is the tension between *Jews and Gentiles,* a dilemma underlying the letter to the Galatians, and Peter's predicament in the incident at Antioch. The Jerusalem council also reflects this concern, with James and Peter advancing differences regarding the law, with still another by Paul. Some groups, like the Jerusalem church, adopt strict adherence to the law; others like the diaspora communities, adapt their life more readily to their surroundings. Even the early Christian apostolic strategy reflects these varying orientations, as Peter goes to the circumcised and Paul to the uncircumcised (Gal 2:8). Dissonance between groups often results, particularly as the Gentiles reflect on their equality in the community. While generally sympathetic to the Jewish tradition, the Gentiles eventually move away from Jewish ritual and circumcision, resulting in variations of Jewish/Gentile Christianity.

Peter and James represent a prelude to the missionary advances of Paul and his co-workers. As the church expands, unity becomes a concern, with the Jerusalem church reflecting an early tendency to conformity as a solution to the problems of pluralism.[26] However, the success of the Gentile mission, with its adaptation to the Hellenistic world, results in vastly

---

[24]Dulles, *Church to Believe in*, p. 102.

[25]See Campbell, p. 34.

[26]See Meeks, p. 113. There was also pressure by some Jews in Galatia to force Gentiles to live like Jews, as indicated by Brinsmead, p. 69.

different communities. At times, the Gentile churches advocate a false liberalism that needs to be tempered, as in Corinth; at other times, the struggle for equality results in new models of community and different structures. While the Christian movement radiates out from the Jerusalem church, believers approach their experience with relative independence and existentially ponder the implications of continuity and change.

Not surprisingly, these diverse manifestations among groups of believers, frequently lead to *opposition and conflict*. However, the understanding of Christian faith is forged out of these conflicts, and what is generally passed on is only what was fought over.[27] Whether it is another gospel introduced into the community, or the spirit of the Hellenistic age as opposed to Judaism, or the varied rates of growth between leaders and the community, this experience of conflict is an essential element in the formation of the early Christian church. Handling these situations well results in growth and integration for the community and a further step in its identity as church.

THE EFFECTS OF DIVERSE COMMUNAL RESPONSES

The early church itself reflects various interpretations of the traditions in its response to situational needs. Some communities adhere to the familiar hierarchical world view with its characteristic male dominance, while other Christian communities witness to an awareness of the freedom of the Spirit to bestow charisms on any person in the community, regardless of sex or status. While tension results because of different emphases, the movement towards egalitarian communities characterizes the household churches in Paul's time.

Differences also exist in terms of how Christians reflect their *equality*. Renunciation of wealth and the choice of a simple lifestyle is one possibility. Another alternative is to use wealth and status for the sake of the gospel while witnessing to an equality in Christ. In the early church, this latter perspective leads to the exceptional contribution of women who could use

---

[27]See Brown, *Churches*, p. 113.

their prominence and their competencies for the benefit of the Christian movement. This new freedom in the churches fosters leadership according to gift as opposed to position, and leads to differences in community structure from the hierarchical norm. However, the Christian churches also vary in their perspective. The Jerusalem church with its pillars—James, John, and Peter—adheres more closely to the synagogue model and Jewish patriarchal organization. The church in Corinth with little formal structure, is intensely alive with spiritual gifts. New forms of ministry and discipleship develop in this context. Thus, early Christianity, consisting of numerous intense groups, motivated by the gospel and conditioned by their environment, represents a cross-section of society and a variety of approaches to life.

An obvious *tension* exists when communities bring together people from different social strata. The conflicts in the Corinthian congregation reflect the difficulty of bridging the expectations of a hierarchical society and an egalitarian community. Rituals like baptism and the celebration of the Lord's Supper reflect these stirrings and call for a resolution. How can the church achieve solidarity while respecting diversity? These rituals also set boundaries for the community in respect to the larger society. Rituals, customs, and language lead to the cultivation of an insider/outsider view in the Christian communities and develop the early Christian movement into a contrast- or counter-group in society.[28] The developments, emphasizing differences and separation, exist alongside the missionary consciousness in the Pauline churches.

The early church reflects pluralism in its community life, integrating many aspects of the Jewish tradition and aspects of the Hellenistic world. While ritual and worship are important, the churches do not focus on priesthood but rather on community life and the ministry of all the baptized according to gift. These aspects of church life are developed in the gospels, while the Pastoral letters draw attention again to the pervading societal perspectives.

---

[28] See Meeks, p. 95; Lohfink, p. 122.

THE EFFECTS OF ESCHATOLOGICAL HOPES

Another variation in the early experience of church comes from the eschatological interpretations of the community. "God is a *faithful* God; therefore, the creation of the true and final people of God must include the fulfillment of every promise he has made. This faithful God is *God;* therefore his oaths to all the fathers will ultimately determine the shape and scope of the eschatological community."[29] While biblical promises affect the new people of God, eschatology has a different focal point for the Christian believers, since the resurrection of Christ marks the beginning of the new age and the process of *transformation.* Christology affects eschatology, clarifying the fulfillment of past promises and anticipating future glory.

Christians also believe that the Lord will come again in glory and that they experience a present realization of the promises in Christ. However, eschatology in the early church offers many interpretations of the parousia, affecting the communities and how they live in the world in various ways. The Thessalonian Christians, a good example of futurist eschatology, expect to be alive at the parousia, and so the death of some members of the community surprises them, and others in the congregation stop working in anticipation of the end. This eschatological perspective also affects the early church's view of marriage, and accounts for its initial appreciation of celibacy. By contrast, however, the Corinthian church focuses on present fulfillment, with its overrealized eschatology reflected in their spiritual enthusiasm and their insensitivity to the cross of Christ.

Some communities focus on the *final judgment,* clothing their Christian hope in the language and concepts of apocalyptic thought (1 Thess 5:3; 1 Cor 1:18; 2 Cor 2:15; Phil 3:19). Historical dualism and a paradoxical tension betwen the already and the not yet affect the consciousness of these communities (1 Thess 5:5; Gal 3:23-29; 4:1-7; 1 Cor 4:5). Opposites, such as spirit/flesh, slavery/freedom, letter/spirit, light/darkness, represent the clashes of antithetical thought and the simplicity of moral decision making in this world view.

---

[29] Minear, p. 111.

The New Testament communities reflect the end-time hopes of the world, either the imminent radical intervention of God or the gradual growth towards the fulness of the kingdom. Eschatology affects both Christian theology and Christian ethics and accounts for pluralistic interpretations in both areas. Consequently, communities represent great *diversity* in their theology and lifestyles because of their differing reflections on eschatological and apocalyptic thought. We observe changes and variations in communities and see ecclesial communities moving from one stage of development to another. Christian life attempts to balance present experience and final fulfillment in a community of faith, love, and hope. Reconciliation, the sign of the eschatological restoration of all things,[30] brings with it an intense and an enduring hope (Phil 1:6) which the churches reflect.

Paul and his co-workers believe they are living in the last days; the appointed time is very short (1 Cor 7:26.29). This realization, though we are dealing with different eschatological views, frees them for *service*. The apostle, entrusted with an eschatological message, proclaims it with urgency and conviction. Believers, challenged by the word, orient their focus and their life in accordance with the views they accept. Pluralism rather than uniformity is again the main characteristic of the churches.

Christian communities begin to develop a *vision of life* as a result of this interaction with traditions and influences. This vision includes a christology of Jesus as Lord, Messiah, Wisdom, Son of Man, and Son of God, reflecting the eschatological nature of Christian faith and anticipating the fullness of the kingdom. Salvation in history heralds the fullness of life in the end times, and a theological and existential freedom pervades the churches. Pluralism describes ecclesial interpretations and lifestyles, while communities continue to identify or affiliate with Judaism in varying degrees. Roots go deep in the world and culture of the period.

Views of the person, of the flesh as characteristic of transitory humanity, of the spirit as the conscious intelligence and

---

[30] See Ridderbos, p. 183.

understanding, of the soul as the vital, purposeful, and living person, of the mind and heart as the source of vision, of the world as the created reality of nature and humanity, struggle to survive and to be refined in the world of contrasts and continuity. Salvation for a people or for all humankind is a point in question, since these issues constitute the search for ecclesial identity in this early period. No one view or vision emerges in the church, rather a rich diversity resulting from the multifaceted interpretations of the Christian communities.

The Jewish community and the Gentile world affect the church in the first century, and each ecclesial community struggles to integrate these influences into an appropriate lifestyle. Since these decades mark a transition for the Christian movement from a sect into a religion we cannot expect uniformity. Pluralism marks the ecclesial communities, so evident in the letters of Paul and in other biblical writings.

Paul in the Letters and Paul in Acts

The authentic letters of Paul to the churches present the apostle to us, whereas the Acts of Apostles present Paul through the eyes of Luke some twenty to thirty years after Paul's actual journeys on behalf of the communities. The different literature reflects certain similarities and considerable differences as well, both contributing to our understanding of the early church. This section focuses primarily on the undisputed letters of Paul and the Acts of Apostles.

SIMILARITIES IN THE LETTERS AND ACTS

Both letters and Acts agree on several points regarding Paul. The conversion accounts reveal common elements, namely that Paul persecuted the church because of his impassioned zeal for the Jewish faith; a change took place when Christ appeared to him as exalted Lord; and the Lord commissioned Paul to be apostle to the Gentiles. The authority and initiative of the exalted Lord make him a witness, and the Damascus experience, containing in seed the core of Paul's preaching and teaching, is transformational in both accounts. Paul's anticipated and culminating visit to the city of Rome represents his theological maturity in the letters and solidifies the universal character of the church in Acts. Both writings concur on Paul's relationship with the Corinthian church, as well as with many other Christian communities, and they draw comparisons between Paul and the prophets, particularly Jeremiah. In some sense, both Acts and letters present Paul as having similar understandings regarding the role of Jews in salvation. In Acts Paul first visits the synagogue in each place, and in the letters describes his own mission as to the Jews first and then to the Gentiles. Also, Paul the missionary, is a leather worker by trade, making use of his occupation in his work for the churches in Luke's account as in the Pauline correspondence.

DIFFERENCES IN THE LETTERS AND ACTS

Notable differences also emerge, for in the letters Paul sees himself as equal to the twelve, while in Acts, Luke is silent about his apostleship and his equality to the twelve, also using the name Saul until Paul receives the Spirit. In Galatians 1:17, Paul travels to Arabia after his conversion, while in Acts 9:26, his missionary work originates in Jerusalem. The historical Paul gives up the law as a means of salvation, whereas Luke tends to present him as the orthodox Jew and Pharisee throughout his writing.[31] They also differ in their views of sin, with Paul perceiving sin as part of the human condition, and so the need for salvation, and Luke seeing it as a defect rectified by repentance. The historical Paul is a poor speaker and a prolific writer (2 Cor 10:10), while Luke's Paul is a great speaker and does not write.

The letters and Acts reflect personal, chronological, and theological differences, developing these into a different ecclesiological sense and perspective. Paul allows conflict, struggle, and diversity to remain in his letters, while, in many ways, Luke presents an ideal picture of the growth of the early church. Paul and Luke also view the community differently,

---

[31]See Bornkamm, pp. 24-25.

with Paul the apostle emphasizing equality and eliminating distinctions, and Luke stressing the status of certain groups and presenting a more organized view of the church. However, both writings must be examined critically to insure a solid foundation for our understanding of the church in this early period.

Letters and Acts offer different perspectives on Paul and the primitive church because their orientation, origins, and purposes differ. In Paul's correspondence situations condition the theological statements, while Luke's prime interests are theological.

Paul readily acknowledges his pharisaic background in the letters, and shows an appreciative understanding of Judaism (Rom 4), but he can also emphasize discontinuity with the Jewish tradition as in the letter to the Galatians (Gal 3). Whether he stresses continuity or discontinuity with Judaism depends on the factors affecting the particular church. In Galatia, the strong position and following of the opponents leads Paul to radicalize his own stance regarding his heritage. He solidly grounds his theological understanding in scripture and uses convincing rhetorical techniques to sway the community in his direction. When under attack, Paul becomes more forceful in his statements, using antithesis to sharpen the issues for the community and to move them decisively in his direction. He emerges as a controversial figure in these instances. While many of Paul's statements can be interpreted in a polemical way against the Jews, his letters, when taken together, actually recount an ongoing dialogue with Judaism.

Luke's theological perspective in Acts conditions the editing of his sources. For the writer Luke, Christ and the Christian community fulfill the promises of Judaism, and so he focuses on the broad sweep of salvation history to set the context for his specific theology and ecclesiology. The author of Acts presents Peter and Paul in relation to salvation history, paralleling their ministries while expanding the outreach of the church. Jerusalem becomes the center of Paul's missionary activity, and the apostolic council, the source of his understanding of the place of the Gentiles in the church. Peter legitimizes the mission to the Gentiles in his baptism of Cornelius, and Paul then carries it out. Luke's theology focuses on Jerusalem, the twelve, and the fulfillment of the promises reflected in the ever expanding ministries in the early church.[32] Paul, however, speaks of an independence from Jerusalem and a unique apostolic call, authenticating the gospel he preaches. While situational conditions affect Paul's emphasis, theological interests primarily affect Luke.

PERSPECTIVES ON THEOLOGICAL APPROACHES.

While Paul's correspondence contains many personal glimpses, changing perspectives, spontaneous and dynamic elements, christology and ecclesiology surface in the issues and in the narrative. But the individual letters do not have a cohesive approach to each topic. Rather, the situation of each community modifies and conditions theological developments.

In Acts, the writer serves the themes of universal salvation and expansion of ministry, by using well-planned journeys, carefully formulated speeches, and literary techniques such as inserting himself as an eyewitness to events in the "we" passages (Ac 16:10). The speeches contain the kerygma of the early church and so proclaim the word more than they reflect the speaker's own personal insights. This kind of redaction is absent from the letters.

Paul's understanding of Christ comes from his unique revelation, although we know that he also relies on the tradition and the kerygma of the early church. In Acts, Luke presents his own christology, reflecting the faith of his community in the 80s. However, imbedded in the narrative are remnants of an earlier christology with its focus on glory rather than the cross. While Paul highlights the law and justification in his letters, Paul's perspective on Jesus as Risen Lord permeates Acts.

PERSPECTIVES ON ECCLESIAL LIFE.

Paul makes strong statements regarding equality in the community of faith; he works with women and men, uses feminine

---

[32] See Doohan, L. *Luke*, pp. 45-66, for an outline of Luke's perspective on ministry.

imagery to exemplify his role and relationship to the churches (1 Thess 2:7), and capitalizes on the household of faith for his mission. Luke shows Paul with prominent women in the community, confirms many of the same co-workers, and has him speaking in the forum and synagogue. He also presents a more organized ecclesial setting with the twelve apostles, the seven deacons, prophets, and other ministers functioning in reasonably defined, though somewhat overlapping ways. The progression, if not the definition of roles, seems important for Luke, as does the movement outward from Jerusalem to the ends of the earth. This view reflects a later period with its theological understandings, different from the authentic letters of Paul. Some of Luke's perspective is akin to the presentations in the Pauline letters to Timothy and Titus.

The letters of Paul give us insights into his ongoing ministry to the churches, while the Acts relate his journey experiences showing little work for the growth of particular communities. Paul in the letters differs from Paul in Acts in this respect. Although these documents mutually support and enlighten each other, the person and his ecclesiology differ in experiences and in theological contexts in his letters and in Acts. However, from the understanding of church rooted in these documents, we can assess the uniquely Pauline contributions to the Christian community.

Unique Contributions of Paul to the Early Church

The apostle Paul makes some unique contributions to the understanding and evolution of the first-century church. While the topic is the subject of the entire book, I would like to offer a preliminary view of his distinctive insights and service to the early Christian community. These will be presented under the categories of Paul's personal approach, his understanding of the gospel, the development of its message, and his perception of church identity, life and mission.

PAUL'S PERSONAL APPROACH

The letters of Paul offer the personal thoughts and approach of the apostle in the earliest documented period of church life. The person permeates the correspondence, with all his human qualities intact. He is the confronting and volatile founder of the community in Galatians; the changing and defensive apostle in Corinthians; and the affectionate and personable Paul in Philippians. He epitomizes the struggle between Jew and Gentile as he integrates the insights of his conversion into his traditional understanding of Pharisaic Judaism. He becomes a dissenter within his own community by condemning legalistic tendencies and offering a new perspective on salvation. To be a real Jew does not mean circumcision (Rom 2:8) or a misguided interpretation of the law (Rom 9:31), for God, whose mysterious plan of salvation includes the incorporation of the Gentiles, is faithful and has not rejected his people (Rom 9:6.27; 11:1.25). Paul's views confront Palestinian Judaism in particular, as he turns away from an outmoded understanding of the traditions of his fathers to their true fulfillment in Christ. In many passages that reflect his background, Paul struggles with the changes his conversion demands and the implications of his decision.

The letters express the thought, religious convictions, and experience of a single person, providing an interesting insight into Paul's ability to blend his Jewish and Hellenistic heritage with his profound Christian experience. The correspondence also reveals a religious leader with his enthusiasm and spontaneity frequently balanced by a more studied approach to community situations.[33] His experience reflects his background and his own personal transformation in Christ.

Paul presents radical views, defends his mission, and offers dissenting views, becoming a controversial figure in his own time. He uses animated argumentation and dualistic extremes to clarify issues, expecting obedience but defending himself when necessary. In Paul's personal approach to the authorities in Jerusalem and to communities, we identify a collaborative

---

[33] See my own *Leadership in Paul*, for a full development of this theme and an assessment of Paul's situational approach.

way of dealing with pluralism and of working through transitions. Despite the fact that he makes mistakes and has limitations, Paul calls for imitation of himself (1 Cor 4:15-16; 11:1). By using the cross of Christ as his vantage point, he assesses his own weakness as strength. He is convinced that imitation can lead the community to a deeper knowledge of Christ, and so presents a challenge unique to the authentic letters. The personal approach of the apostle represents a distinctive contribution in the biblical period.

PAUL'S UNDERSTANDING OF THE GOSPEL

The origin and understanding of the gospel is an early and specific presentation of Paul. His call to be an apostle sets him apart for the gospel of God (Rom 1:1), for God approves him and entrusts him with this gospel (1 Thess 2:2). Paul feels called to preach the gospel, the revelation of Jesus Christ, but not to baptize (1 Thess 2:8; 1 Cor 1:17; Gal 1:11-12). This gospel, universal in scope, offers salvation to all who have faith, to the Jew first and also to the Greek (Rom 1:16), for it is the power of God (1 Thess 1:5).

Paul speaks of "my gospel" (Rom 2:16) and the one gospel (Gal 1:7.9), defending it and proclaiming the word in many lands (2 Cor 10:16). He feels a necessity to preach (1 Cor 9:16; 2 Cor 10:14; Rom 1:15; 10:14), and does it with sincerity (Phil 1:15-17).

The gospel, a fulfillment of all formerly promised in the scriptures (Rom 1:2), is the power and the presence of God (1 Thess 1:5). Its kerygmatic message unfolds in the letters, bringing together the co-workers and the communities. In this sense the gospel is the unifying principle in the early church. While the gospel is the power, presence, and wisdom of God, Jews and Gentiles perceive the preaching of a crucified Christ as a stumbling block and folly (1 Cor 1:21-23). If a veil obscures the gospel for some, Paul considers that imperception as a lack of faith (2 Cor 4:3; Rom 3:24). He defends the gospel in terms of Christ (Gal 1:12.16; 2 Cor 4:4), for it spells out justification as faith in him (Rom 1:16). The gospel has significance for all humanity, and Paul interprets it for particular situations, combining hermeneutics and tradition in his proclamation (Rom 3:24-26; 4:24-25; 8:3-11. 32-34; 1 Cor 15:3-8). His sense of the gospel leads to theological clarification and to his profound insight into Christian existence.

PAUL'S THEOLOGICAL REFLECTIONS

Paul's contributions on a theological level relate to at least three areas: soteriology, christology, and eschatology. The letters of Paul attest to his sensitivity to the theological currents of his day, those vital to Judaism, and those affirmed by the new Christian faith. Basing his understanding of salvation on scripture, Paul rereads the biblical sources and sees Christ in the tradition and in the covenant promises. Through faith, his interpretation changes, although he utilizes hermeneutical techniques similar to those of the rabbis.

Paul's theology is functional, and so he examines each aspect in terms of its meaning "for us" and "for our salvation" (Rom 5:6; 2 Cor 5:14). His understanding of sin is broad, with ritual and personal sins having little interest for him. Christ's death for our sins (Gal 1:4) is probably pre-Pauline,[34] for the apostle focuses on the universal sin situation and the universal need for salvation. While Paul stands for ethical responsibility and a faith response by an upright Christian life, he maintains Christ's role in salvation and does not trivialize sin. If all are in need of salvation, God's saving action and gift in Christ affects all.

Paul's letters reflect the reality of universal salvation but they also contain the language of limited salvation. Paul conveys in myriad ways the fundamental conviction that salvation embraces the whole community unconditionally in Christ, although his understanding is subtle and sometimes confusing. However, his unique insight preserves the centrality of Christ in salvation while in no way limiting the saved to those who confess belief in him.[35] Another distinctive feature integral to

---

[34] See Stanley, "Idealism and Realism," p. 42.

[35] For an interesting treatment of this topic see Boring, "The Language of Universal Salvation," pp. 269, 290-291. Statements of limited salvation include: 1 Cor 1:18; 1 Th

his ideas on justification is his emphasis on God's righteousness (1 Cor 5:21) and faith.[36]

Instead of a focus on the Torah, Paul turns his attention to *christology*. Christ's death and resurrection form the centerpoint of his thinking and his proclamation. Christ, the Messiah and Lord, fulfills the promises to Israel and his resurrection not only vindicates him but promises glory for all those united to him in faith. Paul understands bodily resurrection for Christians much as the Pharisees, but he carefully chooses his language to balance a materialistic doctrine of physical resurrection and a dualistic doctrine of escape of the soul from the body.[37] He also expresses the significance of Christ in terms of wisdom christology and "sending" language, conveying the Son's commissioning, obedience, and special relationship to God (Gal 4:4; Rom 8:3),[38] and preserving the usage of "Abba" in Romans 8:15 and Galatians 4:6 (cf Mk 14:36). Paul's experience of the Risen Lord, siphoned through his background and experience, provides the basic assumptions of his christology.

A link exists between christology and *eschatology*, with Paul's message primarily eschatological, coinciding with the prevailing views of the time. However, his insight that the Christ event is the turning point of the ages, is a fundamentally new idea. The sending, death, and resurrection of Christ constitute the pivotal event that announces the end times.[39] Eschatology permeates Pauline theology but christology guides his thought regarding the expectation and experience of the end.

Not only does Paul center his eschatological views on Christ but his assessment of these hopes and expectations shifts early in his letters. In Thessalonians and 1 Corinthians, Paul expects

---

1:10; 4:13-17; 5:3-9; 1 Cor 1:21-31; 3:16-17; 9:22; 11:32; 15:18; 2 Cor 2:15-16; 4:3; 5:10; Gal 3:10, 23, 29; 5:19-21: Rom 1:16-17; 2:1-16; 3:21-25; 8:5-8; 9:2; 10:1; statements on universal salvation include: 1 Cor 15:22-28; 2 Cor 5:19; Rom 5:12-21; 11: 26-36; Phil 2:6-11.

[36] See Bornkamm, p. 147.

[37] See Moule, p. 201.

[38] See Ziesler, pp. 40-41.

[39] See Bornkamm, p. 199; Beker, p. 262.

the parousia within his own lifetime, but this changes in the later Corinthian correspondence (compare 1 Thess 4:17; 2 Cor 4:14). The final coming of Christ generates an expectancy in the community and it influences Christian life (1 Thess 3:13; 2 Thess 1:10), making the delay of the parousia peripheral to the expectation itself.[40] While Paul consistently sees the fullness of salvation in the next age, the letters attest to a realized eschatology, for Christians experience the powerful Christ event in the here and now, in their newness of life (Rom 6:4), interior transformation (2 Cor 4:16), spiritual existence (1 Cor 15), present abundance (2 Cor 8:2), and sharing in Christ (2 Cor 5:17).[41] A qualitative difference exists in Christian life, for believers actually participate in the victory of Christ.

In developing his eschatology, Paul frequently relies on apocalyptic language and concepts. In his use of the apocalyptic, he identifies forces affecting the human situation: death, sin, the law, the flesh. However, Paul modifies the apocalyptic as Beker notes: "The modification of apocalyptic is evident in the fact that Paul (1) does not employ the traditional apocalyptic terminology of 'this age' in conjunction with that of 'the age to come'; (2) significantly modifies the traditional apocalyptic view of the escalation of the forces of evil in the end time; and (3) rarely uses the terminology 'the kingdom of God' (or the 'day of the Lord'), and when he does, it is mainly in traditional contexts."[42] Paul's contribution is distinct from the prevailing Jewish and pagan apocalyptic views of his time, for he writes as a Christian theologian, creatively interpreting the message of Jesus in light of prevailing views. As an apostle he transmits this developing tradition of the church, to the churches.

Finally, Paul makes a unique contribution in the early church, by conveying a sense of *ecclesial identity* for believers, challenging their community life, and spreading the church through his mission. Paul understands the church both in its relation to Judaism and in its departures from it. Judaism and Christianity are interlocking realities, for the church is a con-

---

[40]See Rigaux, p. 20.

[41]See Braneck, pp. 670-672; Mearns, pp. 138-142, where he identifies the second phase of realized eschatology, as early as 1 Thessalonians.

[42]Beker, p. 145.

tinuation and fulfillment of the historical people of God. However, the identity of the church centers on Christ, and so Paul readily speaks of the community as the body of Christ. Likewise, the Pauline churches bring a different perspective to their self-understanding than the churches of God in Judea, since they consist primarily of Gentile Christians. While Paul appreciates the universal aspects of the church and the shared truth of the gospel, his own experience is with the local churches.

As an apostle, he consistently accommodates himself to changing circumstances, reflecting on the unifying core of church identity, while addressing local issues. Paul's work for unity and his respect for pluralism, mark his contribution in this transitional period, when the community moves away from being a Jewish sect to becoming a Christian church.

In his letters, Paul focuses on community, rather than on priesthood, ritual, or biblical word of God. His emphasis on the internal life of believers startles his Jewish colleagues, but his challenge to the community in regard to structure, equality, growth, responsibility, and ministry, has a solid theological basis. By changing attitudes and lifestyles, the churches eventually impact society, its values and structures. Paul draws out the implications of being the body of Christ and of sharing in the power of his resurrection. He seems comfortable with changes in the communities but always reminds believers of the essence of their commitment. Radical views regarding celibacy, women, conscience, social relationships and structures, constitute the new community. The equality of all persons in Christ and the presence of different gifts for building up the community are essential components of Paul's ecclesial vision.

The apostle to the Gentiles establishes churches in Galatia, Thessalonica, Philippi, and Corinth, preaching the word of the gospel (Gal 2:7). He enlists co-workers, becoming a focal point for many of them in their ministry. He commits himself completely to his Christian call, involving himself in the life of the churches and directing his energy to the mission of the church. He affects the future of the church by his theological insights and his work with the communities in this early period.

Paul reshapes the traditions he receives and integrates them into a new whole, allowing sociological factors to affect his religious ideas, and pastoral situations to modify his theological insights. The Pauline communities more than the Jewish Christian experience, exert an influence on the church today.

The ecclesiology of Paul is our concern and interest and in these first two chapters, we examined the church Paul joins and the church in which he ministers. Paul's conversion to the church and his subsequent journeys to develop the church, provide the basis for understanding his contributions to this early period. His awareness of the church's roots in Israel and his ability to incorporate the influences of the Hellenistic world into his way of thinking, make Paul's ideas appealing to a broad spectrum of people. While many interpretations and understandings of church emerge in the first century, Paul's letters, our earliest written resource, offer a unique perspective on church life. The points addressed in these chapters establish the context for a more detailed development of Paul's ecclesiology in the remainder of the book.

3

Paul's Ministry to the Churches: His Experience of Local Church

"For just as the body is one and has many members, and all the members of the body, though many, are one body, so it is with Christ." (1 Cor 12:12)

Working for unity while appreciating diversity characterizes Paul's ministry to the churches, with its concentration on the local churches, founded by him and nurtured by him and his colleagues. The authentic Pauline letters comprise the prime source of our information regarding the apostle's ministry in the local churches. These letters constitute a personal form of communication and presuppose a previous relationship or knowledge between Paul and the community. However, the letters are also the official acts of an apostle, a substitute for his personal presence, and a vehicle for his teaching. In 1 Thessalonians, Galatians, 1 and 2 Corinthians, Romans, Philippians, and Philemon, the pattern of the letter remains quite constant, with its introductory greeting and statements, thanksgiving (except in Galatians), theological components, exhortations to the community, and closing comments. However, we also see great differences in the content and the context of the individual correspondence, since local situations and experiences differ. Within the letters, a vision of church emerges, a vision enhanced and modified by Paul's reflection on his own experience of these distinctive communities.

Aspects of Paul's Ministry in the Local Churches

As an apostle, Paul proclaims a message and engages in the mission specifically entrusted to him. Paul establishes churches, influences communities, exercises leadership, and reflects theologically on the essence of Gentile mission. He exerts authority in the churches as an apostle, and through his activity in so many communities and by his travels between cities, develops a complex network of relationships. He grows theologically and personally through his ministry in the churches. Pastoral issues, concrete concerns, and the human dimensions of his task, help him to formulate his theological and ecclesiological vision. Paul's relationship to the churches and relationships within the churches surface in the correspondence.

The apostle Paul engages in a unique mission, constantly on the move and having no set geographical base. But his strategy includes not only initiating contacts with communities, but also developing local leadership, and continually supporting the churches in their growth as communities of faith. While the mission of Paul differs from that of the local community, his insights into Christian life are stimulating and provocative. He attempts to draw out the implications of Jesus' message for urban Christians in a Gentile environment, doing "all for the sake of the gospel," that he and others may share in its blessings (1 Cor 9:23).

Each local church has a *tradition* and heritage, either the gospel Paul preaches during his founding visit, the tradition he passes on from those who were apostles before him, or from the community in Jerusalem. Other missionary preachers also pass on the traditions, primarily of belief, but also of custom. The Pauline communities have access to many traditions which they adapt in terms of their own cultural and religious heritage. In his letters, Paul builds on these various traditions and interprets them for changing circumstances, being a bearer and a formulator of the tradition, which is again passed on, interpreted, and changed.

Paul's understanding of *community* parallels his understanding of the church, which he sees as the community of believers in Christ who respond to the gospel in faith and by their lifestyles. The Christian community possesses unique characteristics, among them, mutual love, equality, and freedom, based on their union in Christ. Within the churches, people enter into new relationships and form an alternative environment for their personal growth and the development of the church. Commitment to Christ modifies behavior and through his exhortations the apostle challenges the community to continually grow as church. Being community is equal to being church, and each believing community, while distinctive in its lifestyle, unites with others in the source of its faith.

Communities of believers also share their faith and their new life in Christ, and the letters reveal various *forms of sharing* in the churches. Sharing can focus on aspects of faith, on dimensions of ministry within and outside the community, on revision of ecclesial life, on affirmation or confrontation. Particular forms of sharing result from dialogue within the community and interaction between leaders and followers. The situation of the community conditions the kind of exchanges we see in the letters. Decision making and the beginnings of organization, unique to each community, reflect the growth and maturity of the Christian church.

However, in each of the local churches, *obstacles* surface that impede ecclesial living and personal growth. The problems arise from the environment, different interpretations of the gospel, various rates of growth in the community, conflicting ideas, and incompatible leadership styles. Not only is the identification of the source of conflict important, but principles for dealing with it prove essential for a satisfactory resolution. The early church is a very human church, and its tensions reflect the attempts of communities to integrate the traditions with their own approach to Christian life.

Finally, in each community, Paul seeks collaborators to *build up* the community of faith. He assumes personal responsibility for the churches he establishes, but he also develops a spirit of responsibility in the community so that it maintains the quality of life essential to the gospel. Within the sphere of the local church rests the utilization of gifts and competencies, discernment in faith, and striving for unity. Growth takes place in these local communities as they assume their responsibility to build themselves up in faith. Each church must exist on its own after the missionaries leave, making the building up of the body of Christ essential for the local community.

This chapter examines Paul's ministry in each of the local churches. By using only the authentic letters we can visualize Paul's own personal experience. Each community receives separate attention since the situations differ. My purpose is to identify an emerging vision of church by examining the contributions of the local churches and Paul's experience on this level. For each community, I focus on its tradition and heritage, community life, forms of sharing, obstacles to church growth, and collaboration in the building up of the church.

Paul's Ministry in 1 Thessalonians

Our earliest New Testament document, the letter to the Thessalonians, begins with greetings from Paul, Silvanus, and Timothy to the church of Thessalonica (1:1).[1] The idea of church permeates the letter and establishes the use of the word *ekklesia* for communities of believers in Christ. Paul indicates God's choice of this particular church as he calls the community into his own kingdom and glory (1 Thess 2:12). The newly converted Gentile community soon becomes an example to other believers in Macedonia and Achaia (1 Thess 1:7). In their suffering, the community imitates the persecuted churches of God in Judea (1 Thess 2:14). These references to various congregations seem to indicate a beginning relationship between the churches. Likewise, the missionary spirit in the early church surfaces in Paul's plans, in the activity of Timothy, and in the community's awareness of its responsiblity to outsiders (1 Thess 2:8.17-18; 3:2.6.10; 4:10). Paul's relationship with this congregation is both apostolic and personal. After preaching the gospel, he writes to them as a sign of support and encouragement. This letter becomes our closest connection with the beginnings of the church and offers insight into its spirit and life.

The gospel *tradition* reaches the community through the

---

[1] For background in each letter in this section and the significant issues in the community, see the sections on "situation" in each of the chapters of my *Leadership in Paul*.

preaching of Paul (1 Thess 1:5; 2:8) and in the instructions handed down from Christ through the apostles (1 Thess 4:1-2). Paul mentions the words of the Lord (1 Thess 4:15-17) and freely adapts the Lord's sayings to the situation of the community (1 Thess 4:15-18; 5:2.15). In the autobiographical section of the second chapter, Paul describes apostles as persons of sincerity (1 Thess 2:1-4), integrity (2:5-8), generosity (2:9-10), and concern (2:11-12). This section also conveys the process of evangelizing a pagan community,[2] which is the Thessalonians' background and heritage.

The letter reveals the content of the tradition. Jesus is the savior from heaven whom God raised from the dead to deliver us from the wrath to come (1 Thess 1:9-10). He will come in glory, reuniting believers to himself (1 Thess 3:13; 4:13-17). This focus on the resurrection and parousia characterizes the earliest belief of the church, and Paul demonstrates an intrinsic connection between the resurrection of Christ and the resurrection of Christians (1 Thess 4:14). Apocalyptic language and Hellenistic imagery heighten the awesomeness and drama of the final resurrection and the glorious coming of the Lord. This expectancy and hope have a direct bearing on life in the community, and while the tradition may be the "fairly standard Hellenistic Jewish Mission Christian proclamation and parenesis,"[3] Paul transmits it for all the churches in this letter.

The Thessalonians become a Christian church in God the Father and Lord Jesus Christ, and their lives of faith, hope and love find value in their relationship to the Lord Jesus (1 Thess 1:1-3). Paul affirms the faith and Christian life of this community, giving thanks constantly for them (1 Thess 1:2-3:13). He sees faith affecting every aspect of a person's life and shows his pastoral concern for their growth and development. Underlying the exhortations in the Pauline letters is his vision of *community life*. In 1 Thessalonians, the eschatological expectations of the community influence the quality of its life. While Paul attempts to correct some misunderstandings, his prime purpose is to encourage the community. He asks the

---

[2] See Reese, pp. 16-23.
[3] See Perrin, p. 94.

congregation to live quietly, and to engage in manual work (1 Thess 4:11-12), since their views of the end are modifying their approach to life. More significantly, their life should reflect an active concern and love for one another (1 Thess 4:9), respect and esteem for those who labor among them (1 Thess 5:12-13). Patience, joy, thanksgiving, holiness of life, and appreciation of the gifts of the Spirit, further identify the lifestyle of the community. These exhortations tend to alert believers to their effects on others within and outside the community.

Relationships are a key factor in Paul's understanding of the church and good mutual relationships exist between Paul and the Thessalonians (1:1-11; 3:6). He calls them his brothers and sisters fourteen times and uses endearing images, indicating his affection for them. Paul conveys to this young and enthusiastic church his sense of the importance of continual growth in their life together. He also presents himself and the churches as models for the community, since both persons and communities can reveal the Lord to others (1 Thess 1:6; 2:9.14).

Growth as community implies quality exchanges among believers, with several *forms of sharing* surfacing in 1 Thessalonians. For Paul himself, communication with the church occurs through preaching, during subsequent visits to the community, in the sending of Timothy (1 Thess 3:2), and through the written word. He offers guidance and responds to their questions in the correspondence. In this letter alone, Paul requests that his words be read to the congregation, possibly an indication that the group gathers liturgically (1 Thess 5:27). Other forms of sharing also emerge in this faith community, with prayer, joy, and thanksgiving as the basic Christian attitudes. Since prayer is essential for the Christian community, he exhorts them to "pray constantly, rejoice always, give thanks in all circumstances" (1 Thess 5:16-18). Attitudes such as these, create the atmosphere for mutual growth.

Since difficult encounters must also occur, the community needs the courage to admonish others in a Christian spirit (1 Thess 5:14) as well as to comfort and console one another (4:18). Furthermore, Christians facilitate or hinder the movement of the Spirit and its gifts such as prophecy, thus they discern or "test everything" (1 Thess 5:19-21). These forms of sharing indicate ministries in the community and while ministry varies in the New Testament communities according to needs and gifts, ministry *to* the community is a prime responsibility *of* the community. All these aspects of community life imply mutual respect and an ability to dialogue on matters of importance. Sharing, then, results from an understanding of what Christian community ought to be and its various expressions depend on the circumstances of the community.

Problems arise in the Christian communities whether they be the erring individual, immorality, persecution, or opposition. While Thessalonica exhibits no serious abuses or difficulties, Paul feels the need to reinforce previous teaching and to offer some sound pastoral advice. He anticipates the *obstacles* this newly formed Christian church will face in a predominantly pagan environment. The tone of the letter encourages the community, while challenging its continual growth.

The responsibility for its growth rests within the community, and so "Build one another up" (1 Thess 5:11) indicates the ultimate admonition of Paul. The Thessalonians accept mutual encouragement as the work of the community. Paul, Silvanus, and Timothy, have a role to play, but the local church takes responsibility for the quality of its own Christian life. Their effectiveness in this area is a source of glory and joy for Paul (1 Thess 2:19-20). While he encourages, affirms, and challenges them, the role of the founder of the community differs from that of the members or the local leadership (1 Thess 2:17; 3:5-10; 4:1; 5:12-13). In this community, Paul, the pastoral person, answers questions, delegates to others, reflects on theological issues, and anticipates problems. The local church reflects on the tradition it has received and attempts to live it out as a community of believers, knowing that Paul and others will continue their support and encouragement.

Paul's Ministry in Galatians

Paul writes a disarmingly confrontational letter to the churches in Galatia (1:2). While the Galatian Christians are predominantly Gentile (Gal 4:8; 5:2; 6:12), strong judaizing tendencies surface, posing a serious threat to Paul's gospel.

The resulting letter is a fiery personal response dominated by flashes of controversy. Paul writes as an apostle, addressing a crisis situation. He is decisive in his position and clear in his presentation. Notably, the letter lacks the customary thanksgiving, names of the co-workers, and personal greetings, but the passionate letter includes marvelous pithy phrases and descriptions. It contains an apologetic self-defense (Gal 1:10-2:10), accusation (2:11-21), attack (3:1-5), scriptural midrash (3:6-14), allegorical interpretation (4:21-31), tender appeal (4:12-20), bitter sarcasm (5:12), and an abrupt ending (6:17).[4]

Paul's apostleship is at stake, and he defends its origin and attacks approaches different from his own (Gal 1:1-2:7). Perhaps, these churches epitomize local communities moving in a different direction from their founder. Also inherent in the situation of the Galatian church is the degree of affiliation with Jerusalem appropriate for the Gentile Christian communities, and so Paul clarifies his understanding of being "in Christ" in relation to Judaism and the law (Gal 5:2-3). His personal journey from Pharisee to Christian, as well as the early development of the church, emerges in the fruitful exchange between Paul and the churches in the region of Galatia (1:2). The letter contains few explicit references to church: the church of God that Paul persecutes (Gal 1:13), the churches of Christ in Judea (Gal 1:22), and the new community as the Israel of God (Gal 6:16).

The Galatian communities initially receive the *tradition* from Paul himself (Gal 4:13), the gospel containing the revelation of Jesus as God's Son (Gal 1:6.11.12.16). Paul emphasizes his independence of Jerusalem and of the other apostles (Gal 1:17) in order to demonstrate the truth and authenticity of his gospel. References to the "traditions of my fathers" (Gal 1:14) indicate the background against which he interprets this new revelation.

However, the Galatians receive another gospel, radically different from that of Paul (Gal 1:6-7), emphasizing circumcision and the Jewish heritage (Gal 5:6; 6:14-15). The Galatians question Paul's interpretation and move to another under-

---

[4]See Beker, p. 42.

standing of the tradition. These Gentile Christians appreciate the believer's roots in Judaism and willingly incorporate aspects of the religion into their own Christian life. However, Paul believes that external observance of the law implies acceptance of the entire law (Gal 5:3). He therefore reflects on the biblical tradition, particularly the story of Abraham, and demonstrates justification by faith for Abraham and for the Gentiles (Gal 3:6-9). In this letter, Paul makes the law and the gospel antithetical.[5] Consequently, two contrasting religious views emerge because of the fulfillment of promises in Christ (Gal 3:16).

In Galatians, Paul interprets the tradition in light of the serious situation of the community. To convey his position and the content of the gospel he uses contrast, discontinuity with the tradition, and conditional curse and blessing (Gal 1:8; 6:6). The community must reconsider the meaning of justification by faith in Christ (Gal 2:16; 3:11.26) and the truth of the gospel (Gal 2:14).

The source of the *community's life* is their relationship with Christ, "for as many of you as were baptized into Christ have put on Christ" (Gal 3:27). To put on Christ implies certain characteristics in the community. Love becomes the distinguishing mark of the Christian existence as persons become servants of one another (Gal 5:13). Likewise, life in the Spirit characterizes the community, and visible to all are the fruits of the Spirit: love, joy, peace, patience, kindness, goodness, faithfulness, gentleness, self-control (Gal 5:22-23). Freedom also marks the Christian church as well as mutual responsibility (Gal 5:1.13-15), with the opportunity to do good to all weighing heavily on those of the household of faith. Those within the Christian community have particular claims on the goodness of others (Gal 6:10), as new relationships begin to emerge because of the Christian's relationship in Christ. The community manifests the unity of all and a radical equality despite differences of status, sexuality, or ethnic origin (Gal 3:28). Christian existence enjoys a new relationship with God (Gal 3:26; 4:6). Paul reminds the community of these points as he recalls their initial concern for him (Gal 4:14).

---

[5]See Brinsmead, p. 64.

Because of the vastly different traditions and the strong challenge to the community itself, specific *forms of sharing* develop in this situation of conflict. Abandonment of the gospel elicits Paul's judgment on the churches (Gal 1:6-10). He rebukes and warns them about their choices, while defending himself and his gospel. Paul uses various defenses in this serious situation, but theological reflection underscores the bulk of the correspondence. The arguments in Galatians come from experience (Gal 3:1-5), scripture (3:16-4:18), Christian identity (3:26-28), friendship (4:12-20), and ethics (5:1-6:10).[6] As an apostle, Paul challenges the community and attempts to persuade them to return to the gospel he proclaims. He uses decisive tactics in a critical situation.

The letter evidences the variable relationship between local churches and the Jerusalem church. Paul claims independence in terms of the gospel but accepts mutual decisions in regard to mission and strategy (Gal 1:16; 2:6-9). Ecclesial leaders can oppose each other, as do Paul and Peter in Antioch (Gal 2:11), but Christian leaders exert influence on one another from afar, as does James (Gal 2:12). The Jerusalem leaders confirm, acknowledge, and make suggestions about the ministry of others (Gal 2:9-10), and although a willingness to confront issues and people exists in this early period, so does an affiliation between Paul and the Jerusalem leaders.

Within the community, Paul exhorts members to mutual sharing in the form of challenging those who trespass, supporting those in difficulty, and testing personal work for the sake of the community (Gal 6:1-5). Likewise, Paul encourages mutual support between teacher and those taught (Gal 6:6). Mutual ministry exists within the household of faith and extends to unbelievers as well (Gal 6:10). Perhaps, the strongest suggestion for the community is to assess why they turned away from the gospel in light of the evidence Paul now presents. By using apologetic speech, Paul dialogues with the Galatian church who accept a different theology,[7] entices them

---

[6]See Betz, pp. 30ff.
[7]See Brinsmead, pp. 188-189.

to draw their own conclusions, and asks them to be accountable for their choices.

The Galatian correspondence results from the effects of *opposition* within the community, with the primary factor being "contrast between two religious systems: circumcision—or faith operating through charity" (Gal 5:6; 6:14-15).[8] This issue confronts the Galatians and it is probably the same issue that Paul confronts in Peter (Gal 2:14).[9] In this early period of the church, Paul challenges Jewish legalism, often using antithetical extremes to make his point. But out of conflict situations grow a new understanding and some modifications on both sides. Galatians reflects a movement away from the position of the Jerusalem church by Paul, but a tendency to favor traditional approaches by the community. The apostle projects a cohesive argument to address the problem which the unity of the letter admirably reflects. Galatians attests that problems, opposition, and conflict, are part of Paul's earliest experience in the churches. Although the correspondence does not give the other side of the conflict or its resolution, the questions regarding diversity and division, unity and uniformity, are already significant in the church.

In this serious situation Paul gives little attention to collaboration for *building up* the community. He assumes a theological and confrontational approach, believing that as an apostle, he can persuade the community to again accept his views. Titus becomes an example of the broad interpretation of the church regarding circumcision (Gal 2:3). Paul also indicates the positive encounter of Barnabas and himself in Jerusalem with James, Cephas, and John (Gal 2:9). He centers on broad issues and attitudes in the community, asking that there be no self-conceit, provocation, or envy among them (Gal 5:26). By contrasting life according to the flesh and according to the Spirit, the community can clearly identify its options (Gal 5:16-24).

This letter eradicates sexual or ethnic differences, as equality paves the way for each member assuming responsibility ac-

---

[8] Stanley, *Christ's Resurrection*, p. 159.
[9] See Brinsmead, p. 51.

cording to his/her gifts (Gal 3:28). Paul not only speaks of freedom in Christ (Gal 5:1), but he also allows this freedom to the community, even though his position clearly differs from theirs. The apostle assumes his own responsibility towards the churches in Galatia but he does not personally visit them at this time, nor does he call upon local leadership to correct the situation. Rather, he assumes that the community can listen, assess, and redirect its understanding of the gospel, and so he addresses himself directly to the church.

Galatians provides insight into a heated controversy in the community and offers a solid theological argument for the gospel by its apostolic founder, Paul. This letter signals new directions and issues for the churches in their transition from Jewish to Gentile world by contrasting the Christian gospel with the aspects of the Jewish tradition.

Paul's Ministry in 1 and 2 Corinthians

The Corinthian correspondence begins differently from the two previous letters. Addressed "to the church of God which is at Corinth" (1 Cor 1:2; 2 Cor 1:1), this designation may connote more than simply the local church (1 Thess 1:1), or a number of churches in a geographical region (Gal 1:2), as in the earlier letters. The church in Corinth reflects and manifests the larger reality of church in its own life. Throughout the letters, Paul also refers to other churches (1 Cor 4:17; 10:32; 14:33; 16:19; 2 Cor 8:1.18-19.24; 11:28), the church of God (1 Cor 10:32), roles in the churches (1 Cor 12:28), building up the church (1 Cor 14:12.23; 2 Cor 13:10), and his anxiety for the churches (2 Cor 8:24). Likewise, the church is the assembled community, and the community is the body of Christ (1 Cor 10:16; 12:13.27) or the household of believers (1 Cor 1:16).

The letters to the Corinthians offer exciting reading since Paul writes to them after some difficult encounters, and the correspondence itself reflects misunderstanding and hostility between the apostle and the church. The apostle actually writes four letters to the Corinthian Church: a lost letter referred to in 1 Cor 5:9, our 1 Cor, 2 Cor 10-13, and 2 Cor 1-9. Paul deals with varied and interesting issues in 1 Corinthians, and the short time lapse between the letters indicates rapidly changing situations and moods. 1 Corinthians presents a balanced theology underlying the proliferation of questions and concerns; 2 Corinthians is personal and perplexing correspondence. Paul resolves certain issues in the community by sending 1 Corinthians, but his actual relationship with the church disintegrates.

The Corinthian letters also present figures in the early church, such as Timothy, Stephanus, Apollos, Crispus, Gaius, and Chloë, and highlight some of the travels of Paul and his co-workers (2 Cor 1:15-16; 2:12-13; 7:5; 8:19; 10:16; 12:14; 1 Cor 16:5-9). Excitement pervades the city of Corinth because of its location, population, spirit, and interests, making Paul's encounter with the Hellenistic churches far from dull.

The Corinthians question and challenge Paul, their apostolic founder. Described as quarrelsome, pushy, stubborn, self-satisfied, and proud, they demand a patience and resilience that tests Paul's limits. Influenced by other teachers and possessing an innate spirit of inquiry, the church frequently misunderstands and judges Paul and many of the incidents become personal attacks that are difficult for Paul to accept.

However, these letters offer a unique perspective on the early church. They testify to an over realized eschatology, an exaltation of false wisdom, and an extreme enthusiasm in this community. While the doctrinal problems are minor, the letters skillfully strike a balance between Hellenistic views and Christian belief. Great diversity exists in this church, but a balanced and well constructed theological foundation emerges, particularly in 1 Corinthians. Also striking is the use of the image of the body for the community. In this stimulating and exciting church, Paul renounces privilege and financial assistance, much to their consternation (2 Cor 11:7-8). He continues his relationship with the community through difficult periods, although historians question his ultimate success.

The apostle Paul preaches the gospel and hands on the *tradition* which Christ entrusts to him to the Corinthian community (1 Cor 1:17; 15:3-5). With his commission to preach (1 Cor 9:17; 2 Cor 2:17), not necessarily to baptize (1 Cor 1:16-17), Paul becomes their "father in Christ Jesus through the gospel," not simply a guide (1 Cor 4:15). Because of the problems in this congregation, Paul defends his apostleship, his ministry, and his integrity (2 Cor 11:12; 10:14; 2:17), and although he has the right to expect support for his work, he preaches the word free of charge (1 Cor 9:14-18).

Paul delivers the traditions he has received regarding the death and resurrection of Jesus (1 Cor 15:3-5) and the last supper (11:23) to the community. The latter tradition comes from the Lord, although this statement probably refers to the community rather than to his own personal revelation.[10] In any event, the transmission of the eucharistic sayings of Jesus in 1 Corinthians constitutes the earliest written account (11:23-25; Mk 14:22-25; Mt 26:26-29; Lk 22:15-20; Jn 6:5-10). In addition to the apostolic tradition, Paul notes the customs of the churches (1 Cor 11:16; 14:35b), the commands of the Lord (1 Cor 14:37),[11] and the preaching of others (1 Cor 15:12).

However, the genius of the apostle is not in the transmission of the tradition but in his interpretation of it. While he does not compromise the truth of the gospel, he appeals to the authority of tradition and custom in several ways,[12] and often argues from it (1 Cor 11:2). In certain instances, he goes beyond what he receives, giving his own interpretation (1 Cor 7:8.12.25.40). The church should maintain the Pauline traditions (1 Cor 11:2), and Paul becomes angry if he sees a perversion of the gospel, attributing any blindness regarding the gospel to a lack of belief. The interaction between experience, tradition, and thought, is key to Paul's interpretive approach.[12] In this context, the tradition changes so that it can continually reveal the light of the gospel.

The content of the tradition focuses primarily on the death and resurrection of Jesus, the basic kerygma so central in the major letters of Paul. The resurrection of Christ engenders hope for the final resurrection of Christians, and the cross, although folly to the Corinthians, is the wisdom of God. This letter also contains an early reference to the pre-existence of Christ (1 Cor 8:6). Thus, the content of the tradition includes

---

[10] See Murphy-O'Connor, *1 Corinthians*, p. 112.

[11] The passages are probably interpolated material; see W. Harrington, ch. 11; "Paul and Women," pp. 148-162, for a brief treatment of similar passages.

[12] See Beker, p. 352.

faith and morals clothed in religious language and related to the issues of the day.

Corinth readily adapts traditions since the restored city has little continuity to its own past. Perhaps the community's background partially accounts for the diversity in its *community life*. While the congregation is primarily Gentile, the members are familiar with Jewish teaching. Cephas, Apollos, and Paul provide an exciting perspective for the church, which tends to show its allegiance to one or another apostle (1 Cor 1:12). However, Paul presents Christ crucified as the source of the Christian community, a point he will reiterate throughout the correspondence. This church gathers together for the celebration of the Lord's Supper (1 Cor 11:17-34) and its questions reflect the issues and concerns of its environment.

The stratified Corinthian community consists of the wise and powerful, slave and free, strong and weak (1 Cor 1:26; 7:21; 8:9-13). Inherent struggles and divisions exist in such a community as the members examine their roles and relationships. While the household model fosters patriarchy, the actual situation in Corinth speaks of women's ministry in the community of faith (1 Cor 11:3-5). The most active and dominant members of the congregation possess high social status, with their enthusiasm and resources an asset for the developing community. In conflict situations Paul urges accommodation on the part of the socially and economically secure, and unity among all the members of the body of Christ.

Paul's long experience in this church leads to very specific qualifications for Christian life. He urges responsible behavior (1 Cor 5:12; 8:9; 11:2-16.31-32; 16:1-4), respect for diverse life situations (7:17), appreciation of the gifts of the Spirit (12:1-14:40). Characterizing the community is love (1 Cor 14:1; 2 Cor 5:14), reconciliation (2 Cor 5:17-19), discernment in faith (2 Cor 13:5). Emphasis on conscience formation (1 Cor 10:25), Christian freedom (8:1-13; 9:1-23), unity (12:12.25), and right order (ch 7, 11, 12), consistently underline other issues and problems.

New relationships result among the members of the body of Christ. If one suffers, all suffer; if one rejoices, all rejoice (1 Cor 12:26). Although there are varieties of gifts, the manifestation of the Spirit is for the development and good of the community (1 Cor 12:4-7), and Paul himself challenges the church to reconciliation, mutual love, and communal support (2 Cor 2:1-9). Because of the various Corinthian letters, we glimpse the process of maturation in this church and the changing relationships within the community (1 Cor 3:1-3; 4:14-15; 14:20).

The Corinthians' community life produces *forms of sharing* that reflect the progression in the apostle's ability to work with this church. Paul follows eighteen months of preaching in Corinth with a letter (1 Cor 5:9); receives oral and written information and responds to it with 1 Corinthians. Subsequent letters (2 Cor 10-13; 1-9) and visits by Timothy, Titus, and Paul (1 Cor 4:17; 16:7; 2 Cor 2:12; 7:5), indicate the kinds of communication between the apostle and the congregation. The letters also indicate the results of these forms of sharing. One letter causes sorrow in the community (2 Cor 7:8-9.12) and a visit causes pain for Paul himself (2:1-2).

With the Corinthians Paul faces the ups and downs of prolonged ministry in a difficult church. He relates rather calmly and analytically to the Corinthian letter to him (1 Cor 7:1), but becomes disturbed at the reports he receives (1 Cor 5:1-2).[13] This community questions Paul's teaching and his ability, to which he responds emphatically, "Even if I am unskilled in speaking, I am not in knowledge" (2 Cor 11:6). Between 1 and 2 Corinthians we identify a change in tone and a deterioration in the relationship between Paul and the church which forces him to defend his ministry and boast of his accomplishments (2 Cor 10-13). Later, he appears to experience a change of heart when he pleads for understanding by the community and asks for reconciliation (2 Cor 1:13-14; 4:7; 5:20; 7:2). In 2 Corinthians, Paul challenges himself and the community as he admits mistakes and shares his personal thoughts.

The apostle teaches the community, making his way through difficult and changing circumstances. Not only does he remind them of previous teaching (1 Cor 2:1-2) but he uses the lapses in the congregation as an occasion for developing his ideas (1

---

[13]See Hurd, pp. 62-63, and 82.

Cor 5:1-8; 8:1-13), and his early eschatological views color some of his remarks (1 Cor 7:29). Realism marks Paul's perspective on the appropriate roles in the Christian assembly as he commends, challenges, and instructs the community, while reflecting on traditions and custom (1 Cor 11:1.17.22.33), and providing the framework for Christian behavior with his teaching on love. By clarification, persuasion, and instruction, Paul tailors his developing insights to the changing situation in Corinth, by creatively exploring the meaning of Christ's death, resurrection, eschatology, and Christian life. He also focuses on ecclesial responsibility and reminds the community of the principles for Christian worship and service. The Corinthian ideas, challenged by the gospel, provide a vivid example of living tradition and developing theology.

Within the community, different forms of sharing emerge with a high priority given to ministry and to the spiritual gifts in the community (1 Cor 12-14). The Spirit allocates a variety of gifts such as prophecy, healing, and discernment for the good of the church. Just as the diverse members of the body work together in unity and harmony, so must the apostles, prophets, teachers, administrators, and helpers in the church. Each one contributes according to his/her particular charism but all earnestly desire the higher gifts. Paul provides a model for the members of the congregation when he selects preaching over baptizing as his own ministry (1 Cor 1:17) and assigns greater importance to the gift of prophecy over speaking in tongues (1 Cor 14:5). The trials of ministry are secondary to service on behalf of the community (2 Cor 11:23-28). Each person contributes by ministry and lifestyle to the edification of the church.

The apostle also uses challenge (1 Cor 4:14-21), confrontation (1 Cor 5:3-4; 1 Cor 11:17), admonition (1 Cor 4:14), and warning (2 Cor 13:2-3) with this church. We can attribute part of his directness to the *opposition* in the community. The Corinthians suffer from a reliance on wisdom and a tendency to judgment (1 Cor 1-4). Quarreling, factions, immorality, and idolatry, characterize the community. Likewise, problems arising from social differences, particularly in the liturgical assembly, concern the apostle. Competition between followers of different apostles and lack of support for Paul within the

Corinthian church cause division within the congregation and stimulate Paul's various attempts at resolution in the letters. He concludes that this church needs outside assistance to maintain order, and so he exerts his apostolic authority.[14] Paul also questions their eschatological perspective (1 Cor 4:5) and false liberalism (1 Cor 8:12). However, the Corinthian church continues to cause Paul much anxiety and tension and he becomes overly defensive in his work with them. This church tests the resilience and the creativity of the apostle.

However, Paul continually demonstrates his concern for the Corinthian church (2 Cor 2:4), assisting them in their struggles and remaining unshaken in his hope for them (2 Cor 1:7). *Building up* the community requires collaboration and responsible effort on the part of leaders and the entire church. Toward this end, Paul reminds the church that God has appointed apostles, prophets, teachers, and others for the building up of the church (1 Cor 12:28; 14:12-23). He exercises his own authority for the very same purpose (2 Cor 10:8; 13:10), and he describes himself as a skilled master builder who proclaims Christ for their growth (1 Cor 3:10; 2 Cor 12:19). Paul reminds them that love builds up, calls them to unity, and encourages them to use their spiritual gifts to foster these values in the church (1 Cor 8:1; 12:12; 14:3).

Likewise, Paul seeks to build up relationships among the churches. He therefore elicits their financial assistance for the Jerusalem church, using the collection to foster unity between the Jewish and Gentile church (1 Cor 16:1-4). Paul considers this unity so essential that he travels to Corinth and then on to Jerusalem. Co-workers, such as Titus, accompany Paul as partners and messengers of the churches (2 Cor 8:19-23) and he urges Apollos to visit them again. Paul readily sends emissaries to the church and receives the Corinthian representatives in Stephanus, Fortunatus, and Achaicus (1 Cor 4:17; 16:17-18), and the reports on the community from Chloë's people. In all these instances, the growth of the community is at stake. Paul encourages the community and adds to these concrete

---

[14]See Betz, *2 Corinthians 8-9*, p. 49; Meeks, p. 117; Peterson, p. 299, who speaks of the exercise of local and translocal authority.

actions by his own suffering on behalf of the church (2 Cor 4:8-13).

Moreover, Paul insists that the Corinthians deal with serious moral issues (1 Cor 5:4-13) and make responsible decisions (1 Cor 3:1-20; 6:1-4; 8:1; 10:15.23). He does not solve local problems by telling the church what to do, for the community itself must act. Rather, he shares theological principles and the insights gained from his ministry in other churches, consistently using the extraordinary personal and ecclesial resources at his disposal to guide the church towards maturity in Christ.

The Corinthian correspondence represents a difficult period in Paul's apostolic ministry, however, his acknowledgement of weakness is a sign of strength and his willingness to be reconciled advances the gospel. The church, too, manifests weakness and strength. The Corinthians' inquiring spirit and recurring misunderstanding, while causing considerable difficulty for Paul, foster a continuing relationship between founder and church.

Paul's Ministry in Romans

Paul's letter to the Romans reflects a different orientation from his previous correspondence. He writes to "all God's beloved in Rome, who are called to be saints" (Rom 1:7), never calling this group a church. The term *ekklesia* only appears in chapter 16 with references to the church of Cenchreae (Rom 16:1), the house-church of Priscilla and Aquila (Rom 16:5), and all the churches of Christ (Rom 16:16). If the community's lack of an apostolic founder leads to this omission, Paul still writes them a very ecclesial letter. He plans to visit Rome (Rom 1:10.13; 15:22-24), since his own current work is now complete and he plans to then travel on to Spain.

Paul writes this letter at his leisure, after the conflicts in Galatia and Corinth and does not carry over the previous difficulties into this new situation. Rather, he presents his fullest theological statement to a group that has not met him. Looking forward to a new phase of ministry, Paul goes to Jerusalem before his journey to Rome, armed with the wisdom of his experience and his theological reflections. Romans, written to Gentile Christians (Rom 1:5.13-15; 11:13), contains no major discussion of the resurrection but rather focuses on Paul's prime interest, the theological relationship of Jew and Gentile. In Romans, we expect, and discover, a maturity in Paul and a new integration of his message to the churches.

The Roman community has a Christian history prior to Paul's visit and a unique situation in regard to community membership.[15] However, Paul "set apart for the gospel of God" will preach his gospel to them (Rom 1:1.15), a gospel that recalls the *tradition* of the Jewish community. Chapters 9-11 contain more references to scripture than any other comparable Pauline passage, and traditional confessional formulas throughout the letter identify basic religious convictions. The subsequent interpretation of the tradition captures the imagination of Jewish and Gentile Christians (Rom 1:3; 3:24-26; 4:25; 8:34; 10:9; 14:9).[16] Paul, while recalling biblical promises, proclaims his own gospel as their fulfillment (Rom 1:2). As he stresses continuity of the tradition in Romans, he struggles with the consistent application of this principle in regard to the law (Rom 7:16). Paul writes boldly as a "minister of Christ Jesus to the Gentiles in the priestly service of the gospel of God" (Rom 15:15-16), and the community must interpret his proclamation in terms of their own religious background and development.

Romans 1:16-17 and 3:21-26 contain the essence of Paul's gospel: it is the "power of God for salvation to everyone who has faith, to the Jew first and also to the Greek." God shows no partiality for he extends his righteousness to all those who have faith in Christ Jesus. This priority of Israel in the plan of salvation cannot be misconstrued as exclusive access to salvation (Rom 11:25) for faith widens the possibilities for acceptance of the gospel. How Paul establishes this universal gospel on a strong theological foundation constitutes the genius of Romans.

The letter to the Romans takes a giant step forward in its description of *community life*. Paul connects life and wor-

---

[15] For a discussion of the Roman community and the purpose of Romans, see K. Donfried.

[16] See Reumann, pp. 434, and 450; Conzelmann, *Theology*, p. 166.

ship, centering both ethical behavior and authentic worship in the world, (Rom 12:1) and grounding all his moral prescriptions in terms of charity (Rom 12:9-10). This genuine, persevering, and affectionate love, enables the community to rejoice in hope, be patient in tribulation, and constant in prayer. While Christians meet the needs of all and practice hospitality, they also expect and embrace suffering (Rom 5:3-5; 12:12-15). Their duties include responsibilities within the community, obedience to authority, payment of taxes and of other debts (Rom 13:1-11). The strong members of the congregation show deference to the weak, and Christians avoid those who create dissension in their midst (Rom 15:1; 16:17). This community possesses the life of Christ, is the one body of Christ, and appropriately uses the gifts of prophecy, teaching, exhortation, and mercy (Rom 12:4-8), reflecting the transformation that occurs on all levels because of God's gift in Christ (Rom 6:5-8; ch 8).

The Christian church in Romans incorporates the new relationship between Jew and Gentile in the community of faith and Paul urges mutual love, respect, and unity in this context. His personal anguish regarding his people causes Paul to present Israel in favorable light and challenge the Gentiles to a renewed appreciation of their Jewish heritage (Rom 3:1-3; 9:2-3; 11:11-14). God's call and fidelity provide a basis for hope in the Roman community. The apostle's appreciation of a gospel that unites Jews and Gentiles conditions his view of membership in the Christian community and directs his dialogue with the Roman Christians.

Paul's presentation of theological views and their implications for the community, constitute the prime *forms of sharing* in this letter. The apostle to the Gentiles reflects his personal maturity in Romans as he formulates the universal implications of his gospel and supplies theological foundations for the unique experience of this Christian community. An inner logic dominates the correspondence and contributes to its structure.[17] The new creation demands a different understanding of faith, works, the law, justification, and salvation. Paul dia-

---

[17]See Cranfield, pp. 27, 818.

logues with the Jews, while explicitly teaching the Gentiles and expanding their horizons. He acknowledges the advantages of Judaism (Rom 3:1-2; 9:4-5), the goodness of the law (Rom 7:7-23; 9:31-33; 13:8), and God's fidelity to Israel (Rom 11:1.11.25-26), placing the Gentile's salvation in this context (Rom 11:25). He also realistically assesses humankind's sinfulness and its essential need for God's action in Christ (Rom 7:7-8). Underlying Paul's reflections in this letter is his own personal experience and struggle as a believer.

Frequently, the diatribe (Rom 2:1-20) and a simpler question-answer style of communication (Rom 3:1-8) explicate Paul's argument for the community. He refines topics presented in earlier letters (Gal 3-4; 1 Cor 15:22. 45-49; 56-57), and parallels ideas (Rom 3 & 9),[18] refining, rephrasing, and building on his previous theology. Paradox (Rom 7:14-25; ch 8), individual arguments and vivid images (Rom 9-11) often define his style. Romans persuades and convinces, presenting a balanced discussion of its central issue, the relationship between Jew and Gentile in a changing church. Paul exhorts the community to live according to its faith, in unity, mutual love, and service. Having been transformed in Christ, it can now live according to these theological premises (Rom 6:2-5; 8:15-17).

This community and the broader church face *obstacles* to this kind of growth in identity and self-understanding. The real opponent in the letter, if there is one, is the Jew and the contemporary Jewish approach to salvation.[19] Paul reflects on his response to such people and groups in light of his impending visit to Jerusalem. The larger issue for Paul is the relationship between the church and Israel, and, on a smaller scale, the Roman community reflects this struggle. Likewise, church membership is not an abstract concern, nor is the rejection of Christ by the Jews. Paul attempts to specify the value of the law while proclaiming a new law in Christ, and he interprets salvation history centering on Abraham's faith as significant for both Jew and Gentile. His attempts to solidly

---

[18]Karris, "Rom 14:1-15:13," pp. 165-167, identifies verbal parallels between this section of Romans and 1 Cor, ch. 8-11.

[19]See Sanders, *Palestinian Judaism*, p. 488.

base universal salvation in the history of the Jewish community, constitute the backbone of the letter.

When he addresses the particular Roman situation of the strong and the weak, Paul advocates acceptance of more traditional tendencies, and responsible behavior on the part of all (Rom 14:13). Simple concerns regarding food and circumcision reflect deeper issues for the church since they herald its ultimate separation from Judaism. Romans, then, addresses the issues of the larger church as well as those of the local community. Since Paul has yet to visit Rome, the letter differs sharply from Galatians, with an absence of extreme conflict and confrontation in this correspondence. He can therefore anticipate a different kind of ministry in this community.

Paul's positive tone fosters community growth and facilitates further *building up* of the community of faith. For the Jerusalem church, the apostle demonstrates a change in approach and refinement in his theological presentation compared with the earlier letter to the Galatians. This certainly builds ties with the leaders in Jerusalem. Because of his precise articulation of religious and ethnic relationships, Paul contributes to the understanding of the church in regard to its Jewish roots and Gentile expansion. The newness of the Christian message emerges in this letter and Paul's diplomatic approach leads to its acceptance. In this letter, Paul brings balance and direction to theological issues, paving the way for his effectiveness with a community he will soon visit. The apostle appropriately makes contact with this church and shows himself to be an enterprising religious leader.

In Romans 16, a probable addition to the correspondence, Christians in the various churches exchange greetings and offer commendations. Building the community requires people who collaborate and minister in a spirit of unity and mutual support. The letter to the Romans reflects the apostle's personal resolution of his faith in Christ with his Pharisaic background, reiterates God's irrevocable choice of his people, Israel, and clarifies a key concept of the identity of the early church, its relation to Judaism. Paul also prepares the community to accept his gospel and gains their interest for his proposed missionary activity.

Paul's Ministry in Philippians

The letter to the Philippians, a composite of three separate letters (1:1-2; 4:10-20 = Letter A; 1:3-3:1; 4:4-9, 21-23 = Letter B; 3:2-4:3 = Letter C) constitutes the last will and testament of the apostle Paul (Phil 1:1-3:1; 4:2-9, 21-23), and testifies to his special relationship with this community. While a tone similar to Romans permeates the entire correspondence, the language is considerably more affectionate, joyful, and encouraging. The Philippian church holds a special place in Paul's heart for it is his first congregation on European soil. However, it is not an ideal community for Paul experiences imprisonment and shameful treatment at Philippi (1 Thess 2:2), conflicting teaching still persists (Phil 1:16-17), and the congregation itself struggles with problems and pettiness (Phil 3:2; 4:2-3). In this letter, Paul addresses the entire congregation, "all the saints in Christ Jesus who are at Philippi, with the bishops and deacons" (Phil 1:1). The uniqueness of the church rests in its leadership, particularly the leadership role of women,[20] and in its personal and financial support of Paul. Written from prison, the letter marks a new phase in the life of the apostle and his ministry to the churches.

Paul initially preaches the gospel to this community, so their understanding of the *tradition* can be attributed to him. He draws on his original preaching and example (Phil 4:9), as he exhorts the community to stand firm in the Lord. Surprisingly, Paul rejoices that others proclaim the gospel, even though he might question their motivation (Phil 1:15-18). He also perceives his own imprisonment and suffering as a means of advancing the gospel (Phil 1:12) and a result of his defense of it (Phil 1:16). Paul's confidence rests on his profound understanding of life in Christ, and as a servant of Christ Jesus, he seeks union with him in life or in death (Phil 1:19-26). Paul and this community enter into partnership early in his ministry (Phil 4:15), and he continually displays his confidence in them. In the Philippian hymn (2:6-11), Paul emphasizes Christ as the model for the community, demonstrating

---

[20]See Thomas, pp. 117-118.

again the connection between christology and ecclesiology. The prime focus of Paul's work in this church is the gospel of Christ and its implications for community life.

The Philippian congregation is a refreshing change from the churches in Galatia and Corinth, a change reflected in its *community life*. These Gentile Christians have an unwavering loyalty to Paul, and he devotes himself to them. Joy, contentment, and confidence mark their relationship, with Paul always remembering them with love (Phil 1:3-8) and longing for them (4:1). He shares his experience of suffering and difficulty, and both he and the community find strength in Christ, the source of their life, perseverance, and growth (Phil 2:5.13; 3:15-16; 4:5. 12-13). The apostles' favorite theme of unity, centered in Christ and expressed in the Christian's life together, frequently surfaces in this letter.

The remarkable aspect of community is the mutual love, respect, and support, existing between Paul and the church, that elicits a deep *form of sharing*. Paul shares in a deeply personal manner, revealing feelings of love and longing for the community (Phil 1:7-8; 4:1), sharing his plight with them (1:12) and expressing pleasure at their concern for him (4:10). Chapter 3 of the letter contains a spiritual autobiography in which Paul reveals his deep commitment to Christ and his anticipation of what lies ahead. To have an apostolic founder speak to the church with this intensity and depth witnesses to their mutual trust and respect. Likewise, this letter shows that Paul's personal concerns are secondary to the needs of the church. Rather than focusing on himself during a crucial period in his life, Paul's apostolic spirituality stimulates him to prepare the church for the challenges ahead of it (Phil 2:12; 3:16-17).

The apostle exhorts the community to work out their salvation and to hold fast to the word of life (Phil 2:12.16), exhortations centering on the life and growth of the church. Paul also entreats Evodia and Syntyche to agree to the Lord (Phil 4:2). Singling out these women reminds the church of their role in the community and reinforces the theme of unity. Such confrontation in a spirit of friendship and concern underscores the solidity of their mutual relationship. Paul offers no serious rebukes for this church and gives up debating with his adversaries (Phil 1:18). In these approaches he responds to the situation of the community and may also be influenced by his own incarceration.

Finally, Paul accepts assistance from this congregation and urges them to continue their support. While he can effectively deal with the circumstances of abundance and want, Paul gratefully accepts their monetary gifts and the ministry of Epaphroditus (Phil 2:25; 4:10-20). The human side of Paul filters through his words and action.

Sharing in the community takes on various forms as they personally reach out to Paul with sincerity and love. Faith marks their existence with these convictions tempering their lifestyle. The Philippian church works for unity and strives to restore harmony when it is absent. Their spirit of joy characterizes their acceptance of the gospel and their persevering approach to Christian life. The death and glorification of the Lord becomes the paradigm for their communal interaction, just as it is for Paul.

Few *obstacles* to growth exist in the Philippian church, although opposing preachers become more confident because of Paul's imprisonment, and problems surface because of their activity (Phil 1:27; 2:16; 4:1). The evildoers who mutilate the flesh are enemies of the cross of Christ that the community should not follow (Phil 3:2, 18-19). The existence of another gospel and a rejection of the importance of the death of Christ concern Paul, but he trusts the ultimate response of this church. Within the community, the disagreements between Evodia and Syntyche on ecclesial issues elicit concern. Subtle problems of conceit, superiority, and selfishness, also tend to plague the church.[21] However, this community causes Paul comparatively few difficulties and gives him great personal and ministerial satisfaction. His ability to handle the rigors of imprisonment from the perspective of Christian hope indicates the apostle's spiritual growth and maturity at this point in his life.

With this church, Paul takes active steps to seek out collaborators to insure the *building up* of the faith community in the future. He is not imprisoned by his own limitations but creatively thinks and acts. While anticipating his own fruitful labor

---

[21] See Martin, pp. 31-32.

if the authorities release him, Paul sends Timothy to assess the needs of the church and report the good news back to him (Phil 2:19-24). The apostle builds up this co-worker, indicating an appreciation of his valuable service of the gospel. "I have no one like him, who will be genuinely anxious for your welfare" (Phil 2:20). Continuity in mission is a concern for Paul, and he readily acts in the interests of the church. Paul also accepts the ministry of Epaphroditus and utilizes this messenger for the good of the church. Likewise, the apostle identifies the women, Evodia and Syntyche, as laborers and co-workers for the sake of the gospel, and he presents Clement in a similar way. Paul requests that the community assist, if necessary, in the resolution of any persisting difficulties. In the bishops and deacons of the community, some form of ecclesial order begins to emerge, although the letter does not indicate specific roles or responsibilities.

Finally, the community itself enters into partnership with Paul (Phil 1:5; 4:15), and he acknowledges this long-standing relationship. Because of the quality of collaboration with the community and the cooperation within it, Paul rests secure in his delegation of authority and his hopes for the church's continued growth.

The Philippian church consolidates Paul's experience as an apostle to the Gentiles. He and the community model an unparalleled relationship between apostle and local church, and both Paul and the community deserve praise for their mutual efforts and continued growth in difficult, and changing, circumstances.

Paul's Ministry in Philemon

This unique and brief New Testament letter begins: "Paul, a prisoner for Christ Jesus, and Timothy our brother, To Philemon our beloved fellow worker, and Apphia our sister and Archippus our fellow soldier, and the church in your house" (Phlm 1-2). At first glance, this letter is personal, addressed to the Christian head of a household previously converted by Paul. However, it is also sent to the house-church, and its central issue, the acceptance of a runaway slave, has social and political implications. Paul, imprisoned himself, identifies the plight of Onesimus showing compassion characteristic of the Jewish approach to slavery.[22] The apostle speaks to Philemon, Onesimus' master and a beloved co-worker, making a request on behalf of the slave Paul converted (Phlm 10). The letter offers an interesting perspective on how Paul deals with individuals in the church as well as with issues.

In verse 13, the apostle presents a gentle reminder that his own imprisonment is for the sake of the gospel. This gospel *tradition* proclaimed by Paul to both Philemon and Onesimus, provides the basis for his subsequent appeal. Christian faith and a new identity in Christ constitute the source of life and relationships in the believing community (Phlm 6.8.9.15.20). While the letter does not propose a social policy, it sets the stage for the undermining of the institution of slavery by changing personal attitudes in accord with gospel values. There is neither slave nor free in the Christian church, where all are one in Christ (Gal 3:28). Paul takes this principle and that of forgiveness, applying them to a situation of personal concern. He seeks a Christian response in this specific instance, knowing full well that competing demands persist in the church and in the world.

Since the source of *community life* is the Lord, equality among members should characterize those united to him. Within the house-church, a new reality exists that removes former distinctions, and so the possibility of a slave gaining freedom is realistic, and Philemon can no longer be master in the church or, for that matter, in the social sphere.[23] Paul's request and religious views have social ramifications, if Philemon understands the underlying message in the letter. The Christian community thus creates a new society when it lives out the communal ideal of radical equality: the slave becomes "brother"; and the household structure redefines itself in egalitarian terms (Phlm 16.20).

Some creative and subtle *forms of sharing* indicate how Paul gets across his message. Rather than exercise his apostolic

---

[22]See Cullmann, p. 202.

[23]See Peterson, p. 269, where he provides an interesting analysis of this letter. See particularly pp. 90-93; 269, 290, 295.

right to command what he desires, Paul prefers to appeal to Philemon as an ambassador and prisoner in Christ (Phlm 9). He appeals not only to the head of the household but includes Apphia, his wife, Archippus, his son, and the entire church, consisting of approximately thirty people. Philemon is in a conspicuous position, with local pressure exerted by the community. Paul provokes a crisis for his partner in Christ by presenting this request, and Philemon must choose between two very different worlds by identifying his responsibility to the social institutions of his day. However, the apostle expresses confidence about the outcome, indicating that Philemon will do more than he suggests (Phlm 21). Paul uses persuasion and subtle implication; he also plays on the meaning of Onesimus' name, "useful" (Phlm 11). Likewise, he exercises his authority in regard to a house-church, hoping to modify behavior and change attitudes.

Within the community, prayer and sharing of faith provide the basic openness and insight for change (Phlm 6). Paul expects obedience, but he also wants consent to occur because of free will (Phlm 14.21). He encourages Philemon and the church to receive Onesimus as they would Paul himself and assumes responsibility for any debt (Phlm 18-19). The apostle anticipates that this house-church will remain hospitable to him and hopes to visit them soon (Phlm 20). Obviously, Paul has freedom of communication with this church and with the individuals in it. He shares his views and elicits a positive response.

If there is an *obstacle* to growth and change in the community, societal pressures would be primary. "Standing there on his own doorstep, Philemon is a man on the threshold between two worlds."[24] Society, particularly the Roman world, would justify a particular approach to the situation of a runaway slave. Philemon, however, must make a decision about himself and his responsibility as a Christian. Paul's subtle confrontation provokes a crisis that needs resolution and has far reaching implications for those involved.

For a brief and purposeful letter, we can identify a surprisingly large number of people and relationships. By their roles

[24]Peterson, p. 270.

and dynamic interactions all members *build up* the community of faith. Paul is the apostle, responsible for the Christian life of Philemon and his household. Philemon is a co-worker and partner with Paul. The letter mentions other co-workers, such as Timothy, Epaphras, Mark, Aristarchus, Demas, and Luke (Phlm 1.23-24). Slavery, imprisonment, household roles, and Christian relationships define and describe the intricate patterns of interaction and responsibility. While there is no explicit mention of building up the church, these members of the community are in fact doing just that by their response to Paul's appeal. Philemon feels the responsibility most keenly, but the community itself can influence the direction of his choice. While this letter is brief and focused, it provides us with some indication of Paul's interaction with individuals in the church. As an apostolic leader, Paul takes a stand regarding Onesimus, presents his ideas to Philemon, and indirectly confronts a social issue from the perspective of faith.

Paul's ministry in the local communities provides the basis for his understanding of church and also reflects his perspective. His vision of church results in great measure from his experience, his interaction with others, and his theological reflection. In our examination of the letters, we see that Paul is well aware of the tradition of the early church. He preaches a gospel that rests solidly within the tradition, although he emphasizes that he receives his revelation from the Lord. In his ministry, he freely interprets and expands the tradition to meet the needs of the various communities.

His views on community life, quite radical in the freedom and equality they suggest, stimulate the early church to think beyond the patriarchal structures of the day. Likewise, each community addressed in the letters clearly witnesses basic Christian values in its lifestyle. Relationships develop and various forms of sharing attest to the quality of life in these faith communities. The apostle seeks to maintain gospel values and so he uses persuasion and argument to address deviant situations in the churches. His strong theological approach to pertinent issues presents the church in any age with an effective model for its own use. Discernment affects decisions and determines directions in this early phase of church life.

However, Paul's ministry to the churches is not a panacea, for both he and the community face obstacles within and outside the congregation. Serious problems such as the abandonment of the gospel, and ongoing tensions, such as those existing when diverse people begin to live as church, receive the attention of the apostle. He encourages local churches to address different situations as part of their own Christian responsibility. Building up the community remains an active concern for the apostle and the local churches, leading Paul to seek collaborators in his mission and in the communities. Paul's experience in the churches becomes a formative influence in his ecclesiology, and he articulates and clarifies his vision of church while he engages in his ministry.

Thus, Paul's understanding of church does not develop in a vacuum. Rather, his experience shapes and modifies his theological views. Traditions need adaptation and reinterpretation for changing times and places. Communal life depends in part on leaders, but more significantly on the local church, which bears prime responsibility in this area.

Paul assumes a particular style of relating to the churches, often dependent on the quality of their mutual relationships. However, while he does not renege on his own responsibility as apostle and servant of the gospel, he consistently challenges the churches to discern their direction, utilize their gifts for ministry, and live in a spirit of freedom and love. Crisis frequently leads to creative theological or existential approaches, and collaboration in ministry reflects the vitality of the early church. Paul's ministry in the churches clarifies the meaning of his conversional commitment; his work and his reflection on its significance lead to the ecclesiology we will examine in the next chapter.

4

Essential Components of the Church in Paul

"For as many of you as were baptized into Christ have put on Christ. There is neither Jew nor Greek, there is neither slave nor free, there is neither male nor female; for you are all one in Christ Jesus." (Gal 3:27-28)

The church exists in the gathering together of believers in Jesus, who express their faith in their celebrations, their lifestyle, and their service. As Paul reflects on his experience of these local churches, their diversity must impress him. However, he is also conscious of a unity within, and among, the churches. As apostle to the Gentiles, Paul begins to formulate his ideas about the church as he ministers to these Christian communities. He integrates his own conversional insight regarding the relationship between Christ and Christians, as well as his own background as a Pharisee and a diaspora Jew. Within the letters we discover early expressions and formulations of church identity. We also visualize, as Paul did, that the church is a dynamic reality. Paul engages in a process of interaction and involvement with others, with his theological insight a result of this dialogic experience. As we read Paul's letters, we become keenly aware that we are in contact with the earliest ecclesiology available to the contemporary church.

Chapters 4, 5, and 6, explore Paul's understanding of the church. This chapter deals with the essential components of church life: the sources of church life, its foundation in faith, the experiences of church life with its expressions in worship and service, its structures, and its relational dimensions. Paul refers to these aspects, constitutive of the church itself, in the authentic correspondence. Chapter 5, identifies how Paul envisions and explains this reality of church by examining his models of the church. Chapter 6, presents the ecclesial spirituality, lived out in this early period, that can continue to enrich the church in our own times. The components, models, and spirituality of church, provide a way of coming to grips with Paul's vision, experience, and life in the church.

The Sources of Church Life

In the conversion experience God reveals his Son to Paul (Gal 1:15-16). The Spirit of Christ, always present in the community, further clarifies the apostles experience of the Lord (1 Cor 12:4-11). Although Paul's situational approach to the various churches is foundational for his ecclesiology, he does not succumb to the weakness of this approach, which is an "inadequate appreciation of the transcendent."[1] For Paul, the church, so central to his preaching, is best understood in terms of God's redemptive work in Christ.[2] In fact, Christ is the focal point of his understanding of church and "the glory of the Father and Son in the Spirit of liberty" is its final word.[3] The source of church life is God, whom Paul frequently refers to as Father. Through the Spirit, Christ lives in his church, and this Spirit makes real God's gift to the community. How God calls the church into being, constitutes its identity in Christ, and empowers it through the Spirit, is the subject of this section.

---

[1] Baird, p. 58.
[2] See Ridderbos, p. 327.
[3] Moltmann, p. 19.

CALLED BY GOD

The idea of call is basic to Paul's understanding of church, for God calls the church into being because of his graciousness and his love. "O the depth of the riches and the wisdom and knowledge of God! How unsearchable are his judgments and how inscrutable his ways!" (Rom 11:33). The one God of Israel remains faithful to his promises to Abraham, but now extends his call to all who believe, attaching no conditions to his free gift of eternal life in Christ Jesus (Rom 3:24; 6:23; Gal 2:21). Thus God's call includes the Gentiles who are also the "beloved by God" (1 Thess 1:4), justified and glorified (Rom 8:29-30).

Because of his call, God's righteousness becomes that of the believer (Rom 1:17), whom he reconciles to himself (2 Cor 5:18). Not only does God offer the possibility of transformation, but he provides blessing in abundance (2 Cor 9:8), supplying every need "according to his riches in glory in Christ Jesus" (Phil 4:19). The church responds to this gift by the quality of its life of faith, hope, and love (2 Cor 6:1; 1 Thess 1:3), although Paul continues to pray that God will make us worthy of this tremendous call (1 Thess 5:23-24). Both the call of God and our response result from the grace of God, truly making the church and the Christian, the beloved of God. At the beginning of his letters to the churches, Paul refers to this reality of God's gracious call.

However, we receive and understand God's gift because he sent his Son, who becomes the power and the wisdom of God to all who believe (1 Cor 1:24; Rom 1:16-17). Because of our union in him, we share in the glory of God, becoming sons and daughters in him. God calls us to live a new life because of our union with Christ. This is the beginning of Paul's deepening insight into the identity of the church and his own motivation to "press on toward the goal for the prize of the upward call of God in Christ Jesus" (Phil 3:14).

BAPTIZED IN THE NAME OF JESUS

The theology of Paul is essentially christocentric, since God now reveals his righteousness and offers salvation in Christ

Jesus. Jesus is Messiah, who embodies for us the pattern and purpose of God's dealings with the world. Jesus is Lord, and "every one who calls upon the name of the Lord will be saved" (Rom 10:13). Jesus is the fulfillment of God's promises, and we "are justified by his grace as a gift, through the redemption which is in Christ Jesus" (Rom 3:24). Jesus is the Son of God and as Son enjoys a special relationship with the Father (1 Cor 15:28; 2 Cor 1:19; Rom 8:3.15; Gal 4:4.6).

Although we can identify Jesus in his relationship to the Father, we can also describe Jesus in relationship to the church and to the Christian. Christ is Lord of the church, so let "every tongue confess that Jesus Christ is Lord, to the glory of God the Father" (Phil 2:11). If we do profess belief in him, in faith and in baptism, then we enter into a unique relationship. Baptism incorporates us into Christ and into the community. In baptism, Christians "put on Christ" (Gal 3:27), being also "baptized into one body ... and all ... made to drink of one Spirit" (1 Cor 12:13). Baptism washes, sanctifies, and justifies us (1 Cor 6:11), and through the Lord Jesus Christ, we receive "our reconciliation" (Rom 5:11). However, something more profound occurs. In baptism we "put on the new person," for we "have been baptized into Christ Jesus, ... buried, therefore, with him by baptism into death, so that as Christ was raised from the dead by the glory of the Father, we too might walk in newness of life" (Rom 6:3-4). Through baptism we participate in Christ's death and resurrection, but Christ also transforms our Christian lives, for in him we are the new creation. "If anyone is in Christ, he [or she] is a new creation; the old creation; the old one has passed away, behold, the new has come" (2 Cor 5:17).

Christians live this new life in Christ in community and in the service of one another. In the Philippian hymn Paul reminds us that Christ "though he was in the form of God, did not count equality with God a thing to be grasped, but emptied himself, taking the form of a servant" (Phil 2:6-7). This hymn becomes a paradigm for life in the Christian church: "Have this mind among yourselves, which you have in Christ Jesus" (Phil 2:5), who "though he was rich, yet for your sake he became poor" (2 Cor 8:9). This reality engages Paul's mind and imagination and becomes the essence of life for all who are sons and daughters of God through faith (Gal 3:26). In fact, he goes on to reflect: "Who shall separate us from the love of Christ? Shall tribulation, or distress, or persecution, or famine, or nakedness, or peril, or sword?" (Rom 8:35). Nothing "will be able to separate us from the love of God in Christ Jesus our Lord" (Rom 8:39). Being baptized into Christ marks the beginning of our Christian existence, and as such, initiates our new life in Christ.

SANCTIFIED AND MISSIONED BY THE SPIRIT

As church, we are not only called by God, and baptized in the name of the Lord Jesus, but God also "gives his Holy Spirit" to us (1 Thess 4:8). Paul writes "you are a letter from Christ . . . written not with ink but with the Spirit of the living God, not on tablets of stone but tablets of human hearts" (2 Cor 3:3). Paul identifies the Spirit with God, Christ, the church, and the Christian. The Spirit of God who "raised Jesus from the dead dwells in you" (Rom 8:11). God also sends his Spirit into our hearts but it is "the Spirit of his Son" crying out "Abba, Father" (Gal 4:6). We know the power of the Spirit and by this power we "abound in hope" (Rom 15:13). As Christians, "our sufficiency is from God, who has qualified us to be ministers of a new covenant, not in a written code but in the Spirit; for the written code kills, but the Spirit gives life" (2 Cor 3:5-6). "For this is the will of God, your sanctification" (1 Thess 4:3) and it is the Holy Spirit who sanctifies (Rom 15:16).

Paul closely associates the Spirit with Christ, particularly in his cross and in his glorification (Rom 8:3.17; 1 Cor 2:8).[4] "The Spirit can be identified with Christ in all sorts of ways because it is in Christ's advent and work that the work of the Spirit manifests itself, fulfilling and propelling toward the consummation."[5] Christ and the Spirit define each other, and the

---

[4]See Beker, pp. 291, 293-294, who notes that Paul frames Romans 8:4-16 with two references to the cross but also identifies that the spirit is more closely related to the glory of God and the parousia.

[5]Ridderbos, p. 88.

Spirit communicates Christ to us.[6] "For by one Spirit we were all baptized into one body—Jews or Greeks, slaves or free—and all were made to drink of one Spirit" (1 Cor 12:13).

The Spirit constitutes us as church for God "gives his Holy Spirit" to us (1 Thess 4:8) "as a guarantee" (2 Cor 5:5), and to help us "understand the gifts bestowed on us by God" (1 Cor 2:12). We are "taught by the Spirit, interpreting spiritual truths to those who possess the Spirit" (1 Cor 2:13). Christ works in the church through his Spirit, liberating us to effectively build up the church (Rom 8:2-4; Gal 5:13; 1 Cor 14:12). "The Lord is the Spirit, and where the Spirit of the Lord is, there is freedom" (2 Cor 3:17). This Spirit is the basis of our life as church and the source of our unity, for anyone "united to the Lord becomes one spirit with him," and we all share that same Spirit (1 Cor 6:17; 12:4).

Paul describes Christian life in terms of the Spirit, for in the Spirit, we enter into a relationship with God (1 Cor 2:10-14), and thus can live and walk by the Spirit (Gal 5:25). Paul assumes that all Christians possess the Spirit, since "it is the Spirit himself bearing witness with our spirit that we are children of God" (Rom 8:16). "Likewise the Spirit helps us in our weakness"; and "intercedes for us with sighs too deep for words" (Rom 8:26). Paul associates this same Spirit with spiritual gifts. "Now there are varieties of gifts, but the same Spirit; and there are varieties of service, but the same Lord; and there are varieties of working, but it is the same God who inspires them all in everyone" (1 Cor 12:4-6). These "manifestations of the Spirit" are "for the common good" (1 Cor 12:7). The Spirit of Christ makes us holy, forms us into one body, and gives us gifts for use in the service of the church.

Paul's understanding of God as Father and Son, manifested in the community and the Christian by the Spirit is central to his understanding of church. God will be glorified as this community lives according to its call. Those who are baptized into Christ, live transformed by the Spirit. To apprehend God as the ultimate source of church life, occurs only through faith. Christians share a common faith which becomes the ground of their existence as church.

---

[6] See Ziesler, pp. 45-46.

The Foundations of Church Life

The foundation of our life as church is a faith which all in the community share. This faith, never defined by Paul, is God's gift to the church, a gift that elicits a response of love and service from those who accept it. Christian faith centers on the person, Jesus, and the mystery of his death and resurrection. The Christian's union with Christ and realization of the consequences of faith, lead to a qualitatively different life for the church. This faith foundation of the church directs the Christian's attention to an essential component of church life.

A COMMON FAITH

"If you confess with your lips that Jesus is Lord and believe in your heart that God raised him from the dead, you will be saved" (Rom 10:9). This early confession of faith embodies the core elements of the Christian community. Faith alone begins the process of Christian existence and provides the foundation of the Christian church. Faith is in Jesus, particularly manifested in convictions regarding his death and resurrection. This most basic response in those saved results in our mission as church. Paul frequently speaks of how a community's "faith in God has gone forth everywhere" (1 Thess 1:8) and of his own comfort in that faith (1 Thess 3:7). A common faith binds the community together and Paul thanks "God through Christ Jesus for all of you, because your faith is proclaimed in all the world" (Rom 1:8).

JUSTIFIED BY FAITH

As Paul reflects on this faith, he brings a number of his Pharisaic convictions into his Christian teaching.[7] In Romans 4, he also integrates the faith of Abraham and Christian faith, by demonstrating that "Abraham believed God, and it was reckoned to him as righteousness" (Rom 4:3). Even "the

---

[7] See Patte, p. 117.

promise to Abraham and his descendants" comes "through the righteousness of faith" (Rom 4:13). Now God fulfills his promises in Christ, but continues to justify by faith (Rom 3:26; 5:1).[8] Justification by faith in Christ marks the new community of believers, the community we call church. This faith is always God's gift, expressed now as faith in a person, and as faith that responds in thanksgiving, love, and service.

Our faith as church "in Jesus" marks the "end of the law" and the beginning of the new age (Rom 3:26; 10:4), an assessment resulting not "from a human point of view" (2 Cor 5:16) but from our openness to God's revelation "that depends on faith" (Phil 3:9). Christ himself lived by faith as he expressed his obedience to the Father's will.[9] Paul presents this theme in his gospel and uses Christ's response as a model for the Christian community.

RESPONSES TO FAITH

"Faith comes from what is heard, and what is heard comes by the preaching of Christ" (Rom 10:17). Knowledge qualifies and directs faith, so that Paul can appropriately call for understanding and an enlightened approach in the community (1 Cor 1-4). Faith also elicits certain patterns of behavior for "we walk by faith" (2 Cor 5:7), "stand firm" in faith (2 Cor 1:24), are watchful, courageous, and strong in faith (1 Cor 16:13). An acceptance and obedience to the Father's call characterizes such faith (Rom 6:16; 15:18; 16:19) and allows believers to discover the Lord in the present circumstances of their lives. Faith becomes then, a total response to God's gift in Christ and initiates the new existence in a community of freedom, unity, and love. "For freedom Christ has set us free" (Gal 5:1), and so "let your manner of life be worthy of the gospel of Christ ... stand firm in one Spirit, with one mind striving side by side for the faith of the gospel" (Phil 1:27). Demonstrate your faith by "working through love" and "through love be servants of one another" (Gal 5:6.13).

---

[8] Hanson, *Technique,* pp. 73-74, parallels the faith of Abraham, Christ, and Christians, and the process of justification in outline form.

[9] See Johnson, p. 89.

THE CENTRAL MYSTERY OF CHRISTIAN FAITH

Our shared faith becomes even more explicitly directed, for it is a belief in God's salvific action in the death and resurrection of Jesus. Wayne Meeks reflects on this reality: "The node around which Pauline beliefs crystallized was the crucifixion and resurrection of God's son, the Messiah. This was destined to prove one of the most powerful symbols that has ever appeared in the history of religions; in the earliest years of the Christian movement, no one seems to have recognized its generative potential so quickly and so comprehensively as Paul and his associates."[10] While the death and resurrection are two aspects of the single Christ event, we will examine the significance of each, before looking at their combined challenge on the level of faith.

Paul's preaching in the early church did not consist of the "testimony of God in lofty words or wisdom. For I decided to know nothing among you except Jesus and him crucified" (1 Cor 2:1-2). The *death of Jesus* indicates God's fidelity to the covenant (Rom 3:25) and reveals even further the mystery of God, who "shows his love for us in that while we were yet sinners Christ died for us" (Rom 5:8). God "did not spare his own Son but gave him up for us all" (Rom 8:32). This action grounds our faith not only in the person Christ, but also in a historic event. The cross, however, remains a "stumbling block," "foolishness," and a scandal (Gal 5:11; 1 Cor 1:18.23), when viewed only as death and judgment. However, it also marks the beginning of the new age and the turning point of history for "the Cross of Christ is the place where the sin of [humanity] meets the forgiveness of God."[11]

"All of us who have been baptized into Christ Jesus were baptized into his death" (Rom 6:3). But Paul goes on to say "if we have died with Christ, we believe that we shall also live with him" (Rom 6:8). The death of Christ and our participation in it, enables us to understand weakness and suffering in a different light (Phil 3:8-11). By his death "our old self was crucified" and we are "freed from sin" (Rom 6:6-7). For us

---

[10] Meeks, p. 180.
[11] Perrin, p. 109.

"who are being saved it is the power of God" (1 Cor 1:18). The purpose of the death of Christ is "that the life of Jesus may be manifested in our mortal flesh" (2 Cor 4:11). While the cross as the manifestation of God's love for us must be understood in faith, it is the resurrection that points to the ultimate victory.

The *resurrection of Christ* is a central theme in the early Christian proclamation. Paul hands on what he also received, that Christ "was raised on the third day in accordance with the scriptures, and that he appeared to Cephas, then to the twelve" (1 Cor 15:4-5). Christ also appeared to more than five hundred brothers and sisters, to James, and to Paul himself. These resurrection appearances lead to a conviction in the early church that Christ continues to be with believers. The appearance to Paul confirms for him the veracity of the church's proclamation of faith in the Risen Lord and leads to his insight regarding the union of Christ and Christians. So central is this belief that Paul can say "If Christ has not been raised, your faith is futile and you are still in your sins" (1 Cor 15:17).

Christ's resurrection also holds promise for our own resurrection. "For as by a person came death, by a person has come also the resurrection of the dead" (1 Cor 15:21). "In Christ shall all be made alive," "and we shall always be with the Lord" (1 Cor 15:22; 1 Thess 4:15-17). The questions of how the dead will rise and the kind of body they will possess, are not nearly as important as the reality itself. For the early church those united with Christ in faith share in his glory. However, the Risen Lord "creates for himself his earthly body, ... [and] incorporates believers in his body. The church is the place of his presence only in so far as the Spirit remains the medium of that presence."[12]

The church originates with the resurrection of Christ and continues in existence as believers share his Spirit in faith. Christians draw on the power of the resurrection as the life-principle in the church and the effective force in their Christian lives, thereby experiencing a partial realization of the final eschatological victory of Christ. Furthermore, resurrection faith enables the believer to see the other side of the paradox:

---

[12] Käsemann, *Perspectives,* p. 113.

humiliation becomes exaltation, death leads to life, weakness is power. Paul will translate these realities into the fabric of his ministry and his own approach to church life (2 Cor 4:10-12). "I consider that the sufferings of the present time are not worth comparing with the glory that is to be revealed to us" (Rom 8:18).

The suffering of Jesus leads to a spirit of compassion in the church but the resurrection allows the new creation to flourish. God acts on our behalf in both the death and resurrection of the Lord and we apprehend and appropriate its meaning in faith, as we enter into a new mode of existence.

CONSEQUENCES OF FAITH

Faith remains a constant for the apostle Paul, and the Christian community defines itself by faith. The Christian churches likewise experience the consequences of this faith in their lives of love and service, for within the community of believers we discover a breaking down of the limitations of an exclusive faith. Believers in Jesus are Jews and Gentiles, slaves and free, women and men, with distinctions secondary to unity and equality in Christ. Righteousness is no longer on the basis of the law but salvation is available to everyone on the basis of faith. While the actual relationship between groups needs to be worked out, the reality of salvation for all is the ground of Paul's teaching. "There is no distinction" for through faith the "righteous shall live" (Rom 3:22; 1:17). The death and resurrection of Christ demonstrate for Paul "the absolute inadequacy of the law as means of salvation"[13] and radically changes the meaning of salvation. "Is God the God of the Jews only? Is he not God of Gentiles also?" (Rom 3:29). His answer to the latter question is affirmative since all are in need of redemption (Rom 6:1-7:4). This universal dimension of the church is deeply rooted in the early tradition of the church. Paul explains and pursues this idea and its implications in the churches, with this consciousness affecting the very mission of the church.

The early church is a missionary church and believers pro-

---

[13] Ridderbos, p. 134.

claim the gospel with urgency and enthusiasm. However, a certain perspective emerges in Paul's approach to mission during this early period. He becomes aware that "The mission of the church cannot succeed without the unity of the church in the truth of the gospel."[14] Therefore, as the early Christians evangelize, they also strive for unity in belief, sharing their vision of church with new believers. Likewise, the vocation of the church is not self-preservation but rather being at the service of the larger reality, the kingdom of God. Early Christians attempt to prepare for the final triumph of God in Christ, by being an effective sign of that kingdom in their life together and by extending their influence through the universal mission of the church.

The church in Paul's time shares a common faith. This faith finds its source in its call by God and in its union with Christ through the Spirit. Moreover, the ecclesial community understands its faith in Christ in a particular way. God acts in the death and resurrection of Jesus, which becomes a paradigm of Christian existence and offers grace for the church's new existence. Faith, which is constitutive of the church's life, establishes a radical equality among believers and expresses itself in the universal mission of the church. The gospel proclamation transcends all barriers and creates a unity among believers, a veritable sign of the presence of the kingdom. As we examine the community of believers more closely, we identify how the church becomes this sign of faith and newness of life.

The Experiences of Church Life

The early Christians not only share a common faith but they express their beliefs as they gather together for worship and service. The term *ekklesia* refers to the actual gathering of Christians. Robert Banks notes: "Its chief importance lies in the way it stresses the centrality of meeting for community life: it is through gathering that the community comes into being and is continually recreated."[15] *Ekklesia* encompasses small

[14]Beker, p. 306.
[15]Banks, p. 51.

groups of people with shared values, the households of faith, and the local churches. This term captures more than a human association; it sees the church as a divinely created reality.

THE CHRISTIAN ASSEMBLY

Since *ekklesia* refers to the actual assembly of Christians, we can suppose that the early church has a dynamic quality about it. The social aspects of coming together find their completion in the community's worship. "When you come together, each one has a hymn, a lesson, a revelation, a tongue, or an interpretation" (1 Cor 14:26). Paul also writes "I adjure you by the Lord that this letter be read to all the brothers and sisters," indicating his role in instructing the assembled community (1 Thess 5:27). For the early Pauline churches, gathering together as community is a prime emphasis with language, experience, and ritual, creating and defining their identity. The community celebrates its life in Christ by passing on the traditions, sharing all aspects of its life, building up the church, and worshipping together. All these functions describe the assembly of the faithful. Certain rituals, like baptism and the Lord's Supper, create boundaries for the group and foster the development of its unique identity in relation to non-believers. However, the Christian community gathers to celebrate its life and not simply for worship.

Paul's understanding of spiritual worship sheds light on the broad approach to what constitutes a worshipping community. In his letter to the Romans, the apostle writes "I appeal to you, ... by the mercies of God, to present your bodies as a living sacrifice, holy and acceptable to God, which is your spiritual worship" (Rom 12:1). He goes on to explain the components of spiritual worship: renewal of mind, authentic relationships, using gifts of preaching, teaching, service, exhortation, almsgiving, mercy, genuine love, patience in tribulation, the practice of hospitality, and so on. Paul's view of the person, the spirit, and the body, contribute to his concept of spiritual worship. For him, the fabric of everyday life constitutes the celebrations of the community. Christians present their bodies, themselves, before the Lord, a "living sacrifice, holy and acceptable to God." Käsemann remarks "every activity of the Christian community is to be characterized as charismatic, because in this total activity the 'spiritual worship' becomes real in the world."[16]

Another implication of this perspective emerges, according to Ridderbos: "The New Testament knows no holy persons who substitutionally perform the service of God for the whole people of God, nor holy places and seasons or holy acts, which create a distance between the cultus and the life of every day and every place. All members of the church have access to God (Rom 5:2) and a share in the Holy Spirit; all of life is service to God; there is no 'profane' area."[17]

This perspective helps us to understand the de-emphasis on priesthood in the early church, with the focus on the priesthood of all believers and specified priestly leadership of self-offering, admonition, and instruction (Rom 15:16; Phil 2:17). The implications of our common faith affect every aspect of life and create a new understanding of worship.

BAPTISM

Faith leads to baptism, the sign of the person's incorporation into Christ and the Christian community. "You were washed, you were sanctified, you were justified in the name of the Lord Jesus Christ and in the Spirit of God" (1 Cor 6:11), and you "were all baptized into one body" (1 Cor 12:13). Baptism marks the beginning of the Christian's movement towards Christ and identifies believers as a distinct group. The ritual itself represents a dying and rising with Christ, the "taking off" the old human and "putting on" the new life in Christ. Likewise, baptism establishes a union with Christ and with others who share the same faith. Becoming a member of the believing community demands a particular vision and results in certain behavior.

In the Pauline church baptism is a universally applicable rite, unlike circumcision for the Jews. It therefore elicits language of equality among members of the new community (Gal

---

[16]Käsemann, *New Testament Questions,* p. 195.
[17]Ridderbos, p. 481.

3:28; 1 Cor 12:13). This religious vision offers the possibility of newness of life to Gentiles, women, and slaves, in all their relationships. Likewise, baptism is an initiation into a religious movement that has a mission. Christians, therefore, called to ministry by their baptism, have the gifts for ministry from the Spirit. Service becomes an integral part of church identity because of this rite of initiation. Paul challenges the communities to live according to the light, to encourage one another and "build one another up" (1 Thess 5:4-10). Using varieties of gifts and services for the church is incumbent upon all in the community.

THE LORD'S SUPPER

The community of the baptized gathers together to share a meal and to remember the Lord. "Do this in remembrance of me.... For as often as you eat this bread and drink the cup, you proclaim the Lord's death until he comes" (1 Cor 11:24.26). This ritual imitates the ritual meal Jesus shared with his disciples "on the night when he was betrayed" (1 Cor 11:23), celebrating the meaning of Christ's death for the community and anticipating the end.

Paul presents a startling realism in his treatment of the eucharist. In 1 Cor 11-14, the apostle deals with the issues related to the Christian assembly: the role of women and men, divisions in the community, abuses surrounding the meal, gifts within the community, working together as the body of Christ, the qualities of love, and the responsibility of using gifts appropriately in the churches. The liturgy obviously needs reform in order to be an effective sign of Christ's presence in the community. However, the eucharistic words, framed, as they are in the letter with the gifts, roles, and attitudes of those people who make up the body, are an appropriate arrangement of the material, since the Lord's Supper is a celebration of the community, by the community, for the community, and not an isolated ritual. The unity of the church, so central to Paul's preaching, is the underlying theme. Divisions because of wealth or status mock the meaning and purpose of sharing at the table of the Lord (1 Cor 10:16-17; 11:18-19). The deepening of relationships among believers occurs when the community appropriately celebrates and shares his body and blood.

Moreover, this ritual reveals our participation in Christ and also fosters the full use of gifts in the community. Women participate in prayer, prophecy, and liturgical leadership (1 Cor 11:5), indicating ministry according to the endowments of the Spirit with no restraints based on sex. The Lord's Supper provides an occasion to celebrate Christian identity and to remind the community of the power of the cross. It also links this celebration with life and ministry, another realistic point, since Paul never isolates worship.

The church becomes a sign or sacrament to the world because of how it expresses its faith. The unity of the church reflects the church's union with Christ, a oneness achieved only in love.

PRAYER

Finally, as already suggested, the community shares its common faith through many expressions of prayer. Paul uses prayer of petition consistently and effectively. "What we pray for is your improvement" (2 Cor 13:9). "You also must help us by prayer, so that many will give thanks on our behalf for the blessing granted us in answer to many prayers" (2 Cor 1:11). He urges the community, "let your requests be made known to God" in "prayer and supplication, with thanksgiving" (Phil 4:6). He also gives "thanks to God" for the community, "mentioning you in our prayers" (1 Thess 1:2), "always in every prayer of mine ... making my prayer with joy" (Phil 1:4). Frequently, Paul anticipates his later exhortations to the community in his prayers.[18] He prays for what he commits himself to work toward with his congregation. Prayer among the co-workers creates a bond of unity and enhances ministry; constant prayer constitutes a value for the community of faith. Not only do the letters begin and end with benedictions, but a prayerful apostle contemplates his experience in the churches and his own call, sharing the fruits of his reflection and prayer with the churches.

---

[18]See Wiles, p. 213.

The majority of the examples of prayer occur in the Christian community. As Christians assemble together they pray. "So with yourselves; since you are eager for the manifestations of the Spirit, strive to excel in building up the church," "pray for the power to interpret," "pray with one mind," "sing with the spirit," "let all things be done for edification" (1 Cor 14:12-15.26). Meeks suggests that regular Christian meetings included prayer, exhortations, readings, and homilies, that assisted in the transmission of the religious tradition.[19]

The faith shared by Christians expresses itself in concrete ways: the celebration of life or spiritual worship, in significant rituals such as baptism and the Lord's Supper, in effective ministry within the community, and in various forms of prayer frequently connected with ecclesial life. Living out their communal faith enables the churches to gather together for a purpose. In these assemblies, Christians continually discover and express their identity as church. Since the "body of Christ" expresses a dynamic reality, the possibility of abuses seeping into the community, is a real concern. The early church learns to monitor the quality of its life and to provide structures to enhance its sign value.

The Structures of Church Life

To speak of the structures of authority conjures up for the contemporary reader images of institutions, organizational charts, channels of communication, and even dictatorial approaches and power plays. However, the primitive church presents little or no formal organization and even contradicts society's assessment of authority and its hierarchical world view. Paul certainly claims authority but Jesus is his model. Persons even share authority in the Christian community, as explicitly demonstrated in the collaboration between Paul and his co-workers. The primitive church values orthodoxy and uses discernment to determine the movements of the Spirit within the churches. While the community recognizes its leaders, discipline appears to be as much the responsibility of

[19]See Meeks, pp. 146-150.

the community as it is the role of the apostolic founder or the Jerusalem church. This vibrant portrayal of life in the early church excites, challenges, and offers direction to our more mature and institutionalized church.

Since God calls the church into existence and its life depends on the presence of Jesus' Spirit in the community, religious purpose or motivation determines the use of authority. Religious values permeate the believing community, coloring its views of leadership and responsibility.[20] Meeks notes well: "The Spirit counted as authority par excellence in the Pauline communities"[21] becoming also the principle of church order. The Spirit as the power of God, builds, sustains, and governs the church, so that the church becomes a charismatically structured community with Christ as its Lord.[22] Although organization is minimal, the apostles draw on their authority as do the leaders in the local churches. Authority and charism go together in this context; "all the baptized are 'office-bearers'; they have each ... charisma and, therefore, each ... special responsibility, and it is precisely on grounds of this responsibility that they are challenged in 1 Cor 14."[23]

Christian communities order themselves with individuals contributing through service to the building up of the church. Apostles, administrators, teachers, prophets, and others, function within the communities. Women and men express their authority in the exercise of these gifts. While the New Testament offers limited answers for today's questions about authority, church order, and structure, principles emerge that challenge us to be as creative in our own interpretation, as were Paul and the early church.

The church necessarily differs from society because of its foundation in faith, while constantly learning from its environment. Individuals in the church differ in their roles, responsibilities, experience, and ability to influence others, so

---

[20] See my *Leadership in Paul,* for an assessment of Paul's religious leadership, pp. 161-167 and each chapter section 4, and for an understanding of authority, pp. 168-170.

[21] Meeks, p. 138; Conzelmann, *Theology,* p. 259.

[22] See Dulles, *Church to Believe In.* p. 20.

[23] Käsemann, "Ministry," p. 80.

that the principle of equality in Christ requires a careful interpretation with diversity, not uniformity, providing the framework. Ecclesial authority, exercised within the community, guided and modified by its interaction with the faithful according to the gifts of each one, is an approach that differs from society's hierarchical tendency. However, conflict easily emerges as the church struggles to maintain the rich diversity in the one body of Christ and provide an alternative experience for all Christians.

PAUL'S AUTHORITY

Paul grounds his authority in his experience of the Risen Lord: "He appeared also to me," and in this revelatory experience Paul receives the gospel he now proclaims (1 Cor 15:8; Gal 1:11-12). The apostle is, therefore, a "servant of God," a "fellow worker for God," "your servant for Jesus' sake" (1 Cor 3:5.9; 2 Cor 4:5), who no longer speaks on "human authority" (1 Cor 9:8). Not only does Paul claim an authority from the Lord but he also bases his exercise of authority on Jesus himself, for whom the servant model predominated. Authority expresses itself in the service of others. However, because all are one in Christ, all share in the authority of Christ. This powerful insight creates the dynamic we see in the early Pauline churches. Paul consistently uses his authority, "which the Lord has given me for building up and not for tearing down" (2 Cor 13:10; cf 10:8), but the community also challenges Paul in his approach to them (2 Cor 10:10-12).

Nevertheless, Paul's view of his own authority allows him to "urge you, then, be imitators of me" (1 Cor 4:16). The life of the apostle is clearly a reflection of Christ and demonstrates the possibilities of Christian life for other believers. Models of imitation for the community include Christ, apostles, and other Christians who reflect Christ. Paul also identifies his unique relationship to the community: "For though you have countless guides in Christ, you do not have many fathers. For I became your father in Christ Jesus through the gospel" (1 Cor 4:15). For his own authority, then, Paul leans heavily on his experience of the Risen Lord, his reception of the gospel and apostleship, and the authentic living of his call. The authority of the Jerusalem church does not occupy a central place in his views, although we know of his relationship to the church and of his respect for its leaders. This particular interaction will be examined later.

Paul exercises his authority in a personal manner, recognizing his own abilities for persuasion and conviction. In the churches he establishes the apostle maintains a profound influence, exhorting them to grow in their spiritual, social, ethical, and intellectual lives.[24] He is often the center of attention even though he collaborates with co-workers and local leaders in his ministry. Paul also exercises his authority from a distance, through his letters to the community. In these instances, he fosters responsibility in the community while clearly maintaining his own influence. "Despite his strong missionary sense and personal commitment, as the 'apostle of Jesus Christ,' Paul in no way assumed a position of leadership over the communities he had established that excluded all right to participate in decisions."[25] In this way, Paul respects the community's authority and exercises his own in dialogue with the local churches. While Paul exhorts and appeals to the community, authority in this early period emerges as "interrelated parts of an organic whole."[26]

Authority demands respect, mutual love, reciprocity, and exchange. These qualities exist in the Pauline churches, although groups constantly need to grow in these areas. Paul asks Christian communities to respect those who labor among them and "esteem them very highly because of their work" (1 Thess 5:12). No automatic response occurs because of position or status; rather, the quality of their service to and within the community insures the authority of all persons. This authority of service is an expression of love. As Murphy-O'Connor notes, "To be authentic one must be a vital part in a web of power constituted by the reciprocity of love. The interchange of love is the new being of the believer."[27] For Paul and the early

---

[24] See Holmberg, p. 70; also ch. 3: "The Distribution of Power in the Local Church."

[25] Schnackenburg, "Community Cooperation," p. 14.

[26] Holmberg, p. 193.

[27] Murphy-O'Connor, *1 Corinthians*, p. 121.

church, this interaction becomes clearly visible in the collaborative efforts of the co-workers. We will attempt to identify the principles of collaboration, see how they operate among the co-workers, and specify any distinctive functions that emerge.

COLLABORATION

Working together in the service of the church is another essential component in Paul's vision of church. In 1 Thessalonians we already see the theme of shared ministry within the community, the work of leaders in the local church and among the churches. In subsequent correspondence, collaboration becomes integral to ecclesial life and its effectiveness relates to how well individuals work as part of a whole. Principles of collaboration, which we can apply to our church today, underlie Paul's work with others.

Paul and his co-workers designate themselves "servants of Christ Jesus" (Phil 1:1), indicating their responsibility from the Lord and their attitude towards the community. "Paul's work is essentially a service organization whose members have personal, not structural, links with the communities and who seek to develop rather than dominate or regulate them."[28] The vast number of co-workers of Paul finds no parallel in this early period, with the apostle creatively utilizing full-time and part-time workers, women as well as men, in his missionary endeavors. Paul appeals to those within his social class, entering into partnership with them, or encouraging them to act as patrons and sponsors for his missionary activity. Others remain as local leaders, developing the churches beyond the point of Paul's initial evangelization and providing a point of contact for the apostle. Still others go off on their own, establishing churches and extending the geographical boundaries of the Christian community. Whatever their status and background, the primary commitment of these collaborators is to Christ and the mission of the church, not to the person Paul. "Servants of Christ Jesus" aptly describes them.

[28]Banks, p. 170.

Nevertheless, these collaborators also constitute the circle of friends that support Paul in his ministry. While these colleagues differ in the time spent with Paul and in the way they work with him, their value in terms of mutual encouragement and support is unquestionable. Women, esteemed as his peers, provide essential services in the early church, reminding all believers that equality, mutuality, and coresponsibility mark the new existence in the community of faith. A solidarity emerges while diversity remains intact.

The early church has a complex and fluid network of persons with various gifts, providing visibility, a high degree of participation, and collaboration of these ministers in the service of others. As expected, the visible leaders exhibit exceptional competency and outstanding qualifications. Their extraordinary abilities and resources contribute to the initial phases of church development. Bonds of friendship and love round out the enthusiastic commitment of persons with different social, ethnic, and sexual identities. Paul gathers these people together and facilitates their ministry as well as enhancing his own work as an apostle. Collaboration implies a religious commitment since the church is called into existence by God. It also appreciates the competencies and diversity of all persons who work together in a spirit of dedication and love.

Paul's language in his letters indicates his sense that all colleagues share responsibility for the mission of the church. However, this view does not prevent Paul from challenging their views when he believes misconceptions occur. A hierarchy of service, an appreciation of workers, and a deference to outstanding missionaries exist in the church (1 Cor 16:16; 1 Thess 5:12-13; Phil 2:29). However, this fact should not obscure the larger reality of equality of persons, mutual responsibility, and the collaborative mission that also exist.

Paul frequently delegates responsibility, as with Timothy and Titus, and the churches receive their ministry (1 Thess 2:17; Phil 2:23; 2 Cor 12:18). In other instances, as with Epaphroditus, the church takes the initiative to send someone to Paul, or individuals, like Stephanus, present themselves for service. Ministry expands in terms of relationships between communities and among people. Co-workers also have the freedom to develop their individual abilities and work, indicating that they are colleagues "alongside of" Paul and not working "for" him. Apollos appears to have his own work when Paul urges his visit to Corinth again (1 Cor 16:12).

Likewise, the apostle seriously considers input from his colleagues and works through difficulties with them. This latter point becomes evident in the Philippian situation with Evodia and Syntyche. Paul does not suppress their leadership but attempts to hasten the satisfactory outcome of the situation by identifying further options for the community (Phil 4:2-3). Confidence in the ability of others fosters a good spirit of collaboration in the church and acceptance of new ministers by the community (1 Cor 16:10-11). The churches also have a responsibility to do all in their power to foster a good spirit of working together. Collaboration exists among very high-powered individuals like Paul and Apollos, and also between married couples like Priscilla and Aquila. However, each person has the freedom to move in or out of the Pauline circle, according to the needs of individuals and communities. Priscilla and Aquila work and travel with Paul but also have a church in their house (Rom 16:3-5). Tertius, the secretary/ writer of the Romans letter, and others like him, indicate the variety of workers at the time of Paul.

It soon becomes evident that Paul collaborates with many people on his missionary journeys and in the local churches. He works differently with each person, with his colleagues exercising their own authority according to their own gifts and service. The resulting picture is of a marvelously vital church because of the various levels of involvement that consistently build up the community of faith. Paul's own work is intimately connected with the ministry of others. Local leaders serve the overall mission as well as their own Christian communities. Sosthenes and Crispus, synagogue rulers, and Erastus, the city treasurer, Gaius and Stephanus make an essential contribution to the Corinthian church as they maintain relationships with Paul. Collaboration marks Paul's style of interaction with the co-workers. As a religious leader, he effectively calls forth the gifts and competencies of others. These principles of facilitation, encouragement, respect, and mutual ministries, offer timeless guidance for working together in the church.

THE CO-WORKERS

Paul's mission includes the gathering of persons with specific gifts to collaborate in his ministry. These co-workers preach the gospel, establish churches, and provide assistance for the developing communities. Their background varies, Jewish, Greek, and Roman, as does their status. "Not many of you were wise according to worldly standards, not many were powerful, not many were of noble birth" (1 Cor 1:26). Although the tentmaking and leather work of Priscilla and Aquila sound like a simple manual occupation, they have the means to travel and their home is large enough for the church to gather. Others like Erastus, Stephanus, Fortunatus, Achaicus, and Chloë's people, also travel from the Corinthian church, indicating reasonable financial resources and connections, as well as Christian dedication (1 Cor 1:11; 16:15-18; Ac 18:18; 19:22). These envoys provide a service to Paul for "they refreshed my spirit as well as yours," and sacrifice themselves for the Pauline mission (1 Cor 16:17-18). Priscilla and Aquila "risked their necks" for Paul; Epaphroditus becomes "ill, near to death" while engaged in ministry (Rom 16:3; Phil 2:26-27).

During his turbulent periods of imprisonment or when other reasons prohibit his visits to the churches, Paul sends his co-workers in his place. "Timothy's worth you know, how as a son with a father he has served with me in the gospel (Phil 2:22). Timothy goes to Thessalonica "to establish you in your faith and to exhort you," and also to Corinth (1 Thess 3:2; 1 Cor 4:17). Titus also visits Corinth to "complete among you this gracious work" (2 Cor 8:6). He bears Paul's letter to the church and begins arrangements for the collection (2 Cor 8:16-23).

Some of the co-workers present a challenge to Paul. Apollos certainly does. He has his own following in Corinth and his own ideas about priorities in his ministry (1 Cor 1:12; 16:12). Barnabas, an important Christian missionary in Antioch, responsible in part for Paul's missionary activity, eventually leaves Paul. "Barnabas was carried away by their insincerity," Paul tells the Galatians (2:13). Silvanus disappears from the group of co-workers after the second missionary journey, probably to work independently.[29]

Women share leadership in the Pauline churches; they labor strenuously, and independently, for the Christian mission (1 Cor 16:16; Rom 6:6.12). Tryphaena, Tryphosa, Julia, Nereus' sister, Rufus' mother form only a partial list of women involved in the churches. Phoebe, "a deaconess of the church at Cenchreae," "a helper of many and of myself as well," has influence, social position, and credibility in the church (Rom 16:2). Paul identifies Junia and her husband Andronicus, who "were in Christ before me" (Rom 16:7), as apostles, indicating the breadth of the ministry of women in this period.[30] Although references to second-class citizenship creep into the scripture and similar status for laity develops in the history of the church, this early period witnesses to the hosts of co-workers in the various communities and on mission in the church. We have living examples of the principles of collaboration and equality at work in the Pauline churches. Everyone assumes responsibility for ministry according to the gifts of the Spirit and through his/her mutual ministry contributes to the unity of the church.

FUNCTIONS OF LEADERSHIP

Throughout this early period, the correspondence establishes collaboration among Paul, co-workers, and the community, as the operating principle in the churches. The gifts of the Spirit, rather than "offices," dictate the functions and roles in the congregations. Christians continually respond to needs and to circumstances, building up the body of Christ in creative and enterprising ways. Ministry and community become mutually inclusive in these groups. Gifts and ministries may be prioritized, "first apostles, second prophets, third teachers," but the guiding principle is the manifestation of the Spirit for the common good.

---

[29]See Holmberg, p. 65; also ch. 2 for a description of the various functions of the local church and co-workers.

[30]Lohfink, p. 97: "Without exception the fathers of the church took Junia to be *a female apostle.*" See also Fiorenza, *Memory,* p. 172.

The primary apostle in the Pauline churches is Paul himself, "called by the will of God" (1 Cor 1:1) and entrusted with a mission. Paul preaches Christ and, through his preaching during the missionary journeys, establishes churches. While many preach the word, the apostles known to us are Paul, Andronicus, Junia, Barnabas, and Silvanus,[31] whose work transcends their own churches. Apostles work with relative independence, could enlist their own co-workers, and provide services of preaching and teaching.[32]

Prophets exist in many places, including Corinth, Thessalonica and Rome. Women prophesy in the Christian assembly, and this gift indicates the presence of God's Spirit in the community. Many of the co-workers also possess this gift.

Preaching the gospel and teaching become appropriate functions of the co-workers, and a means of transmitting the faith to the various Christian groups. Frequently, missionary couples provide services, another indication of sexual equality in these significant forms of ministry. Paul indicates that this missionary work is a labor and a difficult task, for which he commends Phoebe, Mary, Tryphosa, and Persis (Rom 16:6.12).

Other leadership functions fall to the co-workers and to members of the community (1 Cor 12:8-10; 28-30; Rom 12:6-8). These ministries become a constitutive element of the early church and a sign of its vitality and growth.

ORTHODOXY

With such a rapidly developing church, the concern for orthodoxy is essential and Paul reflects his concern each time he speaks of the unity of the church and the truth of the gospel. He understands the different approaches to teaching and preaching in the communities. However, he also challenges the communities if they turn away from his gospel, as did the Galatian churches. "There are some who trouble you and

---

[31] See Schmithals, p. 89, where he indicates the following references: Phil 3:5; Rom 16:7; Acts 4:36-37; Gal 2:1ff; Acts 15:22, and claims the apostles known to us by name are all Jewish Christians.

[32] See Ellis, pp. 12-13.

want to pervert the gospel of Christ" (Gal 1:6-7). Nevertheless, it becomes difficult to clearly identify orthodoxy in such an early period, when the churches are still struggling to understand themselves in relation to Jew and Gentile. The principle emerges, while the content continues to develop.

DISCERNMENT OF SPIRITS

One option Paul consistently advocates for his churches is the testing of spirits. He believes that Christians are "taught by the Spirit, interpreting spiritual truths to those who possess the Spirit" (1 Cor 2:13). The spiritual person "judges all things," and the community has "the mind of Christ" (1 Cor 2:15-16). Just as God "tests our hearts" (1 Thess 2:4), Christians can test their response and their direction (1 Cor 10:15), for "God has revealed to us through the Spirit" and "the Spirit searches everything, even the depths of God" (1 Cor 2:10).

Paul sometimes offers his own assessment of the situation, "this persuasion is not from him who called you" (Gal 5:8; cf 1 Cor 11:29). However, more frequently the community discerns. This ability to discern in faith tempers a strong position of authority (1 Thess 5:21; Phil 1:10; 1 Cor 11:28, 2 Cor 13:5; Gal 6:4). Personal and communal decisions that meet the criteria of discernment are important for the Pauline churches, with building up communities becoming a consistent criterion for authentic charisms.[33] "Examine yourselves, . . . test yourselves" (2 Cor 13:5); "there must be factions among you in order that those who are genuine among you may be recognized" (1 Cor 11:19). This ability within the church community contributes to its maturity and entails a capacity for independent decisions.[34] The churches identify true and false apostles (2 Cor 11:13; 12:12) and choose appropriate actions (Gal 4:8-9). Paul prays "that your love may abound more and more, with knowledge and all discernment" (Phil 1:9), indicating that charity is indispensable for true Christian life.

---

[33]See Stanley, "Authority," p. 560; "Idealism and Realism," p. 45.
[34]See Holmberg, p. 81.

DISCIPLINE

Conflicts emerge in the churches as Christians and leadership persons attempt to discern appropriate directions for the new community. Discipline, while essential, bases itself on an understanding of authority as service, and a sharing in the authority of Christ by all the baptized. Faith becomes the constitutive element in the authoritative teaching and discipline in the churches. Paul sends his letters to an enthusiastic and "undisciplined" Corinthian church, as consultations for the church, indicating a particular approach to discipline. He also states the community's responsibility to settle grievances. "When one of you has a grievance against a brother [or sister] ... why do you lay them before those who are least esteemed by the church?" (1 Cor 6:1-4). The community can and should deal with these difficulties and affirm the truth of the gospel. Edification is always a principle for behavior (Rom 14:13; 15:2; 1 Cor 14:26), but hard choices must also be made. "Admonish the idle, encourage the fainthearted, help the weak, be patient with them all" (1 Thess 5:14).

The community mediates the demands of the gospel and its reflection on the lifestyle of the group. This aspect of church life resonates with Paul's own experience in the churches. While he never abdicates his own responsibility to the churches, he always challenges each one to contribute gifts and to assume responsibility. Discipline preserves the integrity of the church, and the church itself has the power to upbuild itself. Paul nowhere directs "himself over the head of the church to the office-bearers. Even in so severe a case of discipline as that intended in 1 Corinthians 5 he reproves the church that it has not taken action, and he wants the exercise of discipline still to take place 'when you are assembled, and my spirit is present with the power of our Lord Jesus Christ,' (1 Cor 5:4)."[35]

Judgment and discipline come from the community; obedience belongs to the community and so does forgiveness (2 Cor 2:6-8). Paul's comments are sometimes strong, "I wrote you not to associate with anyone who ... is guilty of immorality or greed" (1 Cor 5:11). However, he also states: "But with

---

[35]Ridderbos, p. 473.

me it is a very small thing that I should be judged by you or by any human court.... Therefore, do not pronounce judgment before the time, before the Lord comes, who will bring to light the things now hidden in darkness and will disclose the purposes of the heart" (1 Cor 4:3.5).

Discipline belongs to persons and to the community in a tenuous way. Ultimate judgment is the Lord's. Paul's respect for conscience and his identification of the elements that comprise ecclesial living, provide a broad basis and a different focus for the contemporay church.

Paul's understanding of authority and its exercise is another component of his vision of church. Principles and guidelines emerge rather than rules and commands. These principles establish the parameters of church life for the community of faith.

The Relational Aspects of Church Life

In all aspects of its life, a common faith binds the community together. This faith colors relationships between the church and society, within the Christian community, between Jewish and Gentile groups, local church and the churches, and key leaders in the church. The apostle Paul continuously works at maintaining good relations with communities, as is indicated in his relationship with the Thessalonian community. He uses familial terms, such as father, nursing mother, and child, to create a sense of intimacy and interdependence. Paul's missionary activity creates a complex network of relationships. The letters offer a glimpse into one phase of these ecclesial relationships, but these interactions began before the correspondence and continue beyond it. The focal point of the early church is a set of relationships, since embracing the gospel means joining the community.

A new set of human relationships replaces the old, for the "gospel calls into being the church as the discipleship of equals that is continually recreated in the power of the Spirit."[36] Relationship becomes constitutive of church life, with its equal-

[36] Fiorenza, *Memory*, p. 345.

ity resulting from the divine origin of the community, not from aspects of the human personality or social influences. This transformation and freedom in relationships foster the spirit of collaboration and growth in the early church. The community's lifestyle witnesses to society that believing in Christ makes a qualitative difference.

RELATIONSHIPS WITH SOCIETY

The ecclesial community has a responsibility to the social world of its day. The approach Paul pursues is to transcend the social order and create an alternative environment. His way of dealing with societal ills is by changing attitudes within the believing community. Rather than attack the institution of slavery, Paul speaks of barriers broken and a new spirit among believers in Christ. He directs his energy to the Christian community and not against social or political issues. "Let every person be subject to the governing authorities. For there is no authority except from God, and those that exist have been instituted by God" (Rom 13:1).

The eschatological perspective of the community partially explains this emphasis. The new social reality within the ecclesial community appropriates Christ's victory and anticipates the end. Thus, Christian life takes precedence over social transformation, although the ecclesial community challenges patriarchal structures and society's transgressions by its very existence. While the early church creates its own boundaries and counter culture, it also indirectly assumes responsibility for the good of all.

RELATIONSHIPS WITHIN THE COMMUNITY

While the Pauline congregations represent a cross-section of urban society, these communities reflect a breakthrough in terms of how different people live together. While Christians celebrate their oneness in Christ, they do not obliterate their distinctions. These early ecclesial communities recognize diverse gifts and ministries within the church. Equality never means uniformity; neither does diversity mean hierarchy.

Diversity such as we find in the human body marks the new set of human relationships, since we can comprehend differences as well as unity in this powerful analogy. The challenge to live as part of the whole remains with each community member as he/she grows more fully conformed to Christ.

Likewise, congregations, while respecting leadership and striving for the higher gifts, attest to the responsibility of each member for the development of ecclesial life. Responsibility to build up the community resides within the community. Enrichment of communal life, comfort, and confrontation constitute the dynamics of interaction between believers. Ministries emerge as the community discerns needs and gifts. With this understanding of mutual responsibility, the possibility of a cohesive group becomes a reality.

Christian life is not only worship and service but the community relationships formed by the process of interaction in all the situations of life. Christians understand and know Christ through one another. They live out their faith precisely through their communal relationships of mutual love and service. This point constitutes an essential component of Paul's ecclesiology and accounts for his many exhortations on Christian life. Growth in church life depends on people and the practicalities of the moment. That communities will differ presents no major problem for Paul, providing that the essential components of equality in Christ and mutual responsibility remain intact. Communal relationships account for the dynamic element within the early church.

RELATIONSHIPS BETWEEN THE JERUSALEM CHURCH AND THE GENTILE COMMUNITIES

The early church goes through its transition from Jewish sect to separate entity before our very eyes in the letters of Paul and the early gospels. Hastening the separation is the incorporation of the Gentiles into the community in large numbers and the adaptation of a Palestinian-based movement into the Hellenistic environment. The Jerusalem church changes in its relationship to the Pauline communities as leaders of both groups communicate their experience in very different environments. However, a relationship between the various wings of the church comprises an essential component of church life with Paul and others working conscientiously towards this end.

Paul reminds the congregations that they "became imitators of the churches of God in Christ Jesus which are in Judea, for you suffered the same things from those in your own country as they did from the Jews" (1 Thess 2:14). He also emphasizes their relationship to the mother church in Jerusalem when he takes up the collection, a token of financial support and a sign of the unity of the church. He tells the Romans, "at present, I am going to Jerusalem with aid for the saints" (15:25). The apostle also maintains the priority of Israel in salvation history, stresses continuity with Judaism for the Gentile Christians, and respects the various religious traditions of his people (Rom ch 4, 9-11). The Jerusalem church incarnates these traditions to a great degree. Likewise, Paul relies on the Jerusalem kerygma, knows the church leaders, and "on a number of occasions it appears that he is permanently dependent in some aspects on this centre of the church."[37]

However, Paul strives to maintain a delicate balance between the Jerusalem church and the Gentile communities. With the strong foundation at Antioch and its separation from Jerusalem, it becomes acceptable to speak of the churches rather than the church. While Paul maintains a primacy of honor, he also creates a distance between himself and the Jerusalem church. He says "I did not go up to Jerusalem to those who were apostles before me" (Gal 1:17). Paul stresses his independence in the gospel while acknowledging his appreciation of their recognition and their delineation of ministry. "James and Cephas and John, who were reputed to be pillars, gave to me and Barnabas their right hand of fellowship, that we should go to the Gentiles and they to the circumcised" (Gal 2:9).

As an apostle, Paul also challenges the Jerusalem church's observance of the law in the incident at Antioch, and his ministry to the Gentiles contributes to the outcome of the Jerusalem council. Paul has little desire to lean on the authority

---

[37]Holmberg, p. 194.

of this church and so carefully plans his contacts. His relationship with the Jerusalem church is elusive at best. He works independently while maintaining only the amount of interaction necessary to preserve the essential unity of the churches. Paul models this kind of relationship for the Gentile communities and for his co-workers. The focus seems to be the development of local churches from the grass roots, rather than mandates from the mother church down to the newly formed communities. Paul epitomizes the relationship between the Jerusalem church and the Gentile communities in his own relationship with the church. However, this fact does not deny the reality of both a local and a more universal church.

RELATIONSHIPS BETWEEN THE CHURCHES

The development of the early churches consists in the establishment of the local communities by apostles and missionaries. These churches mature under the guidance of its leaders in conjunction with their membership and with some intervention from their apostolic founders, as in the Pauline communities. Young fervent communities develop according to the tradition they have received, and their interpretation of the traditions in their communities establishes their faith identity. The missionary circuit assures interaction between these communities and creates a unity in faith.

Paul's use of *ekklesia* usually indicates the local congregation or an aggregate of communities. However, in some instances, difficulty persists in uncovering the primary meaning of the term (Rom 16:23; 1 Cor 6:4; 10:32; 12:28; 15:9; Gal 1:13; Phil 3:6).[38] While *ekklesia* refers to the gathering or assembly of believers, the letters attest to the seeds of a fuller understanding of church. A universal sense of church seems to be present since the particular community embodies the essence of God's call to all believers in the local community. The church, then, as the gospel, has a breadth and a life that transcends the local experience.

The mission of the early church contributes to this fuller

---

[38] See Beker, p.315.

notion of universal church. Through frequent and ongoing contacts, a unity of purpose, traditions, and understanding begin to develop. The sense of the body, or organic whole, goes beyond the local experience of church. While there is no overriding organization, a vital organism results from the union of all believers in Christ. Each local church reflects the essence of the universal church in a unique manner and an interdependence results among the communities.

Paul's own conversion prepares him for the universal aspect of his ecclesiology, since his conversion is to the church, not to a particular congregation. However, his experience is in the local churches, founded because of his universal mission to the Gentiles. The interplay between local community and universal church comes easily for the apostle. He emphasizes one dimension or another, depending on the situation at hand. However, unity within the community and among the churches, while an essential aspect of his vision and ministry, becomes difficult to insure. Distinctiveness can have its drawbacks as well as its assets.

The church represents a reality constituted in Christ and distinct from the Jewish synagogue. In fact, we see no connection between the Pauline communities and the synagogues, since the Christians focus on their local churches which they build up in the spirit of the gospel. Interestingly, while Paul appreciates the broader dimensions of church, he, too, focuses his attention on these local communities. Here Christians live out their faith commitments; in the local setting transformation in Christ becomes visible; in this realm new ideas emerge and the discipleship of equals expresses itself in concrete ways. The local church impacts the lives of believers in a more significant way than does the universal dimension. In the local church we have the concrete manifestation of what it means to be Christian. However, as in the Antioch incident, what happens locally matters to the Jerusalem church and the other communities. While a fluid relationship exists among the churches, their sense of being the one body of Christ develops in breadth and depth in this early period.

RELATIONSHIP WITH PETER

Finally, we glimpse Peter's relationship to church as it emerges in Paul's understanding of his role in the churches. The apostle acknowledges his own indebtedness to Peter, gaining a unique perspective of Jesus from this Galilean Jewish disciple of the Lord. "Paul could recognize Cephas as a church authority, but this need not have meant Cephas' ecclesiastical superiority over Paul."[39] Paul in fact stresses their equality in terms of the gospel and in their ministry. Peter may be the focal point for unity because of his relationship to Jesus, but Paul challenges his action and his theology in Antioch. He attacks the self-righteousness, legalistic and cultic attitudes in Peter, probably remembering his own pre-conversion stance. This Antiochian incident reflects an enlightening aspect of relationships in the early church. A willingness to confront colleagues and leaders on their basic understanding of Christian life exists. Peter chooses one approach to the dilemma of an appropriate relationship between Gentile and Jewish Christians, Paul another. While Peter remains the dominant figure in Antioch after Paul's departure,[40] Paul's reading of the issues survives in the long run.

The value of this encounter is that confrontation could happen and did happen in the early church. Relationships in the Christian community are so integral to the church's self-understanding that no pain is spared for their authentic development. This timeless lesson insures the growth of the church in our own century. Whether it entails a relationship to society or relationships within the communities or between churches or leaders, how we relate to one another as women and men of faith reflects our basic commitment.

Paul's vision of church includes what he perceives as the essential components of its life. The source of the church's life is God and its foundation is faith. The community lives out its commitment in the various experiences of Christian life, particularly in its ecclesial celebrations. The structures of church

---

[39] Brown and others, *Peter*, p. 29.
[40] See Brown and Meier, p. 24.

life and its relational dimension round out Paul's view of the church. These constitutive elements of church life result directly from Paul's ministry in the churches, and the models of church that he utilizes in the letters reflect and further explain this reality.

5

Pauline Models of Church

> "Therefore, if any one is in Christ, that [he/she] is a new creation, the old one has passed away, behold, the new one has come. All this is from God, who through Christ reconciled us to himself and gave us the ministry of reconciliation." (2 Cor 5:17-18)

From his extensive ministry in the churches, Paul develops a vision of church that inspires and unifies the believers in Christ. The essential components of his ecclesiology surface again and again in his letters. However, a vision must be accessible in part to the ordinary believer, and toward this end, Paul uses images to describe his understanding of the church. Some of these images or metaphors have symbolic meaning and become models that effectively explain the reality of the church. The people of God, the new creation, the body of Christ, the mystical person, capture the imagination of the early communities and speak to their experience and their hopes. These few models emerge from the myriad ways Paul describes the church. They reflect the essence of the community of faith, emphasizing certain aspects of its identity. Paul uses, what we recognize as models, in a dynamic and flexible way. In fact, we see an overlapping of ideas as well as a progression of insight of these descriptions.

Paul not only uses innovative metaphors for the church but also traditional images which he imbues with new life. Discourse accompanies the use of these images, and even in Paul's use of analogy, practically synonymous with model, the picture itself has no independent significance.[1] His interpretation and explanation provide the context to understand the development of the model. Some of the models go beyond the sociological and cultural understandings of their day, thus, the new humanity incorporates cosmic beginnings and future destiny.[2] At times central images have a particular function or purpose, either confirming what we know or leading us to new theological insights. Likewise, some descriptions reflect the Hellenistic world, like the runner, prize, race, or game; others the diaspora Jewish world, as the temple, blessing cup, people, elect; still others earthy and familial images, as in the seed, bread, table, bride. While the picture may condition our understanding, each metaphor or model must be viewed from all possible angles. All too often our way of seeing "is wholly dictated by a single controlling picture which excludes all others.[3]

Paul uses a plurality of images, each with its own inner logic, and each beginning a chain of inferences and implications. What Paul really means is difficult to ascertain since models emerge from a particular social environment and cultural milieu. At best the power of models is to challenge us to be, or to do, something different; they do not immobilize us. Likewise, Paul selects and develops each model in relation to his understanding of Christ, for his christology is always at the center of his understanding of church.

This chapter focuses on the models of church used by Paul in the authentic letters. Each model will be explored in terms of its origin, meaning, and potential for growth. While there is no best model, some will speak more eloquently to the contemporary church than others. However, the significance of these descriptions of the early church can enlighten our present experience and open us to further developments.

---

[1] See Gale, p. 91.
[2] See Minear, p. 67.
[3] Boring, p. 290.

Descriptions of the Church in Paul

The apostle Paul uses images to convey his understanding of Christ and his church. These images often elicit a powerful response in the believer and the community, and thus, function as symbols. Some symbols can potentially serve as models, when they not only elicit a response, but can be used critically to understand and explain the reality of church. While few models emerge in Paul, some symbols and metaphors still hold this potential for the contemporary church. Models are extremely significant for they synthesize what we tend to believe and lead us in new theological directions. These are the explanatory and exploratory or heuristic models.[4] In Paul's letters, we discover powerful descriptions and images, some drawn from the created universe or the environment, others emphasizing humanity and the relational aspects of life. Many of the descriptions which Paul applies to the church have biblical foundations.

In his correspondence Paul uses agricultural and architectural images. He speaks of planting, seeding, watering, growth, the field, the olive tree. The building images, with foundations, materials, and the work of the laborers, are vivid and realistic. These metaphors remind believers of their dependence on the Lord as well as their own roles and responsibilities in the community. God gives the growth, although Paul plants and Apollos waters the field of the community. Likewise, Paul lays the foundation, another builds, but the foundation itself is Christ Jesus (1 Cor 3:5-11). We will explore some of these images in more detail.

THE BUILDING

"According to the commission of God given to me, like a skilled master builder I laid a foundation, and another person is building upon it. Let each one take care how he [or she] builds upon it" (1 Cor 3:10). Paul develops this metaphor,

---

[4]See Dulles, *Models of the Church,* chapter 1 "The Use of Models in Ecclesiology," pp. 19-37; and pp. 22-23 for these kinds of models.

identifying the foundations of "gold, silver, precious stones, wood, hay, stubble." In the end the quality of work "will be revealed with fire, and the fire will test what sort of work each one has done" (1 Cor 3:12-13). As the apostle expands the metaphor it becomes a description of the church. However, the emphasis in his usage is on the source of the community's life in God, for the foundation is Jesus Christ, "we are co-workers for God," you are "God's building" (1 Cor 3:9). Paul also reminds the community that they are a special building, "God's temple" (1 Cor 3:16).

This image of building or temple opens us to another perspective on the church, for "God's Spirit dwells in you" (1 Cor 3:16) and "your body is a temple of the Holy Spirit within you" (1 Cor 6:19). Paul uses the image of the spiritual temple for the community, whose holiness rests in being set apart by God. Likewise, the temple refers to individual Christians who belong to God in a special way, and in whom God or Christ dwells (Rom 8:11). The images of the building or temple filled by the Spirit of God open some important perspectives in a view of the church. It not only permits a better grasp of the eschatological nature of the church, but allows a more penetrating view of its inner structure and life.[5]

God equips the church with gifts and ministries for its upbuilding (2 Cor 10:8; 13:10; Rom 12:3.6-8; 1 Cor 12:4-11). The building image no longer remains static, but refers to persons, the community, and their growth. Mutual upbuilding is a key concept in Paul, for whom a right relationship between the community and the individual is a central consideration. For the apostle, "each one is ever to place the good of the church above [his/her] own preference and ability."[6] The concept of upbuilding elicits from all in the church, a response which includes gratitude and service.

Finally, Paul also uses the tent to demonstrate the fragility of life for the Christian. "The earthly tent" may be destroyed, but "we have a building from God, a house not made with hands, eternal in the heavens" (2 Cor 5:1). Here, the dwelling

---

[5]Schnackenburg, *Church,* p. 158.
[6]Ridderbos, p. 432.

image focuses on what happens after death, since life for believers has an eternal quality about it.

THE EKKLESIA

The image describes the process of coming together and the actual gathering of Christians, reminiscent of God's assembly (*qahal*) in the desert. The Pauline churches are congregations called by God in Christ Jesus (1 Thess 2:14; Gal 1:22). *Ekklesia* refers to the local community of believers assembled together for worship and service. However, while the focus is on the local church, *ekklesia* is also "the description of the church in its totality, irrespective of its being scattered over various localities."[7] It is the total community and the total church insofar as the local church fully represents the church. "The local church does not merely *belong* to the Church, the local Church *is* the Church."[8]

For Paul, the *ekklesia* is more than an association of churches for it describes the various communities in their different localities. *Ekklesia* emphasizes the gathering and interaction of believers. When Paul writes to the churches of Jews and Gentiles assembled in the name of the Lord, he identifies the unity expected within the communities and among them.

The church of God also identifies the local church in a particular place, "the church of God which is at Corinth," or the "churches of God in Christ Jesus which are in Judea" (1 Cor 1:2; 1 Thess 2:14). These churches acknowledge in faith their communal bonds, receive the gospel, and share in the mission of Jesus Christ. The church of God specifies the religious orientation of the community and its origin in the Lord.

Paul speaks of the Jerusalem church as the "church of God," and encourages imitation of this church and the churches of God in Judea, indicating their priority in time. In addition to respect and imitation, all the churches offer particular financial support for the Jerusalem church. In fact, the Jerusalem church becomes a focal point for the Jewish and Gentile churches,

---

[7]Ridderbos, p. 328.
[8]Küng, p. 85.

creating a unity among the communities.

Ekklesia becomes a concrete expression rather than a conceptual description of the Christian community, since it describes the assembled congregation constituted in faith. Paul also speaks of believers in the congregation as "saints" (Rom 8:27; 16:2; 1 Cor 6:1), a term closely related to "elect," "beloved," "called." Likewise, the community is a "holy people" and the church a "holy temple." Rather than isolate believers, these descriptions specify their distinctive lifestyle, a sign to a society in need of conversion. The saints in Jerusalem receive aid from Paul and the Gentile churches (Rom 15:25), indicating the early use of this special description for believers. It becomes integral to the church's understanding of itself as a community with a special call, lived out in its organic unity and mutual relationships.

THE HOUSEHOLD

The house-church is a basic unit and subgroup of the local church. In the early period, the mission of the church prospers because of the Christian households in various places.[9] Within these house-churches, equality in Christ represents the norm, and the emergence of women gains momentum. The house-church consists of family and converts, reflecting a religious association more than a patriarchal family.[10] Leadership develops in this setting, alongside of the leaders in the local church and the itinerant apostles and missionaries. The Christians assemble in these homes that become centers of hospitality and of missionary endeavors. "Now [brothers and sisters], you know that the household of Stephanus were the first

---

[9]Elliot, p. 149., identifies the following households in Acts and the letters: Jerusalem and Judea: Acts 1:12-14; 2:1-4, 42-47; 4:23-31; 5:42; 8:3; 9:43; 12:12-19; Caesarea: Acts 10:1-11:18; Damascus: Acts 9:10-19; Philippi: Acts 16:11-15, 25-34; Thessalonica: Acts 17:5-6; Corinth: Three households: Stephanas (1 Cor 1:16; 16:15-18); Gaius (1 Cor 1:14; Rom 16:23); Crispus (Acts 18:8; 1 Cor 1:14); Cenchreae: Rom 16:1-2 (the patron Phoebe); Troas: Acts 20:7-12; Ephesus: 1 Cor 16:19; 2 Tim 4:19; Colossae: Philemon's household; Laodicea: Col 4:15; Rome: Five households: Aquila and Prisca (Rom 16:3-5; Acts 18:2); Aristobulus (Rom 16:10); Narcissus (Rom 16:11); and the groups mentioned in Rom 16:14-15.

[10]See Fiorenza, *Memory*, p. 179.

converts in Achaia, and they have devoted themselves to the service of the saints" (1 Cor 16:15). The house-church tests relationships within the community and also between the house-church and the local church. Structures of authority and the beginnings of organization find their basis in this expression of church life. Opportunities for women multiply because of the Christian household, causing tensions between these communities and the pagan patriarchal households.

Likewise, an intimacy develops within this environment as well as a high degree of commitment. These patterns of life contribute to the developing understanding of church. While Paul relies on the house-churches for his missionary work, he moves away from the household image to a sufficient degree that it does not emerge as a model. However, it has the potential to speak to our time because of its small mixed community with varied relationships. Even in Paul's time, the household serves as a sign of the new family of God, where boundaries break down and a new community emerges.

THE FAMILY

Closely associated with the household image is the description of the church as family. Paul describes his relationship with the churches in terms drawn from family life, such as father (1 Cor 4:14-15), mother (Gal 4:19), nurse (1 Cor 3:2), speaking in tender and endearing ways. The family reveals the essence of Paul's thinking about community. Use of the homes of Christians for the gathering of the community reflects the family character of the early church. The atmosphere and attitudes in the community speak to fundamental family values, with trust, respect, love, patience, tolerance, resilience, and generosity, insuring the kind of interaction essential to being church. These qualities develop in a family context, a significant insight for the early Christian community. With this metaphor, the church again becomes a concrete and real experience rather than an abstract concept.

Christians live out their commitment as church by being a family of faith. Banks notes: "All Paul's 'family' terminology has its basis in the relationship that exists between Christ, and as a corollary the Christian, and God. Christians are to see themselves as members of a divine family; already in his earliest letters Paul regards the head of the family as being God the Father."[11] The family image could potentially become a model for Paul, since he focuses on relationship, unity, and love, rather than priesthood and ritual.

In addition to the usual family images, Paul speaks of the church as bride and Christ as husband. "I feel a divine jealousy for you, for I have betrothed you to Christ to present you as a pure bride to her one husband" (2 Cor 11:2). This exclusive image conveys another aspect of what it means to be church.

Paul's varied descriptions of church and the images he uses, convey certain aspects of church life to the believing communities. The building, the *ekklesia,* the household, and the family, describe something of the reality of church for Paul. He focuses on the process of development and growth in the building images, also identifying the community's special relationship to the Lord, its foundation and its life.

In the *ekklesia* the gathering of the local church receives attention, while the household images indicate the usual meeting place for the Christian communities. Underlying so many references in the letters is family imagery with its varied and intimate relationships.

These descriptions identify some dimensions of the character of the early Christian churches. Notably, the images relate to the ordinary life of believers. A few of these images become the basis for models of the church.

Models of the Church in Paul

While many potential models emerge in Paul's descriptions of church, only a few key models actually specify and illuminate his understanding of church. These models originate in the various traditions and take on new meaning

---

[11]Banks, p. 54, and chapter 5; also L. Doohan, Ch. 3: "The Church as Family," *The Lay-Centered Church.*

in light of Christ. Furthermore, they represent a clear direction in Paul's thinking and a development of his ideas regarding the ecclesial community. We will explore the meaning of four of these models, the people of God, the new creation, the body of Christ, and the mystical person.

THE PEOPLE OF GOD

An early fundamental model of the church is that of the people of God. Designations such as "saints," "beloved," "elect," and "called," lead to the realization that believers in the gospel are a chosen people. The idea of a people indicates separation from the world but also communion with one another. For the *origin* of this concept and an indication of its meaning, we return to the Jewish roots of Christianity.

People of Yahweh is a theological statement reflecting Israel's self-understanding. Yahweh, the God of Israel, calls this people to himself in a preliminary way through the covenant made with Abraham (Gen 12:2) and in the exodus event. "I am the Lord, and I will bring you out from under the burdens of the Egyptians, and I will deliver you from their bondage, and I will redeem you with an outstretched arm and with great acts of judgment, and I will be your God" (Ex 6:6-7). Yahweh makes of this people "a kingdom of priests and a holy nation" (Ex 19:6). He promises his continued presence: "I will walk among you, and will be your God, and you shall be my people" (Lev 26:12). With this call of Israel goes also a stipulation, "if you will obey my voice and keep my covenant, you shall be my own possession among all the peoples" (Ex 19:5).

Israel becomes Yahweh's people because of his gracious call, and both "the gifts and the call of God are irrevocable" (Rom 11:29; cf 10:21). However, when Yahweh calls his people it is "as a covenant to the people, a light to the nations, to open the eyes that are blind, to bring out the prisoners from the dungeon" (Is 42:6-7). A burden of responsibility falls upon Israel to be this sign to the nations and to serve those imprisoned and in darkness. Likewise, "a tension can be detected between a 'particularism' and 'universalism' with respect to Israel's being People of God—especially in the late prophetic literature (Ho 1:9-10; Zach 2:11; Is 2:1-5; 42:6)."[12] The priority of Israel remains intact, with the Jewish community symbolizing God's dealings with humankind. However, while God's promises remain in effect, there emerges the possibility for the Gentiles to share these promises. As indeed he says in Hosea, "those who were not my people I call 'my people,' and one who was not my beloved I will call 'my beloved'" (Rom 9:25).

This idea emerges full force in Paul, with the apostle building upon his understanding of the people of God to clarify and to unfold the fuller identity of the Christian church. Linked to this idea is the reminder of the covenant now fulfilled in Christ (Gal 3). However, Paul does not use the term "new Israel" for the believers, except for a reference to the "Israel of God" in his letter to the Galatians (6:16). While the church is a fulfillment and continuation of the historical people of God, Paul remains concerned about the future of Israel and its place in the overall scheme of salvation history. His models reflect that bias and concern.

People of God provides a rich term and a breadth of *meaning* for the early church. Since Paul's primary description of the essence of the church draws heavily on the people purposely formed by God in history, the first level of meaning stresses *continuity with Israel*. The church is the historical entity standing in relation to the biblical people of Yahweh. Expressions applied to Israel become connotations for the church. God's elect becomes a designation for the Christians and for the church. The call of Abraham and the promise made to his descendents find their fulfillment in the new people of God, those who believe in Christ.

In this new people, the Lord manifests himself through the Spirit. The fulfillment of God's election and covenant also modifies the traditional theological interpretation of justification. Hence, a relationship exists between the people of God and the process of justification. While Paul refrains from directly identifying the church as the true Israel, he indirectly expresses this reality in his use of the people of God.

---

[12]Worgul, p. 24.

Continuity with ancient Israel gains importance for Paul as he works with the various churches. While the Jerusalem community could lay claim to the designation people of God, Paul applies it to the entire church. He draws on the tradition and expands it (2 Cor 6:16//Lev 26:12; Rom 9:25-26//Ho 2:23; 1:10; Rom 10:21//Is 65:2; Rom 11:1-2//Ps 94:14). The apostle also demonstrates *discontinuity with Israel*, since justification which constitutes the people of God occurs by faith in Christ (Gal 3; Rom 1:16-17; 3:21-26). The loving graciousness of God remains intact but now all who believe in Christ become his people.

This point leads to the significant expansion of this model for the New Testament communities. While Israel opened itself to the Gentiles (Rom 15:10-11//Dt 32:43), Paul extends the interpretation of Abraham's posterity to include both *Jews and Gentiles*. His assessment focuses on God's choice of believers and not on being an Israelite by birth (Rom 9:8). Therefore, the uncircumcised become an integral part of the people of God. While his universalizing of the concept has foundations in Judaism, in Paul's understanding Gentiles respond to God's call directly and become believers without the acceptance of Jewish ritual and observance.

The new people of God, then, is an entirely new reality. While its roots may be in Judaism, its identity emerges in the form of a truly new community. In this sense, universalism wins out over the particularism inherent in the original meaning. People of God becomes a spiritual concept, supplanting the national and the political aspects of its Jewish meaning. Likewise, the possibility of a universal people of God establishes the extensive *mission of the church*, for the missionary character of the church is coextensive with this self-understanding of being open to all people.

Futhermore, the *radical equality* in the believing community finds its basis in the people of God. Since God's call is paramount, and he constitutes the community because of his salvific action in Christ, a leveling of persons, a true equality, and a mutual respect, result. No longer Jew nor Greek, other distinctions disintegrate as well, for people of God explains the reality of being church, conceptually and existentially.

Finally, the description focuses on the *communal aspect of church life.* Relational dimensions are significant but so is the growth of the community. God may call a people to himself but there is always the challenge to become that people. Thus, essential to this model is growth as community and building up the community of faith. People of God is more corporate and personal, rather than simply a collective image.[13] It, therefore, understands unity as essential to its identity and incorporates a dynamic interaction among its members into its life. The Christian community also describes itself as a people in relation to the kingdom. While the people of God refers to the Christian believers, the kingdom of God is a larger reality than the church and extends beyond earthly existence.

People of God means the entire church, not simply the local church. However, in its *response* to the call to be a people, the church offers worship and service, both essential aspects of living according to the covenant originally established by God. Privilege is not important, but rather the opportunities for service. In accepting this relationship with God, the church assents to live out its righteousness in relationship to one another in commitment of love and service.

Paul uses people of God as a model for the church in his authentic letters. The analogy sheds light on his *theological understanding* of church and underlies his many challenges to the communities. The model itself has great potential for the church since it explains what the church is and opens believers to even fuller theological insights. People of God challenges the church to appreciate its roots in Judaism, to understand the points of continuity, but to also identify the theological distinctions and uniqueness of the Christian experience. In order to develop the points of departure from Israel as God's people, the church necessarily reflects on the difference Christ makes in the scheme of salvation history. Paul does this effectively in Galatians 3.

Because this concept focuses on God's choice and action in Christ, it opens the possibility for thanksgiving as a Christian response. Likewise, the celebration of life and the worship of a people seems an appropriate response to God's gift.

---

[13]See Minear, p. 229.

Since people of God means community, the responsibility to be a visible sign of unity, to exercise responsibility for building up the community, and to create an atmosphere conducive to growth, becomes integral to the model. However, people of God establishes a tension between who we are and who we are to become. The resolution of this tension is in the realization that in being God's people, we can also draw on his power available to the community through the Spirit of the Risen Lord.

People of God is a *dynamic image* of the church. It has historical roots in Israel, emphasizes the present reality in Christ, and moves us to the future as church. The Second Vatican Council recognizes its potential as a model for the contemporary church by placing this image before its treatment of the church in its hierarchical or structural manifestations.[14] Paul capitalizes on its potential and people of God becomes the foundation of his other descriptions. We too can reflect on this model to reinforce and reorient our thinking on the essentials of being church. The new people of God comes into existence because of Christ, and reflection on the significance of Christ for all humanity develops into another Pauline model, the new creation.

THE NEW CREATION

"In the beginning God created the heavens and the earth. The earth was without form and void, and darkness was upon the face of the deep; and the Spirit of God was moving over the face of the waters" (Gen 1:1-2). This creation story in Genesis marks the initial episode of beginnings in the Hebrew Bible. Noah, Moses, David, and Jeremiah, signify new beginnings for the Jewish community and a new relationship with Yahweh, the God of Israel. Paul's use of the concept of new creation *originates* in this Jewish tradition. He refers to previous signs of the covenant but explicitly identifies another new beginning. "For neither circumcision counts for anything, nor uncircumcision, but a new creation" (Gal 6:15).

---

[14]See document on "The Church."

This new age, effected by God in Christ, heralds a personal, communal, and cosmic transformation. The old world passes away; the Spirit again moves over the waters and realizes a new world in Christ. The new creation is not exaggerated imagery in Paul, but rather the basis of his reflection on the significance of Christ and possibilities of Christian life. In order to identify the qualitative difference Christ makes in this new age, Paul reflects on the time before Christ, particularly in relation to sin and the law.

The biblical *notion of sin* originates in Genesis, where its powers inhibit the full development of the original creation. Sin comes into the world created by God, through human fault. Adam is the representative figure characterizing the effects of sin and also the solidarity of humankind in sin. "Therefore as sin came into the world through one ... and death through sin, so death spread to all ... because all ... sinned" (Rom 5:12).

Throughout the scriptures, the pervasiveness of sin calls for a universal need for redemption. This power of sin marks our humanity's mode of existence in the world (Rom 6:14). All persons share in a common humanity, and therefore, in the weakness and transitoriness of human existence. Furthermore, these negative powers actually enslave persons. Individuals are responsible for their own actions, and inauthentic existence reflected in the vice lists in the Pauline letters becomes a distinct possibility (Gal 5:19-21; Rom 13:13; 1 Cor 5:10-11; 6:9-10; 2 Cor 12:20-21).

Just as sin exists in the world, and individuals can choose sin, it also has social ramifications. The vice lists, known to the Hellenistic world and used by Paul, address communal as well as individual attitudes and orientations. Opposed groups in society reflect this phenomenon of inauthentic existence (Gal 3:26-28; Rom 10:2; 1 Cor 12:13). Since sin is universal and pervades all levels of human life, the biblical writers establish a universal need for redemption (Rom 1:18-3:20). "We know that the whole creation has been groaning in travail together until now" (Rom 8:22). This bondage of individuals and communities is part of our heritage, but sin is also part of our responsibility.

Prior to Christ, humankind was powerless to effect a qualitative change in their world and so corruption prevailed. "Who will deliver me from this body of death? Thanks be to God through Jesus Christ our Lord!" (Rom 7:24-25). With Christ, a new existence becomes a possibility, even a reality. However, while Paul reflects on this sinful situation of humanity, he does not infer that human nature is corrupt nor does he focus on forgiveness of sins. Rather creation is very good (Gen 1:12.18.25.31), even though the power of sin continues to enslave us. While Paul identifies the practical consequences of sin (Rom 7), he does not trivialize sin, but uses broad strokes to create his understanding of sin and to establish a setting for his radical understanding of Christ's role in salvation.

Closely related to his understanding of sin is Paul's *assessment of the law*. His statements appear to be contradictory: "The law is holy, and the commandment is holy and just and good" (Rom 7:12), but "no human being will be justified in his sight by works of the law, since through the law comes knowledge of sin" (Rom 3:20). While Paul affirms the goodness of the law and the fact that God gives the law to his people, he also connects the law and sin. In his unusual assessment of the law, "It is the conclusion which is consistent, not the treatment of the law: all are condemned; all can be saved by God through Christ."[15] In certain passages, the law becomes the symbol of unredemption (Gal 3:13; Rom 4:13-16). The law itself cannot lead a person to salvation, for righteousness is from God, apart from the law. In fact, the law loses its splendor because of Christ (2 Cor 3:10); what was gain, changes to loss (Phil 3:7). The negative role of the law paves the way for Paul's evaluation of God's action in Christ.

God achieves his ultimate salvific purpose in an entirely different way. If there is any law for the believer, it is the "law of Christ" (Gal 6:2). External observance gives way to the power of love, for "love is the fulfilling of the law" (Rom 13:10). Furthermore, "sin will have no dominion over you, since you are not under the law but under grace" (Rom 6:14). Paul sees the law in a new perspective because he understands righteousness in a different way. "For the law of the Spirit of

---

[15]Sanders, *Paul, the Law*, p. 81.

life in Christ Jesus has set me free from the law of sin and death. For God has done what the law, weakened by the flesh, could not do" (Rom 8:2-3). In fact, the apostle could say, "you have died to the law through the body of Christ" (Rom 7:4). While the period under the law reflects God's purpose, the law itself becomes part of the old creation that is passing away. "Now the righteousness of God has been manifested apart from law, although the law and the prophets bear witness to it" (Rom 3:21). Thus, Paul draws on his own tradition to develop the exciting model of the new creation, symbolizing life for all humanity. The meaning of this description of Christian existence goes beyond any previous understanding, with sin and the law providing the springboard for the dawning of the new age.

The pivotal point of the new creation is the *radical difference Christ effects* by his death and resurrection. The recreation of humanity in Christ means a new existence for the believer, which is new life in the Spirit. Because the Christ event is the turning point in history, the last Adam replaces the first Adam by releasing a new power that supplants the power of sin. Reconciliation constitutes the foundation of this new creation, restoring harmony, peace and unity. Newness embraces every aspect of human life and the apostle affirms the universal scope of salvation in Christ.

In the new creation, justification belongs to all who believe in Christ, both Jew and Gentile, and this gift releases humanity from its former enslavement to sin. "But if Christ is in you, although your bodies are dead because of sin, your spirits are alive because of righteousness" (Rom 8:10). The guarantee of new life also implies the present realization of that life signified in freedom from the law. Furthermore, this gift of God in Christ gives birth to a new community of equals with the transformation of old alienations, becoming a distinct possibility. "Do not be conformed to this world but be transformed by the renewal of your mind, that you may prove what is the will of God, what is good and acceptable and perfect" (Rom 12:2). Life becomes satisfying and complete since a new power and presence of Christ establishes the community in faith. "Paul's 'high ecclesiology' suggests not only a messianic lifestyle within the church but also a revolutionary impact on the values of the world, to which the church is sent out as agent of transformation and beachhead of the dawning kingdom of God."[16] The new creation includes both an individual and a corporate transformation in Christ. Individual believers and the church draw on the power of the Spirit and so live differently.

A distinguishing mark of the new creation is *love,* for faith expresses itself through charity. Without love, the Christian is nothing (1 Cor 13:2). In fact, Paul says "Let all that you do be done in love" (1 Cor 16:14), "for you yourselves have been taught by God to love one another" (1 Thess 4:9). The consistent admonitions to love find their basis and most eloquent expression in the cross of Christ, through which God conveyed his love for us (Rom 8:28.35.37.39). This fullness of love provides a model for believers and for the church.

Christians attempt to discover new ways to express their love and to expand the sphere of their influence. Christian love implies fidelity to the Lord and obedience to his will. Qualities of active and persevering love emerge throughout Paul's letters, making this aspect of the new creation a concrete witness to its presence. Agapé implies qualitatively different relationships within the church since this love is a gift of the Spirit which brings us into a new relationship with God and with one another. It is the essence of Christian life and accounts for Paul's somewhat exalted view of the potential of Christian existence. "Complete my joy by being of the same mind, having the same love, being in full accord and of one mind" (Phil 2:2).

Furthermore, "you were called to freedom" and challenged "through love" to "be servants of one another" (Gal 5:13). "The centrality of love, rather than of a moral or legal code, self-control or self-abandonment, particularly marks off his concept of freedom from that of Judaism and Hellenism."[17] While *freedom* includes risk, it also offers new possibilities and new criteria for actions. Individual conscience becomes an important feature in the community. A person discovers the

---

[16]Beker, pp. 318-319.
[17]Banks, p. 31.

self, and becomes directly involved in his/her own destiny through decision-making.

However, in the Christian context, responsibility for oneself becomes tempered by responsibility for others. True liberation in Christ actually builds the new community into a striking herald of new values and new existence. This freedom challenges authority and sharpens the church's insight regarding its inner dynamics. Neither legalism nor license holds any sway if the church understands the meaning of Christian freedom.

Notably, the church can create an alternative lifestyle, steering its way clear of extremes. Freedom from fear and freedom for service lead to growth in the Christian community. Faith and obedience become enlightened responses when conditioned by love and freedom. The strong and the weak, women and men, apostles and local leaders, take these aspects of the new creation and integrate them into their communal roles and structures for ministry. "For freedom Christ has set us free, stand fast therefore, and do not submit again to a yoke of slavery" (Gal 5:1).

Paul's model of the new creation explains the reality of being church and being Christian. *Theologically,* the apostle uses the image to reflect on the significance of Christ in terms of Adam, sin, and the law. He also uses the creation stories and covenant relationships as a prelude to the new creation established in Christ. The symbols of creation, light, darkness, earth, life, water, and spirit, provide the basis for the rich Christian usage and development.

The new creation includes the created world, all humanity, and the universe, opening the possibility for futher reflection and analysis. This image heightens the believer's awareness of the power of the Risen Lord and his presence through the Spirit residing in the person and in the church. Contrast between old and new, first and last, clearly identifies the distinctive characteristics of the new creation. The community becomes this new creation in fact, if it understands the transformational implications of this model.

With love and freedom as the foundation of life within the church, the creation image touches all the basic relationships, decisions, and ministries in the community. *Principles* emerge which believers now apply to new situations. Responsibility becomes the cornerstone of action, and mutual liberation the greatest challenge. Inherent in this model is conflict and tension since believers work out the practical consequences of this vision for themselves and their communities. This particular understanding of the church offers continued potential for growth in our own age. In fact, this model touches timeless values, sparks an excitement, and constitutes an appealing vision for the contemporary church. Human aspirations resonate with the new creation and expand with this vision of reality, perhaps heralding another new age.

THE BODY OF CHRIST

The church as the body of Christ is a typically Pauline description and "unfolds a part of Paul's unique theological vision of the Christian church."[18] This image allows the apostle to reflect on dimensions of his ecclesiology and christology that might otherwise remain hidden. Body of Christ specifies aspects of the new creation better than the more general image of the people of God. While the church as people continues and fulfills God's promises to Abraham, the body of Christ expresses its special character and identity, for it focuses on the community's relation to Christ.

For the *origin* of this concept, rabbinic ideas about Adam influenced Paul.[19] His own conversion experience plays a part, for this experience identifies the basic union of Christ and the Christian. Some reliance on the Hellenistic concept of unity affects the apostle and his hearers, leading to the theme of unity in diversity. However, this development also emerges from his understanding of the body, *soma*. Paul moves away from the Corinthian enthusiasts who regard the body as an inferior part of a person and understands *soma* to signify the self, the whole person, the living being, the complex living organism, as would his Jewish contemporaries. This perception of the person includes the potentialities of the living person

[18]Worgul, p. 25.
[19]See Davies, p. 53.

(Rom 6:12-13; 12:1; 1 Cor 6:15; 12:7; Phil 1:20).

The human person is a unity that expresses itself, its vitality, purpose, and consciousness, through its spirit, *pneuma,* and its soul, *psyche.* However, in Paul these designations refer to the human spirit and the living person, not to a higher or spiritual part of the human being. Flesh, *sarx,* expresses the reality of the human condition, with its frailty and transitoriness, but *soma* is the basic understanding for Paul's designation of the community as the body of Christ.

When Paul describes the church as the body of Christ, he goes beyond the metaphorical or collective understanding to the "real" and "personal" sense.[20] He explicitly dwells on the *special bond* existing between Christ and the church, constituted by the Spirit. Paul draws attention to the community itself. "Now you are the body of Christ and individually members of it" (1 Cor 12:27). Our incorporation is into Christ, and because of this union, we are one body. Relationship within the community take their direction from the church's relationship to Christ.

The body of Christ model fosters reflection on the presence and activity of the Spirit among the believers, the communal life of the church, reflecting both its unity and its diversity, mutuality in relationships, and active participation of the members. The image also clarifies the mission of the church, responsibility for its development, and the gifts of the Spirit available to the church. The full meaning is expansive since the body grows, changes, and matures. The church as his body, actualizes Christ's presence in the world.

Membership in the body of Christ occurs through baptism, which initiates the process of union and participation. Through baptism believers share in Christ's life and become part of his body. Our communal incorporation expresses itself further in the celebration of the Lord's Supper. "The cup of blessing which we bless, is it not a participation in the blood of Christ? The bread which we break, is it not a participation in the body of Christ?" (1 Cor 10:16). This celebration effects, realizes, and

---

[20]See Ridderbos, chapter ix, "The Church as the Body of Christ," particularly pp. 362-369, for a development of this understanding in the Catholic and Protestant traditions.

expresses our unique identity as believers, insofar as we emulate the unity and solidarity of the body. The body of Christ is a bold expression conveying our common existence in Christ. Its significance as a model is without parallel since it includes an appreciation of our unity, gifts, functions, and mutual responsibility, based on an understanding of Christ and his continued presence through the Spirit.

The primary meaning of the community as the body of Christ is the special relationship and communion existing between Christ and his church. Christ acts through those whom he calls to union with himself. The many members become one body because of Christ, not because of their own efforts. The community that is the church exists because of its union with Christ; the church manifests this union in the unity of its members.

Christians baptized into the one body of Christ live out their commitment as *community*. Being a body implies an organic unity and a unique set of relationships: "If one member suffers, all suffer together; if one member is honored, all rejoice together" (1 Cor 12:26). This unity manifests itself in the ritual meal where all share in the one bread (1 Cor 10:17) and in our communal life that visibly reflects our unity as Christ's body. Many of Paul's admonitions spring from this conviction. "Live in harmony with one another," "live peaceably with all," "contribute to the needs of the saints, practice hospitality" (Rom 12:13-18).

The apostle also challenges opposing attitudes. "I appeal to you, ... that there be no dissensions among you" (1 Cor 1:10). He forces the church to address this issue by asking, "Is Christ divided?" (1 Cor 1:13). Unity among the members portrays the church's union with Christ; any separation or divisions become absurd according to the body image. In Paul's writings, local communities express this reality, as do all the churches together.

Within this analogy, worldly distinctions become obsolete; equality in Christ the norm. The universal image of one body of believers includes Jew and Gentile. However, the body model allows for the diversity which makes true unity possible. How inconceivable for parts of the body to alienate themselves or to desire uniformity (1 Cor 12:14-21). "If all were a single organ, where would the body be?" (1 Cor 12:19). "For the body does not consist of one member but of many" (1 Cor 12:14). A body does not tolerate diversity, it actually depends on it. So it is with the body of Christ.

Because of Christ we become his body, and he insures our development through the *presence of the Spirit.* The church shares the one Spirit whose gifts, given to everyone, nourish and nurture the body of Christ. Paul uses the body as a starting point for his understanding of *charisms and ministries* in the Christian community. Unity in diversity, harmony and peace are possible within the dynamic organism that is Christ's body. Charism concretizes and particularizes the gift of Christ's life to the church. For Paul, God endows each person within the Christian community with gifts that contribute to the building up of the community. Each person has the responsibility to use and to develop these gifts in the service of the church.

While the identification and prioritizing of charisms occur in the letters of Paul (1 Cor 12:8-10; 28-30; Rom 12:2-8), Robert Banks notes that the gifts actually encompass every aspect of community life.[21] Some gifts promote the growth of understanding in the community, such as prophecy, teaching, exhortation, discernment of spirits, and interpretation. Others address the psycho-social well-being of the community, its integrity and its harmony, such as the pastorally oriented gifts of helping and acts of mercy. A third group insures the physical welfare of the community, such as financial assistance and healing. A fourth group directs itself to the unconscious life of the congregation, such as speaking in tongues. All these charisms manifest the one Spirit and benefit the entire community. Likewise, each person has his/her "own special gift from God, one of one kind and one of another" (1 Cor 7:7). Paul welcomes all these gifts of the community although he does order them, first apostles, second prophets, third teachers (1 Cor 12:28-30). He also exhorts Christians to "earnestly desire" the higher gifts (1 Cor 14:39).

Moreover, Christians use all their competencies for service, with generosity, zeal, and cheerfulness (Rom 12:6-8). The

---

[21]See Banks, p. 103, for the four groups of charisms.

manner of utilizing the gifts of the Spirit actually establishes the quality of life in the churches, and the process of identifying these gifts and facilitating their development builds the relational bonds within the churches. Likewise, Paul "refuses to draw distinctions between members of the community according to the measure of 'holiness' they possess. The exclusion of any leading caste in the community of a priestly or official kind extends to a rejection of any spiritual aristocracy within it as well. For a start all genuine members of the community possess the Spirit."[22] The richness of the body of Christ lies in the true diversity of the gifts of all its members.

Describing the church as Christ's body also allows for a particular *understanding of authority*. Authority for the believers expresses itself in the service of the church, primarily in the recognition and utilization of the endowments of the Spirit. All members share in the authority of Christ which becomes crystallized in service. Charisms, the source and foundation of the various ministries in the community, provide a solid basis for the involvement of every person, albeit in very different ways. Paul maximizes the competencies of the co-workers, those of the local leaders, and those of the community itself. A healthy body lends itself to such an approach. Likewise, the development and use of gifts for the church implies personal growth and self-development.

Discernment of spirits and identification of need also contribute to a healthy organism. "All the members do not have the same function" (Rom 12:4), but they do have obligations and responsibilities. Participation on every level of community life is essential to being church. "To each is given the manifestation of the Spirit for the common good" (1 Cor 12:7). Leadership, administration, prophecy, and teaching complement almsgiving, hospitality, and the other gifts. Communities offer respect and esteem, when leaders function appropriately in the church and "because of their work" (1 Thess 5:12-13). Status counts for little; mutual respect is the ideal atmosphere for facilitating the contributions of all members of the body and for realizing authentic unity.

The community as the body of Christ is *a formidable model*

[22] Banks, p. 137.

that affirms the unique relationship between Christ and his church and results in unity among the members. The image expands as Paul reflects on different aspects of being a body. With its focus on Christ, this model affords the apostle an opportunity to explore the significance of Christ for believers. The fact that he uses the body image allows Paul to articulate his views on the church as a living organism rather than as an institution or organization. With Christ as the source of its life, Christians can adopt appropriate attitudes towards their own existence and acknowledge their total dependence on the Lord. Likewise, Paul's understanding of the human person, with its notable absence of dualistic tendencies, offers a healthy, wholistic, and realistic view for the Christian.

This model also emphasizes the unity of the body, the origin, the purpose, and the diversity of the gifts of the Spirit. Leaving little room for uniformity, inferiority, or pride, this description teases the mind into the creative *application of principles* to the actual situation of the early church. How does one preach one gospel and maintain unity, while at the same time allowing local churches to apply these principles of church life? How does the church appreciate all the gifts, while challenging people to grow in their service of the church? How does a Christian utilize and affirm differences while maintaining an egalitarian approach to communal life? How does local leadership facilitate the gifts of others?

Furthermore, this particular model of church encourages all members to assume their responsibility in the church. Ministry results from baptism, and each one serves according to their charisms. While the Spirit guarantees ministries essential to the church, members of the church need one another to express and to develop their life as the body of Christ.

The body model provides first-century Christians with a *theological reason* for undermining the patriarchal structures embedded within religion and society. It continues to do the same for the contemporary church. Furthermore, the body of Christ places a primary emphasis on relationship, rather than ritual. This perspective has timeless significance since the human and personal dimensions of being church are most satisfying and fulfilling, yet the most tenuous in their authentic development. Body of Christ touches the heart of being church

THE MYSTICAL PERSON

and continues to have potential for growth in our own experience.

In the letter to the Romans, Paul reminds the community, "you are not in the flesh, you are in the Spirit, if the Spirit of God really dwells in you. Anyone who does not have the Spirit of Christ does not belong to him. But if Christ is in you, although your bodies are dead because of sin, your spirits are alive because of righteousness. If the Spirit of him who raised Jesus from the dead dwells in you, he who raised Christ Jesus from the dead will give life to your mortal bodies also through his Spirit which dwells in you" (Rom 8:9-11). The notion of corporate personality gives rise to such a rich theological statement. In 1 Corinthians, Paul is more concise, but his point is clear: Anyone "who is united to the Lord becomes one spirit with him" (1 Cor 6:17). Likewise, in chapter 12 of the same letter, the apostle uses again and again the phrases "the same Spirit," "the same Lord," "one and the same Spirit," "one Spirit." It is the "same God who inspires them all in everyone." "All the members, though many, are one," since "all were made to drink of the same Spirit" (1 Cor 12:6.13). Paul derives his understanding of the church as the one mystical person from its *origin* in the corporate person.

The biblical connotation of the *corporate person* sounds quite foreign to the contemporary Christian. Yet it explains why all persons share in Adam's sin, and all believers in the covenants made with Abraham, Moses, and David. The Hebrew conception understands that the human personality could be expressed in the word, in a personal name, and in one's offspring. Likewise, "the group to which [one] belonged and in which [one's] life was merged was not confined simply to its present members but was extended to include past and future members, the whole group forming a single unity. This whole group could 'function as a single individual through any one of these members conceived as representative of it'."[23]

---

[23]D.S. Russell, *Between the Testaments,* p. 116, includes a quote from H.W.

Adam and Christ become representative figures in Paul. What occurs in each of these figures affects those united to them. In fact, the life of the one permeates the life of the many; when one acts, all participate, since all share the same life.

This particular perspective sheds light on the identity of the church. Not only are Christians united to Christ but believers are "in Christ," sharing his life and his Spirit. Paul assumes that the Spirit is the gift given to all Christians. This Spirit is the same Spirit that is in Christ, and so, the one Spirit animates and vivifies both Christ and Christians. The church becomes then, the one mystical person, the total Christ, as St. Augustine called it. "He has shared with us His Spirit who, existing as one and the same being in the head and in the members, vivifies, unifies, and moves the whole body. This He does in such a way that His work could be compared by the holy Fathers with the function which the soul fulfills in the human body, whose principle of life the soul is" (Dogmatic Constitution on the Church 7, 8). In this document, the Second Vatican Council draws on this early imagery, reminding us that the mystical person still constitutes a profound model for the Christian church.

Paul, convinced of this union and unity between Christ and believers, clarifies its meaning for the congregations. Reflected in the expressions "in Christ" and "in the Spirit" is a way of thinking fundamental to Paul's preaching and writing. The many become the one Christ, for they share the same inner life principle. What is predicated of the one, Paul presumes to be understood for all. Life in Adam becomes transformed by our life in the new Adam, Christ. This life affects the church since we form one person with Christ, and for this reason, the term, total Christ, can be used of church.

The apostle draws on a number of expressions to connote different levels of *incorporation into Christ:* through Christ, into Christ, with Christ, in Christ. However, the term "in Christ" comes closest to conveying his idea of the mystical person. To be in Christ expresses the intimate union of Christ and the Christian and the dynamic influence of Christ on

---

Robinson, "The Hebrew Conception of Corporate Personality," in *Werden und Wesen des Alten Testament,* 1936, p. 49.

those baptized in his name. This pervading influence affects the believer's life and conduct in practical ways. The person who is in Christ is a new creation, participating in, and belonging to, a new world. This participation in a qualitatively different life does not occur in special moments, rather this communion is an abiding reality, determinative of the entire life and behavior of the Christian. The believer can draw on this reality at all times. This presence and life in Christ enables the believer to live differently and is the ground of a truly new existence. Paul is so caught up with this possibility that the expression "in Christ" occurs 165 times in his correspondence. His exhortations challenge believers to become who they are in Christ. His mandates rest on his conviction that the one life of Christ and his power, integral to the identity of believers, permeates the church. The apostle says with confidence, "I can do all things in him who strengthens me" (Phil 4:13), for nothing is impossible.

This vital union constitutes the church's life and Christian existence. All that is said about Christ and the new creation becomes a reality for believers who share the one Spirit, the same Spirit as Christ. Every aspect of life is an opportunity to reflect this union. Nothing is secular for believers since transformation becomes the perspective for understanding Christian existence.

This union in Christ occurs because Christians share the *same Spirit,* "his Spirit which dwells in you" (Rom 8:11). Believers receive "the Spirit which is from God, that we might understand the gifts bestowed on us by God" (1 Cor 2:12). Apart from this Spirit we remain ignorant of God's greatest gift, his life that we share. "If we live by the Spirit, let us also walk by the Spirit" (Gal 5:25), for the "Spirit shows that Christian existence is based in the life of God and not in ordinary human possibility."[24]

Authentic human existence becomes a reality as Christians draw on the energy within themselves. Sharing the one Spirit enables them to realize in the present something of the fullness of life. "We all, with unveiled face, beholding the glory of the Lord, are being changed into his likeness from one degree of

[24]Ziesler, p. 96.

glory to another; for this comes from the Lord who is the Spirit" (2 Cor 3:18). This solidarity in the Lord belongs exclusively to believers who share the one Spirit, and thereby participate in the life of Christ. The model of the church as mystical person goes deeper than the body of Christ for it actually touches on the nature of our union. The statement of Paul, "For to me to live is Christ" (Phil 1:21), expresses his fundamental belief about our life as Christians.

Because of this profound union, Christians assess the exigencies of life in faith and view *Christian existence* in hope. "We are afflicted in every way, but not crushed; perplexed, but not driven to despair" (2 Cor 4:8). We "abound in hope" (Rom 15:13) because we share the risen life of our crucified Lord. This hope makes us bold (2 Cor 3:12), "and hope does not disappoint us, because God's love has been poured into our hearts through the Holy Spirit which has been given to us" (Rom 5:5). The concept of the mystical person, the one-in-the-many and the many-in-the-one, creates an opportunity for Paul to reflect on the quality of the relationship between Christ and his church. Likewise, sharing the one life allows Paul to develop a remarkable view of Christian life, full of potential and of hope.

The *model* of the church as the *one mystical person* provides many avenues for growth, clarification, and reflection. For the early Christians, this understanding explains why and how we are the new people of God, a new creation, and the body of Christ. Likewise, it accounts for the qualitative difference expected in Christian life and in the church. When we live this life, abiding in the Spirit of Christ the new Adam, we also discover there is no need to "spiritualize" our actions. Thus, a spirituality of integrated human Christian existence results from this model. Furthermore, Christian influence permeates every sphere of human activity in which Christians participate, for the life we live is Christ's. However, the human person is not submerged into another identity but reflects the influence of Christ and the Spirit.

This model challenges us to be aware of the life we share and to draw on the abiding presence of the Lord. The church with Christ forms a new reality, the mystical person, the total Christ. Many Christians set false limits to their potential, making a mockery of Christ, behaving like those who have no faith or hope. In Paul's day, the church understood the significance of the corporate personality, and the idea of the mystical person gave communities an extraordinary impetus to live the new life that was theirs in Christ and in the Spirit. Potentially, it can do the same for us as we search out new reasons for living and hoping.

The Dynamic Use of Models in Paul

As we have seen, Paul uses a great variety of descriptions to express his ideas about the Christian community. Many of these images, taken from the daily life of the people, convey the values of growth, holiness, and working together. You are a seed, a field, a building, a temple. Paul also describes the process of growth or of building, emphasizing the various roles and responsibilities within the community, and bringing out dynamic elements in potentially static images. The building itself is a prelude to building up the community; the field becomes important when Cephas, Apollos, Paul, and the community respond according to their own instincts regarding God's action in them.

Relational images become extremely significant. The *ekklesia* is the actual gathering of the community; the household adjusts its relationships to the radical truth of the gospel; the family and its members describe the quality of human/Christian relationships.

A few of the descriptions capture the imagination of the early church and emerge as models. People of God, the new creation, the body of Christ, and the mystical person clarify, assess, and expand the meaning of church. Each of these models originates in the Jewish and/or Hellenistic world. Each one speaks to a broad audience in various ways. Each analogy reveals a potential for expansive thinking and creative application.

THE UNDERLYING MEANING OF THE MODELS IN PAUL

The models, like the compelling images of Paul, are not clearly defined and delineated. They overlap in their meaning, and they often describe similar realities from only a slightly different perspective. For example, all the models demonstrate the radical difference Christ effects in terms of salvation and Christian life. God calls his new people in Christ; the new creation results because of God's salvific action in Christ; the body of Christ and the mystical person reflect the kind and quality of the union between Christ and his church. Also all the models imply a purpose or mission for the church. The people of God are called for a purpose. The body realizes its unity through the utilization of gifts expressed in service. Likewise, both the new creation and the mystical person reflect the actual transformation in Christ that creates this new reality of an ecclesial community.

These models also convey distinct aspects of the church's identity. Continuity with Israel is most clearly demonstrated in the people of God. However, the body of Christ pursues an entirely different dimension of church, its actual union with Christ. This description also specifies how we become the people of God in the local church and in our primary communities, thereby concretizing the broader image of God's people.

While the new creation and the mystical person draw on ways of thinking within the biblical tradition, their impact is far greater than any previous conception because of the underlying faith convictions regarding Christ himself. Union with God, sharing the one Spirit, living a new life in Christ, take on qualitatively different understandings for the believer. Paul often uses these images to inspire hope and challenge the community to new levels of existence.

All the models thus address some dimension of the reality of life in Christ; all are communal images rather than individualistic ones. However, they speak to both persons and communities because of the underlying perspective of the corporate personality. These models focus on essentials, convey vision, knowledge, and understanding. They elicit a response and thereby force us to apply these insights to particular situations.

THE APPLICATION OF THESE MODELS BY PAUL

Paul uses these models in each of his letters, conveying the essence of being church but being somewhat selective in his application. In Galatians and Romans, he draws on the understanding of people of God and the Jewish tradition to expand his ideas of the uniqueness and universal appeal of the Christian community. In Galatians he uses God's call as a starting-point for the new life in the Spirit. In Romans, he not only develops the idea of new creation but also that of the body of Christ. The prolific Corinthian correspondence draws on the greatest number of images and models, calling the Christian church to live out its identity in concrete ways within the community of faith. The Thessalonians reflect on their present identity and new life within the Christian assembly but also in terms of their future participation in Christ's life. The Philippians translate life in Christ into his pervasive influence on their community life and their hope for the future. Philemon brings attention to the practical consequences of being Christian in the household of faith.

The apostle Paul addresses significant issues in the early church through his use of models, such as the people of God, the new creation, the body of Christ, and the mystical person. He clearly identifies the place of Israel and areas of continuity with the tradition, appreciating the church's roots in the historical people of God. However, Paul also proclaims the newness of God's action in Christ and expands his vision of God's people to include Gentiles as well as Jews. Paul not only looks at universal and exclusive membership but also universal and local church, using the various models to emphasize one aspect, then another.

Furthermore, the apostle is not interested in a purely conceptual understanding of church. His ecclesiology emerges from his experience in the churches, and he confronts the local churches in terms of their actual life. He addresses the issue of unity, even though divisions exist. He appreciates diversity, even though actualizing this aspect of community is a monumental task. He confronts stereotypical roles, even though he and the churches struggle to integrate all persons and different views into their own experience as church.

The question of ministry takes on a new perspective with little emphasis on traditional forms such as priesthood, and great importance given to the gifts of all members of the churches. With the use of his models, Paul squarely faces the building up of the community by discernment, collaboration, and authentic response to the gospel. He provides a vision and a basis for working out problems and insuring the quality of life demanded by the gospel. The creative tensions he provokes expand the self-understanding of the church.

Finally, Paul identifies the presence of the Risen Lord through his Spirit within the community itself. He bypasses ritual as the core experience and focuses on ecclesial life in all its dimensions, including worship. Faith touches every aspect of life, and faith provides insight into issues of concern. The essential meaning of church for Paul is our identity in Christ, which signifies not mere improvement of our condition but transformation. It implies visible unity, mutual responsibility, and continued growth in the Spirit.

THE MESSAGE FOR THE CONTEMPORARY CHURCH IN PAUL

While the images and models used by Paul have great significance in the early church, some of them still constitute a major challenge for the contemporary church. The equality of all in the body of Christ and the essential ministry of each person according to gift, provide the basis for our dialogue on the role of women and laity in a very different model of church. The new creation can expand into care for our environment, our world, and its resources. It can appeal to the cosmic consciousness of our age. The understanding of the mystical person can solidify our bonds and give us new hope for effectiveness and for quality life. The various models of body and new creation, when applied critically to the church itself, will sensitize us to new forms of oppression, slavery, selectivity, inequality, and exploitation. They also provide an insight into the dynamics of collegial relationships and allow us to rethink the hierarchical and institutional emphases of our churches. Human existence and sexuality take their rightful place when we understand the implications of the mystical person and the new creation. A rethinking of the values of the human person and the human body seems essential for the church today.

Furthermore, some early images are potential models for today. The household, with its varied relationships based on extended family ties and faith commitment, could speak to our basic ecclesial communities and neighborhood groups. This potential model invites experimentation and could effect radical changes today as in the early Christian experience. Perhaps, the time has come to affirm the family model. In the lay-centered church, this experience of family resonates with many believers and its values of intimacy, love, creative development, and growth toward maturity, need reaffirmation. What we learn in the family can help us address some of the issues of a divided church. Perhaps urban images will take on a new meaning as we identify architectural advances and reflect on the cosmopolitan flavor of our large populations centers and our changing technological world.

Several questions come to mind. What models appeal to us and capture our imagination? What are the images that speak to our world? What are the new models emerging from our experience as church in our different environments? Just as Paul's vision of church and his models grew out of his experience and his tradition, so must ours.

The models critically explain the reality of church and contain many points for further growth. Paul, while not committed exclusively to any one model, conveys a similar realization through all his models and images. In Christ, you are a new creation; in his Spirit, you form one person. The early church attempts to live according to its identity, drawing on the one Spirit that is its life and witnessing to the unity of the body of Christ. Today's church must do the same.

6

Paul's Spirituality of Ecclesial Dedication

> "Never flag in zeal, be aglow with the Spirit, serve the Lord. Rejoice in your hope, be patient in tribulation, be constant in prayer." (Rom 12:11-12)

Spirituality is about life and maturity, living and growing in authentic relationships to God, the world, and one another. In the letters of Paul, the apostle's vision of church, and the models he uses serve to challenge Christians to live as church. The spirituality of Paul's writings is a spirituality of ecclesial dedication. Little interest in individualistic piety emerges in the correspondence, rather, the conversion experience is primarily a conversion to the church. Therefore, Paul challenges Christians to understand their call to be church and to respond accordingly with lives of faith, hope, and service. Christian spirituality enriches the life of the church; the spirituality of Christians visibly presents the church to non-believers. Likewise, the ecclesial spirituality of the letters incarnates the mission of Christ and his church.

Paul always reminds his communities that the gospel he preaches comes from "a revelation of Jesus Christ" (Gal 1:12). Faith leads to an understanding of this gospel, a faith that marks the end of the old existence and the beginning of new life. Faith permeates every aspect of a person's life and challenges the believer to respond in line with convictions (1 Cor 16:13; Gal 5:1; Phil 1:27; 4:1; 1 Thess 3:8). Holiness of life includes this visible and social dimension, which becomes a sign of our true holiness as church.

Paul believes that he embodies many qualities of Christian life, and so he frequently urges Christian to imitate himself (1 Thess 1:6-7; Phil 3:17; 1 Cor 4:15-16; 11:1), knowing that others need concrete examples of Christian values. Example itself thus becomes a powerful exhortation. However, communities must extract principles from the apostle's example and then adapt them to their own situation and experience. Paul does not advocate slavish imitation but rather an appreciation of God's action in him and a sensitivity by the community to God's similar action in their own personal and communal experience. Faith affects all the activities of believers, and Christian faith challenges believers to be church in new ways.

This chapter examines the characteristics of spirituality in Paul. It then identifies various aspects of this spirituality of eccesial dedication, namely, a constant dialogue with God, the centrality of Christ, a common vision, the place of prayer, ethical principles, union with the dying and rising of Christ, a common service of others, evangelization and the empowering of church life in others. Paul's insights into ecclesial living constitute the most challenging and exhilarating aspects of his rich legacy, for he presents the practical consequences of belief in a dynamic portrayal of authentic ecclesial existence.

Characteristics of Spirituality in Paul

Paul's spirituality and that of his converts focus on being church together. Growth as a community of believers constitutes the most appropriate response to God's call in Christ. In fact, Paul insures Christians against a privatization of faith by his emphasis on community and through his models of the church. While the apostle does not minimize the value of the individual, he consistently maximizes the impact we have on one another and our mutual responsibility.

Paul's own conversion includes an appreciation of the community dimension of faith. His own christological insight paves the way for the appreciation of the potential of the church's union with the Lord. Because of this realization, Paul challenges believers to live as church and to think as communities of faith. Necessarily, the spirituality emerging in Paul's letters to the churches takes on the distinctive characteristics of being church.

KEY ASPECTS OF SPIRITUALITY IN THE LETTERS

The Christian's response in faith results in a spirituality of *ecclesial living*. Our communal life identifies us as a people and as church. Living and growing together as a community of believers is the most appropriate response for the Christian. Personal faith grows as the individual matures in relation to God and to others. An authentic response to the values of the world occurs when the church thinks through situations, needs and responsibility. Being church and witnessing to this reality is the prime commitment of disciples. Paul invites us to develop our relationships in light of this call to ecclesial living. "We beseech and exhort you in the Lord Jesus, that as you learned from us how you ought to live, and to please God, just as you are doing, you do so more and more" (1 Thess 4:1). This aspect of spirituality reflects our unity and the essential insight that we are the body of Christ.

Spirituality means *holiness* of life for the believers in Jesus. Paul's understanding of holiness is far from elitist. He sees all Christian as God's beloved, as saints. Furthermore, holiness becomes a reality in our own particular situation of life. "Let every one lead the life which the Lord has assigned to [him/her], and in which God has called [him/her]. This is my rule in all the churches" (1 Cor 7:17). "Every one should remain in the state in which [that person] was called" (1 Cor 7:20.cf:24). The Christian discovers God's will in the circumstances of life and grows in holiness in these practical life situations. Paul's insight that sanctification occurs in the experience of daily life challenges Christians to seek the transformation of their lives in Christ.

At times, the apostle contrasts different realities to clarify a point, using the Spirit and the flesh as representative of two possible modes of existence.[1] Paul demonstrates that a personal

---

[1] See Ridderbos, p. 66.

choice in either direction is always possible and constantly affirms a dynamic concept of holiness for all believers. Holiness is the result of our response to God's call, worked out in our individual lives and with others. However, the apostle also sees holiness as God's gift to the church itself, since it shares the Spirit of Christ. In Paul's understanding growth in holiness occurs as love increases (1 Thess 3:12-13) and as the one "who began a good work in you" brings it to completion (Phil 1:6). Holiness, a reality for the church, becomes intimately connected with the daily lives of all believers.

This perspective of holiness leads to a unique *view of Christian existence*. "Whether you eat or drink, or whatever you do, do all to the glory of God" (1 Cor 10:31). Such a positive view of Christian existence is refreshing. God's gift of life, expressed in the concrete existence of the human person, is life animated by faith, love, and hope, that takes on new value. Being human is our mode of being in the universe. Spirituality recognizes this fact and relegates nothing to the purely "secular" sphere. Sexuality, family life, service of others, personal growth, and work, provide the framework of our Christian/human existence. These tangible realities are the vehicles for manifesting our life in Christ. This wholesome approach reverences all life and allows God's life to channel itself through every avenue of human experience. Furthermore, this understanding of Christian existence provides for the appreciation of all life and experience, making this expression of spirituality catholic and universal.

The apostle's view of Christian existence also enables us to identify the *attitudes and qualities* essential to our life as church. A basic assumption for Paul occurs in his powerful statement: "You are all one in Christ," designating the radical equality of all persons in the believing community. Paul also suggests, "Give thanks in all circumstances; for this is the will of God in Christ Jesus for you" (1 Thess 5:18). Thanksgiving and joy are basic attitudes of Christian life. Other qualities include generosity, confidence, trust, hope, and patience. 'We do not lose heart" but "rejoice" in "perfect confidence" (Gal 6:9; 2 Cor 7:16). Christians reflect in their personal and communal attitudes the "God of love and peace" who calls and nurtures them (2 Cor 13:11). In fact, *the* quality of the new existence is love. "Make love your aim" and let this love be genuine (1 Cor 14:1; 2 Cor 8:8). Love that is gracious in giving, free, spontaneous, and mutual, characterizes authentic Christian existence. When the church consistently reflects this love among its members, it reflects the love of God manifested in Christ.

Spirituality rightly becomes an *apostolic spirituality* since a spirituality that centers itself on Christ unites itself to the mission of Christ. Paul directs his own attention to the service of others. Even when he is in prison, the apostle reflects on the churches, their growth and development. Community life becomes the concern of Christians as they use their gifts for building up the church. Although limitations exist, interest in others, communal growth, and the mission of the church are basic aspects of Christian existence and a life of service becomes the distinctive mark of apostle, prophet, and every believer. Continuous conversion to the mission of the church occurs in ministry since it is here that we clearly identify both the needs and the gifts of others.

A spirituality that incorporates ecclesial dedication certainly reflects the *tensions* that exist in our Christian experience. So much is possible since we are transformed in Christ. So much is still ahead of us since we must continuously appropriate salvation in Christ and express our hope in the fullness of life. Living as church remains a creative impetus to development and change.

Finally, a spirituality of ecclesial living challenges us to *grow as church*. "Do not be children in your thinking; be babes in evil, but in your thinking be mature" (1 Cor 14:20). Paul often expresses his own commitment to nurture fledging communities: "We were gentle among you, like a nurse taking care of her children" (1 Thess 2:7). However, growth as church requires us to consider all the aspects of experience that prod us to new levels of thinking and being. These include affirmation, teaching, exhortation, confrontation, mutual support, and patient love.

In his letters, Paul identifies a number of consistent characteristics of Christian spirituality. This spirituality embodies ecclesial life, holiness in our situation of life, a positive view of Christian existence, attitudes and qualities conducive to living as church, an apostolic orientation, tension modified by hope, and a challenge to continually grow as church. Paul develops these basic characteristics as he clarifies the fuller meaning of a spirituality of ecclesial dedication.

Components of Paul's Spirituality of Ecclesial Living

A CONSTANT DIALOGUE WITH GOD

If spirituality concerns itself with perennial values, then Christian spirituality rightly focuses on God, the ultimate source of its life and convictions. Paul acknowledges this fundamental relationship to God in several ways. "By the grace of God I am what I am, and his grace toward me was not in vain" (1 Cor 15:10). He also states, "Not that we are sufficient of ourselves to claim anything as coming from us; our sufficiency is from God" (2 Cor 3:5). The apostle acknowledges the wisdom of God's ways. "We know that in everything God works for good with those who love him, who are called according to his purpose" (Rom 8:28). This confidence in God, response of love on the part of the Christian, and understanding of God's purpose, come through the intuitive insight of the contemplative. Paul believes that all Christians have access to this mystical life and union in all its depths. They can receive the revelation of God and speak to God (2 Cor 12:1; 1 Cor 14:28). In fact, a profound contact with God is the presupposition of Christian life and of effectiveness in ministry. "If we live, we live to the Lord, and if we die, we die to the Lord; so then, whether we live or whether we die, we are the Lord's" (Rom 14:8).

The level of belonging to the Lord and understanding his ways results from a constant openness and dialogue. Christians believe that God does reveal himself and communicate his purposes to them. His revelation comes in a variety of ways: in the word of scripture, through the wonders of nature, in the person Jesus, through the presence of the Spirit, through others, and in our personal experiences. Receiving this revelation requires sensitivity to the diverse forms of God's presence and communication, with listening, trust, and patience, the prerequisites for a true dialogue.

Quiet reflection prepares us for the gift of insight. However, in Paul's understanding of this basic component of spirituality, God's ways emerge in and through our life situation, our ministry, and our contact with others. A Christian cannot limit or confine the source of revelation to certain sublime moments or special experiences. A viable spirituality attunes itself to a constant dialogue with God, with its ongoing revelation, and our continual responsiveness. Perhaps the glance of love, the attentiveness of mutual love, and self-gift of love, prepare us most fully to receive the God of love and to experience the union that is possible.

The Spirit of God dwells in us (Rom 8:9), and we have access to this Spirit and to its movements, as we become sensitive to its presence and to its working in ourselves. This indwelling presence becomes part of our growing awareness and ongoing dialogue with God who is the ground of our being and who communicates his life to us. Our spirituality bases itself on this revelation and this life principle.

THE CENTRALITY OF CHRIST

Since God communicates himself most clearly in Christ, Christian spirituality centers itself on the person Jesus. Paul acknowledges this focal point as he writes to his congregations. "I give thanks to God always for you because of the grace of God which was given you in Christ Jesus" (1 Cor 1:4). God now acts in Christ, in fact, God in Christ is "reconciling the world to himself" (2 Cor 5:19). Indeed, "while we were yet helpless, at the right time Christ died for the ungodly" (Rom 5:6). Because of this action the love of Christ controls the believer (2 Cor 5:14). Through Christ, God leads us in triumph (2 Cor 2:14). Nothing in fact "will be able to separate us from the love of God in Christ Jesus our Lord" (Rom 8:39).

So central is Christ for the apostle Paul, that he claims, "what we preach is not ourselves, but Jesus Christ as Lord, with ourselves as your servants for Jesus' sake" (2 Cor 4:5). Believers have the mind of Christ and find their strength in him (1 Cor 2:16; Phil 1:21; 4:13). Christ becomes the model for church life in his self-gift, and so Paul invites Christians to conform to the pattern of the Lord's life (Phil 2:6), as he becomes the firstborn of many brothers and sisters who share in his life through baptism (Rom 8:29; 1 Cor 15:49; 2 Cor 3:18).

The centrality of Christ and union with Christ dominate Paul's understanding of his new life after conversion. Christian spirituality not only takes note of God's action in Christ, but realizes that Christian life itself takes on meaning because of this mystery of faith. To be Christian is to be in Christ, to be one with him and with those he calls to be his body. Realizing the place of Christ is the backbone of Christian existence and our life as church. Understanding this aspect of salvation commits us to being church since Christ and believers form one mystical person. Integral to New Testament spirituality is an ecclesial spirituality. While our comprehension of being Christian is a personal appropriation, our actualizing of this reality is more than a private affair, it is being church. Thus, Christ brings us new life, affects every aspect of our lives, and challenges us to live in union with him and with one another.

A COMMON VISION OF COMMUNITY

Touching the mystery of God and of God in Christ, introduces believers to a new vision of reality. This common vision emanates from the common source of our life and our union in Christ. As we touch the mystery of God and of Christ, we begin to understand the mystery of the church. We articulate our common vision when we describe ourselves as God's people, a new creation, Christ's body, and when we live as one mystical person. This sense of church forces us to think as "we" since we are united to one another in Christ. Our personal lives of faith become intimately connected to the community of faith, and our actions affect one another, not simply ourselves. A new spirit emerges as Christians realize that their basic identity calls them to live and work together as community. In this ecclesial experience, all are one in Christ, and all are are endowed with gifts for the building up of community. Baptism becomes the leveling experience as we begin to appreciate our basic equality and unity in Christ.

Love, the basis of our existence, becomes the hallmark of

our life together, "Let all that you do be done in love" (1 Cor 16:14). Not only love, but mutual love that balances freedom and responsibility. Furthermore, just as Christ was at the service of others, so are we as members of the church. A shared vision enables us to express our identity while appreciating the various gifts and diverse roles in the one body. Individually, Christians can discover a unity of life and purpose, communally we do the same.

In an ecclesial spirituality, the vision itself is inadequate. What is essential is a common or shared vision, solidly based on the authentic interpretation of God's action in Christ. Since the mystery of the church gradually unfolds as the understanding of Christ develops, so too should we expect a continually unfolding perspective of church. No individual, no local community, and no particular age, fully grasps the meaning of our ecclesial identity. As we identify the essentials of our life as church, we also continue to interpret and adapt these principles to local situations.

A common vision actually becomes something that unites many different people, witnessing to our unity in diversity, as Paul so wisely noted. Our vision grows from believer's constant dialogue with God in their lives, and dialogue with one another in the Spirit of Christ. A Christian vision results from the corporate views of the members of the body. Insofar as this is so, the church authentically incarnates the new creation and remains a sign of Christ's transforming Spirit in the world. Our common vision, then, is one we all share in Christ, since we all contribute to that vision according to our God given competencies and insights.

THE PLACE OF PRAYER

Vision results from insight, and a vision of church requires an ability to articulate personal views and to process the ideas of others. Articulation and processing are skills that can be acquired. However, the insight itself comes from a profound contact with reality and reflection on that experience. A vital avenue towards that insight is prayer.

Prayer opens us to the possibility of an intense contact with

God and a new appreciation of his presence and activity. Prayer enables us to develop other dimensions of our human personalities. It is also the vehicle that enables us to appreciate the richness of the lives of others. Furthermore, prayer puts us in contact with the mystery of God, ourselves, and others, since through prayer we pursue an unending wealth of possibilities and experience.

Paul's prayer engages his entire personality, has universal scope, and offers practical implications. Not only does the apostle plead for his needs and those of the churches, he acknowledges that the spirit "intercedes for us with sighs too deep for words" (Rom 8:26). His prayer is full of thanksgiving and joy (Phil 1:4.19). He never ceases to pray for the churches (Rom 1:9), also urging them to be constant in prayer (Rom 12:12), "praying earnestly night and day" (1 Thess 3:10). A prayerful life offers practical results, such as inner peace, by reducing anxiety, since our requests are made known to God (Phil 4:6). More importantly, prayer puts us in touch with ourselves and with the Lord, culminating in the praise and glory of God. (Phil 2:11).

The contemplative insight that sparks the imagination of believers results from the quality of these moments of profound contact with the Lord. This kind of openness to the divine becomes essential to our personal faith lives. In fact, we move from personal prayer to a quality sharing of faith together in word and worship. Prayer together creates and deepens the bonds of unity among believers, thereby enhancing the life of the church. Likewise, in Paul's conversion experience and in his own diverse experience of prayer, the fruits of prayer, rather than the experience itself, are significant. Religious experience and prayer result in mission and ministry, forming in believers an apostolic spirituality.

ETHICAL PRINCIPLES

Spirituality, while understanding its core as the experience of God in Christ, necessarily expresses itself in Christian life and behavior. Guidelines for action constitute an important aspect of a viable spirituality. The letters of Paul reveal the basis for moral and ethical behavior, principles for action, and specific exhortations to concretize their meaning for the early Christians. Paul's thinking contrasts sharply from that of the Pharisees, a formative influence in his own moral development, and from the perspective of many other Jewish Christians. He presents a level of thinking that could easily be misunderstood, since he focuses on broader issues rather than simply on whether a given action is right or wrong.[2] Because of this approach, Paul's ethical principles have significance beyond the religious and cultural milieu of the first century.

Paul's ethics are strongly christocentric, finding their criterion for action in righteousness in Christ.[3] Holiness of life originates in God's act of justification, for we "obtain salvation through our Lord Jesus Christ" (1 Thess 5:9). Righteousness determines the conduct or activity appropriate to our relationship with God and others in Christ,[4] and we can identify two aspects of ethical behavior for the Christian. The justified person necessarily responds to God's gift and brings forth fruit, described as an ethics of expansion. Likewise, the Christian takes care not to fall back under the yoke of slavery, an ethics of watchfulness.[5]

Underlying the basis of behavior is the realization that Christ actually transforms our Christian lives. This reality of the newness of life conditions our Christian responses and makes them qualitatively different from the responses of others. Not only is righteousness the basis of ethical behavior but more significantly the motivation for God's action in Christ stimulates a new level of thinking. The center of Paul's ethical thought, and the guiding principle in ethical behavior, is love. This realization marks a new stage in moral reasoning and provides a relational foundation for behavior.

Paul writes during the initial developing period of the church's life. Reflection on the scriptures, the ethical traditions, and the kerygma of the early church lead to an evolution of

---

[2]See Brunt, p. 121.

[3]See Baird, p. 57; see also Byrne, chs. 9 and 10.

[4]See Williams, p. 241.

[5]Goguel, p. 429, identifies these dualistic aspects of ethics, noting a similarity between Paul and Jesus.

principles of behavior and specific moral exhortations.[6] The apostle frequently focuses on attitudes that clearly reflect our faith in Christ. Through letters and dialogue, he shares ideas that eventually emerge into a consensus of beliefs and goals. Wayne Meeks notes that "The fluid but recognizable set of beliefs, attitudes, and dispositions that constituted the common ethos of the Pauline groups would tend to produce a certain level of consensus about most behavior expected in these communities."[7]

However, Paul provides more of a service to the church when he deals with complex and sensitive issues by extracting the *principles* that should direct Christian behavior. He considers the one life we share in the Spirit and advocates that we walk in the Spirit. Rather than dictate the faith response of others, he points out the basis of his instruction, invites the community to participate in his reasoning or judge for themselves, and reminds them of what they already know.[8] Paul instructs, persuades, commands, and challenges his communities to incorporate Christian values into their daily lives. His concern is the actualization of these values, and so he identifies several basic principles of behavior to guide the communities. "Only let your manner of life be worthy of the gospel of Christ ... stand firm in one spirit, with one mind striving side by side for the faith of the gospel" (Phil 1:27). Paul develops this fundamental challenge in several ways, mindful of the expectancy and enthusiasm of believers and respecting their possession of the Spirit.

A vital principle of ethical behavior surfaces in Galatians 3:28. The *radical equality* of believers in Christ, and the elimination of social and sexual distinctions in the community of faith, mark a different lifestyle for the Christian churches. Not only do stereotypical and traditional roles lose their force, but the ideas and leadership that develop community life become

---

[6]Whiteley, pp. 205-206, notes that Paul connects every article of the kerygma with specific moral exhortations and gives examples.

[7]Meeks, p. 136.

[8]Westerholm, p. 245, also gives the following references: respect for the faith of others: 2 Cor 1:24; 8:8; 1 Thess 2:7; Phm 8f; basis of instruction: 1 Cor 7:40; participate in decisions: 1 Cor 10:15; 11:13; reminders: Rom 15:15; 1 Cor 4:17.

everyone's responsibility. Likewise, the church itself sets its direction and its ethical standards, based on the insights of all. This principle, so basic to a collegial environment, results in a different way of approaching ethical behavior. Ecclesial life becomes the context for personal decisions and all members of the community contribute according to their gifts. Equality of believers in Christ prepares the way for dialogue rather than legislation, even in regard to moral behavior.

Freedom of conscience is another principle emerging from the letters, particularly in 1 Corinthians 8-10. Interestingly, in the issue of eating food offered to idols, the operative principle is not the individual's inner consciousness or personal judgment regarding the action. The relationship between people is the real ethical question.[9] Paul underscores responsibility towards others rather than the simpler right or wrong criteria for behavior. The principle of behavior resides in an ecclesial spirituality, so firmly in place in Paul's letters. In fact, attention to the effects of behavior on others is a guideline for Pauline ethics. 'If your brother [or sister] is being injured by what you eat, you are no longer walking in love. Do not let what you eat cause the ruin of one for whom Christ died" (Rom 14:15). Christians always seek "the good of the neighbor" (1 Cor 10:24), a special responsibility of the "strong" and the mature in the Pauline communities.

However, the key principle in moral or ethical behavior is *Christian love*. "Paul deserves the credit for having originally constructed the synthesis of all moral prescriptions in terms of charity."[10] God acts in love, and he pours his love into our hearts (Rom 5:5). Paul advocates that believers make love their aim, and he places love above faith (1 Cor 13:2.13). For the apostle Christian love emanates from the cross, the perfect manifestation of God's love for humankind. Love directs our life as a community. Love is the source and the criterion for our actions and our decisions. For the early church, continual clarification of the meaning of love, challenged Christians to truly center this virtue in the mystery of Christ's death and

---

[9]See Horsley, pp. 586-589; Brunt, p. 115, who speaks of "principled ethical thinking" that transcends the rightness or wrongness of the act itself.

[10]Spicq, p. 90.

resurrection, so that his self-gift becomes the paradigm for community life.

Paul draws on a few basic principles to guide his churches in their moral and ethical responses. The equality of all persons in Christ, freedom tempered by responsibility to others, and Christian love, direct and modify the behavior of believers. Communities adapt and apply these principles to their own situations, and Paul suggests ways of insuring the growth of the churches through his own exhortations to the churches.

The placement of the *exhortations* within the Pauline correspondence is itself a point of teaching. Generally, the exhortations follow the theological or dogmatic sections of the letters, indicating that only when the churches understand the essence of their faith can they be challenged to live it out in concrete ways. This principle of knowledge conditioning behavior enables the church to reflect on its identity in Christ and to draw out the implications of their belief for their daily lives.

Culture conditions the exhortational examples of what constitutes authentic Christian existence. Many of the exhortations are actually responses to specific questions or the part of an ongoing dialogue with the community, and thus they need to be interpreted in this light. Some admonitions emerge as vice lists in the letters, already known to the Hellenistic world, covering areas of social, religious, sexual, and personal significance (Rom 1:29-31; 13:3; 1 Cor 5:10-11; 6:9-10; 2 Cor 12:20-21; Gal 5:19-21). Likewise, Paul exhorts Christians to perform the duties of their life, obey authorities, pay taxes and debts, and love one another (Rom 13:1-11). In some instances, the ethical admonitions seem to contradict Paul's own theology and ministerial experience. "He does have a myopic view of marriage. His theology is unexceptional, yet in his insistence that the married are less free for the Lord he fails to entertain the possibility that the married can do something for him better than the single, giving hospitality for instance. Nor does he allow that a couple's commitment to each other need not compete with their commitment to Christ but may be a way of fulfilling it."[11] Paul's teaching about marriage and slavery is for

[11] Ziesler, p. 115

an interim period, for they are examples of how his belief in an imminent end directly affects his ethical perspective.

Paul uses exhortations as concrete examples of his theological and ethical principles. Some of these admonitions and challenges provide new areas of application for his converts. However, the specific qualifications take on importance insofar as they reflect the basic principles of equality, freedom, responsibility, and mutual love. Furthermore, when communities accept specific suggestions and begin to incorporate them into their own experience of church, they necessarily struggle with creative adaptation. In areas of ethical and moral behavior, local situations and communal relations influence how the general principles become part of the Christian experience. Legal codes give way to a new understanding of behavior. An appreciation of the law of love creates the community as it establishes guidelines, urges new attitudes, and suggests appropriate behavior. "Whatever is true, whatever is lovely, whatever is gracious, if there is any excellence, if there is anything worthy of praise, think about these things" (Phil 4:8).

UNION WITH THE DYING AND RISING OF CHRIST

Christian spirituality adheres to a difficult and often contradictory paradigm for Christian life, our union with the dying and rising of Christ. Although "a stumbling block to Jews and folly to Gentiles" (1 Cor 1:23), Paul decides "to know nothing among you except Jesus Christ and him crucified" (1 Cor 2:2). The cross and the death of Jesus are the redemptive center of Paul's thought, since, while we were still sinners, Christ died for us (Rom 5:8-11). The cross profoundly reflects God's love for humanity, for he sent his Son that we might live (1 Cor 15:45; 2 Cor 5:21).

However, Paul does not dwell on the death of Jesus as an isolated event. The death and the resurrection of Christ effect salvation for the Christian. While the two events cannot be fused into one, death/resurrection together constitute the salvific event. New life in the Spirit and present realization of our ultimate victory in Christ, become possible for the Christian because of this central mystery of our faith. The resurrection provides such a startling realization for the church that the earliest Christians believed they were already risen, with many not expecting death for themselves (1 Thess 4:13-18). However, the real impact of the Risen Lord rests in the fact that we are "in Christ" and receive his "life-giving Spirit" (1 Cor 15:45; 2 Cor 3:17-18). Christians actually share Christ's power, victory, and life, a reality affecting the quality of their lives.

Paul's contribution, however, is not in his reflection on the cross or resurrection, but in his explication of the Christian's union with the dying and rising of Christ. Believers share Christ's condition: "for if we have been united with him in a death like his, we shall certainly share in a resurrection like his" (Rom 6:5). Furthermore, "if we have died with Christ, we believe that we shall also live with him. . . . So you must consider yourselves dead to sin and alive to God in Christ Jesus" (Rom 6:8.11). Paul's prolific statements about the union of Christians with the dying and rising of Christ, provide a simple basis for Christian existence. This foundation is realistic and powerful. Paul centers his ethics in this paradox as union with, not imitation of, Christ, and this becomes the criterion for Christian behavior.

This union with the dying and rising of Christ enables Christians to make sense out of their lives. *Suffering* becomes an anticipated part of our reality, since Christ "humbled himself and became obedient unto death, even death on a cross" (Phil 2:8). He impoverished himself, taking on the form of a servant. Paul takes this model and demonstrates how these very same attitudes must permeate community life, for the churches have the same mind as Christ.

However, while suffering becomes comprehensible in light of Christ's suffering and death, Paul also reflects on the growth possibilities of Christian existence. Since we have put on Christ, we can now live differently. Since Christians share his Spirit, they also draw on his abiding presence and his love. The exhortations in Paul's letters indicate the possibilities of Christian life. If they seem relentless in their quest for authentic existence, they also embody the realism of Christian existence, our transformation in Christ. Christian spirituality never lets go of the tension between death and life, since baptism unites believers to Christ's dying and rising. This paradox provides a balanced and integrated approach to life.

If our union with Christ in his death and resurrection means anything, it forces us to realize that as believers, we cannot wallow in suffering without hope or settle for mere optimism instead of hope. Christian life solidly bases itself in an unusual model, one that explains our existence, yet challenges us to continually move to new beginnings.

A further realization of the significance of our union with Christ coincides with Paul's statements on *reconciliation*. "God was in Christ reconciling the world to himself, not counting their trespasses against them, and he committed to us the message of reconciliation" (2 Cor 5:19). Reconciliation refers to the change in relationship between God and humanity, the renewal of our existence in Christ. For Paul, reconciliation affects Christian life and denotes the transformation of existence, so that the love of God controls us (2 Cor 5:11-15). Peace and joy results, even though believers still live the paschal experience. The process of reconciliation and our full response to God's graciousness remain the ongoing work of the Christian. Community life reflects our progress and our struggle as the church allows Christ's healing peace to bridge differences and to encourage creative dialogue. Believers are dead to sin (Rom 6:2) but must continously remove the remaining obstacles to authentic existence. Thus our spirituality rests on a realistic hope, for we understand both the struggle and the goal.

Forgiveness exemplifies the believers approach, forgiveness of oneself and of others in the community. Certainly, this component of spirituality characterizes Paul's experience with the Corinthian church. The spirit of mutual forgiveness must permeate the community, and the community's forgiveness of others becomes effective for the apostle. "Any one whom you forgive, I also forgive" (2 Cor 2:10). This forgiving action is a concrete result of being an ambassador of reconciliation (2 Cor 5:10). Paul and the communities energetically work towards unity by eliminating divisions and building up the bonds of trust, love, and harmony. While Paul uses broad strokes to convey his understanding of reconciliation and forgiveness, he demonstrates its practical consequences in the lives of the early Christians.

Related to the mystery of our union with Christ's death and resurrection is a new approach to power and *weakness*. The height of the paradox in Paul's letters is his understanding of the significance of weakness. "For the foolishness of God is wiser than men [women], and the weakness of God is stronger than men [women]" (1 Cor 1:25). Paul states "when I am weak, then I am strong" (2 Cor 12:10), and he boasts of things that show his weakness (2 Cor 11:30). Furthermore, he reminds the community that "we have this treasure in earthen vessels, to show that the transcendent power belongs to God and not to us" (2 Cor 4:7).

If Christians are united to Christ, then their lives reflect this union in suffering and in weakness. Weakness and transitoriness comprise our human existence. Weakness allows God's powerful action to be visible in us. It also demonstrates the human side of the church and of ministry in the church. "For Paul God's Spirit is not the supernatural power that enables a [person] to transcend [one's] earthly life and limitations: instead, it is the power of God who shows himself mighty in lowliness and weakness."[12] This aspect of spirituality signals a difference for Christians between success and effectiveness. Criteria differ since our model in Christ's death and resurrection supports different assessments. We may be most effective in apparent failure. "We are fools for Christ's sake, but you are wise in Christ. We are weak, but you are strong" (1 Cor 4:10). This kind of language confirms our total dependence on God, which is the true empowering of the Christian. Christ's power becomes effective in weakness and in the ordinary circumstances of our lives. Paul endures weakness for Christ's sake and actually expects it in his life and ministry.

However, weakness for Paul is not a denial of the power of God available to him. Rather, the cross of Christ radically changes Paul's perception of where true power lies. Limitations and greatness often go hand in hand. Death frequently means growth and new life. The treasure and the earthen vessel are but two aspects of our Christian existence. A Christian spirituality recognizes the paradox in our personal lives and in our experience as church.

[12] Bornkamm, p. 181.

A COMMON SERVICE OF OTHERS

An authentic Christian spirituality identifies closely with the model the Lord Jesus presents. Therefore, just as Christ came to serve others, Christians express their spirituality in ministry.[13] While ministry is a response to needs, the New Testament also presents ministry as the responsiblity of all the baptized, who serve according to their gifts for the building up of the community. This service occurs in an ecclesial context, and Paul's image of church provides the framework for both the emergence of roles and the dynamics of relationships within the community of faith. Likewise, ministry as service of the church as well as service to the church, becomes the shared responsibility of all believers.

In Paul's letters, the realization of the Christian's call in Christ always leads to its actualization in ministry. For the apostle himself, the pattern is similar—the manifestation of Christ followed by a commissioning for service. This service, primarily a response to the needs of others, "supplies the wants of the saints but also overflows in many thanksgivings to God" (2 Cor 9:12). For the believer, this service in Christ takes on many forms, with evangelization being a primary task. The Christian exercises the privilege of service, as Jesus did, for the advent of the kingdom. Likewise, service is to real people with concrete needs best understood in the presence of dialogue and mutual love. Ministry thus builds the relational bonds within the community and helps set its direction.

Christian ministry is the *responsibility of all* persons baptized into Christ. Paul frequently challenges his congregations to assume responsibility for one another and for their growth as church. No matter what the role, whether public or within the smallest household of faith, the attitude of responsible action permeates the early church. Every activity assumes significance and people discover their particular service for the benefit of the church. Their Christian ministry confirms their faith. "Under the test of this service, you will glorify God by your obedience in acknowledging the gospel of Christ, and by the

---

[13]See my book, *Minister of God,* chapter 3: "Developing a Spirituality for Ministers," also chapter 5 and chapter 6 for the ministry of Jesus and Paul.

generosity of your contribution for them and for all others" (2 Cor 9:13). Interestingly, the quality of Christian life as well as the sharing of resources, solidifies the Christian's dedication to the Lord and each contributes to the church's growth.

Ministry in the Pauline writings results from the believer's call in Christ and finds its grounding in the Spirit, allowing service of others according to the *charisms* received from the Spirit. "For Paul, to have a charisma means to participate for that very reason in life, in grace in the Spirit, because a charisma is the specific part which the individual has in the lordship and glory of Christ; and this specific part which the individual has in the Lord shows itself in a specific service and a specific vocation. For there is no divine gift which does not bring with it a task, there is no grace which does not move to action. Service is not merely the consequence but the outward form and the realization of grace."[14]

The gifts of the Spirit include everything necessary for the life and growth of the church. While Paul ranks the charisms according to their effects, he always presumes a manifestation of all the necessary charisms in the assembled community. While the exhortation to strive for the higher gifts opens the community to new growth, Paul does not impose certain types of ministries on the believer. Rather, ministries result from the recognition of personal gifts used for the benefit of all. These charisms, freely given by the Spirit, represent the presence of the one Spirit vivifying the church.

"There are varieties of service, but the same Lord" (1 Cor 12:5), and the purpose of these gifts of service is to build up the body of Christ. Personal growth is not an issue, rather, the focus becomes the growth of the community, with the individual's growth the anticipated byproduct. The early church develops through its ministry. Persons become intimately connected to the church because of the service they offer. Authority too expresses itself as service to the church. Mutual service builds up the community if it reflects the freedom and love we share in Christ. Since persons within the churches exercise a specific ministry on behalf of others, each one becomes essential to the whole body of Christ.

---

[14]Käsemann, "Ministry and Community," p. 65.

Paul's persective on ministry demands an *ecclesial consciousness* and context for understanding its focus and relationship. Ministry emerges from the community itself and incorporates many functions for the benefit of all. To be church implies more than worship. It requires the active involvement of all believers, with members contributing according to their competencies in the daily circumstances of their lives. However, while rhythms of life may differ, as well as roles and responsibilities, all persons share in the community's life in some way. A relationship with the Lord implies a commitment to be church through the exercise of ministry. Paul does not differentiate between ordained and non-ordained ministers. Service does not become elitist in this early period nor is passivity among the members allowed to exist. Ministry is ecclesial and all believers not only share this awareness of their call but contribute earnestly and actively to the development of the church.

The models of the church identified in the previous chapter insure a common service of others. Ministry becomes the hallmark of the churches who see themselves as the new people of God and the body of Christ. Likewise, realizing the new creation and acting as one person in Christ requires an ecclesial consciousness with its sense of responsibility and appreciation of the life available to us in the Spirit. None of the models used by Paul stereotype ministry. All of them create a dynamic within the community that attempts to balance gift and need. Ministry operates in the early church much like an organism in that the activities vary but each one contributes to the whole. Ministry in the church must also be ministry as church, so that those outside the circle of faith will recognize the presence of the kingdom. Christian spirituality thus incorporates this common service of others into the lives of all believers.

EVANGELIZATION AND THE EMPOWERING OF CHURCH LIFE IN OTHERS.

Paul makes concerted efforts in evangelization and the spread of the church by enlisting co-workers and communities into service for the sake of the gospel. He enters into partnership with others to advance the gospel, and he understands how to use everyone's gifts for the benefit of the church. Paul becomes a model for the ministry of others, and he also effectively facilitates ministry within the churches, thereby insuring a vital ecclesial community.

The apostle exemplifies the qualities of effective service to the church as he ministers to the various communities. Paul always connects his call to be a follower of the Lord with his reception of the gospel and his mission to the Gentiles. Being Christian means being at the service of the church. For Paul, it means proclaiming the word and establishing new faith communities. Likewise, Paul embodies creativity in his ministry, embraces suffering for the sake of the gospel, and demonstrates remarkable effectiveness in his endeavors. However, he balances his limitations and weaknesses with a persistent awareness of the power of God working through him. He experiences joy in his ministry, even with difficult communities, and appreciates the gifts of others. Paul's primary concern is the preaching of Christ and the growth of believers as church. His purpose becomes clear as he repeats these consistent points in his letters to the churches.

The apostle recognizes the contribution of others, particularly on the level of their work in the local churches. Creating an atmosphere conducive to growth along the lines of Jesus' message is no easy task, but Paul conscientiously pursues his task, enlisting the service of others to develop these faith communities. The church recognizes and utilizes the gifts of the Spirit available to all Christians. Building up the community is only possible from within the community, as members assume responsibility for their life and service.

Paul recognizes the Spirit frequently distributes gifts rather unevenly among believers and that some persons are more eager to assume responsibility than others. With this insight, Paul capitalizes on the gifts of leadership, the ability to travel, preach, offer hospitality, and challenge others. Likewise, prophets, teachers, administrators, and helpers, contribute according to their gifts. While community life is essential to being church, Paul and his co-workers live out their ecclesial commitment differently from the smaller households and local churches. Appreciation of diversity in ministry and lifestyle marks the early experience of the Pauline communities.

Furthermore, the apostle to the Gentiles models a *collaborative response* in his service of the church. He works with the Jerusalem church, his own converts, women, Gentiles, and Jews. While he utilizes his own strong personal qualities for the sake of the gospel, he knows how to work with others committed to similar values but with different gifts. As Paul speaks about his preferences and his approaches to the gospel, we can admire even more his ability to stand by the decisions of others and of communities, as they discern the appropriateness of particular actions. Paul truly becomes a servant of the gospel and his sense of church overrides his own personal tendencies.

Paul guides the expansion of the church's mission and the development of ministry in others in several ways. Not only does he recognize gifts and competencies, but he readily affirms these qualities in others. He is lavish in his praise, recommending co-workers to communities with remarkable ease and sincerity. He engenders a spirit of collaboration by his style of ministry, encouraging cooperation with communities and working together among the various churches. Exhortations abound, so many dealing with unity and service in the church. Likewise, Paul sees ministry as a constantly growing aspect of church life. "Never flag in zeal, be aglow with the Spirit, serve the Lord" (Rom 12:11). Service determines leadership and authority, and surprisingly, flourishing ministering communities exist with little reliance on the hierarchical framework of the day. As Paul approaches the end of his life, the letter to the Philippians attests, he becomes increasingly concerned about the future development of the churches and takes steps to insure their self-reliance. His theology and ecclesiology lead Paul to empower others to live fully as church. Dedication to be church and to live as church is integral to the spirituality of Paul and the early Christians. Ministry, evangelization, and giving others freedom to serve according to their charisms, are prime works for everyone in the churches.

Christian spirituality as presented in the letters of Paul provides a fascinating context for our personal growth and development. The ecclesial community is the setting for Christian life, and ecclesial dedication is the cornerstone of an authentic spirituality. While Paul addresses the usual components of spirituality, our relationship to God and a life of prayer, he jolts the contemporary Christian by his consistent emphasis on living as church.

For Paul, religious experience leads to an identifiable Christian existence, ethical behavior grounded in Christ, and service of others. An essential dimension of our Christian commitment is empowering others to live authentically as church, utilizing their gifts, and contributing to the growth of the faith community. Spirituality directs itself towards others, with deepening relationships to the Lord and to the people in our lives. The focus shifts from an emphasis on personal growth to our life in Christ and as church. Our personal dedication moves us to labor energetically in the service of the church, by the witness of our lives and the testimony of our words and works.

Spirituality is always a movement to, and through, beginnings as we attempt to live out our call in the new and changing circumstances of our lives and our world. Paul's unique contribution is his identification of the ecclesial dimension of our personal quest. His insight might well challenge Christians today to widen their perspective regarding how to live as believers. In this new age of the church, the principles and guidelines of Paul can redirect and refocus our attention. His emphasis on our shared life and mutual responsibility might move us toward a more collaborative stance within the local communities and the universal church. His identification of ministry and ecclesial dedication as essential to our Christian commitment, may reopen the doors closed to many Christians today. With its centering on Christ and its appreciation of the movements of the Spirit, a spirituality of ecclesial dedication resonates well with the yearnings, needs, and aspirations of the contemporary church and can serve to effectively meet the needs of our church and our world.

7

The Interpreters of Paul

> "He is the image of the invisible God, the first-born of all creation; for in him all things were created, in heaven and on earth, visible and invisible, whether thrones or dominions or principalities or authorities—all things were created through him and for him. He is before all things, and in him all things hold together. He is the head of the body, the church." (Col 1:15-18)

The primary focus of our work has been the earliest ecclesiology available to us, the church in the authentic letters of Paul. Only the letters whose Pauline authorship is unquestioned were included in the body of the book. However, the correspondence from the next generation of Christian writers shed considerable light on Paul's impact on the early church. Solidly based in this category are Ephesians, 1 and 2 Timothy, and Titus. More open to question regarding authenticity and dating are 2 Thessalonians and Colossians.[1] However, each of these deutero-Pauline letters offers a fascinating perspective on the developing church. At times the letters build on Paul's ecclesiology and in other instances seem to turn from his perspective.

This chapter addresses 2 Thessalonians and spends more

---

[1] Authenticity and dating of these letters is widely discussed; see Kümmel, for a basic presentation of the various positions, and Roetzel, ch. 6: "The First Interpreters of Paul." 2 Thess and Col make the strongest claims for inclusion among the authentic letters, but I place them here since their authenticity is in doubt.

time on Colossians, Ephesians, 1 and 2 Timothy, and Titus, attempting to identity the development of Paul's understanding of church within their cultural and religious environment. New trends begin to emerge, some that enhance the church's understanding of itself and others that need to be reassessed by later generations. Paul's interpreters attempt to do what he also attempted to do, reinterpret the message of Jesus for new times and new places. However, for many of these writers the church is already separated from Judaism, and so one aspect of the struggle of self-identity is behind them. The delay of the parousia, the beginning threat of gnosticism, the increased possibility of persecution, and a developing christology contribute to the new set of circumstances of the deutero-Pauline correspondence. These writers face a different future from Paul and respond accordingly.

2 THESSALONIANS

This letter can be understood as an imitation of Paul's previous correspondence to the community, addressing a different and a later situation. An early dating may be indicated by the reference to the temple of God in 2 Thess 2:4. The writer addresses the "church of the Thessalonians" who supply reasons for his boast to "the churches of God" (2 Thess 1:1.4). Two main issues emerge, the apocalyptic enthusiasm of the community and their experience of persecution,[2] points affecting the content of the entire letter.

2 Thessalonians contains references to the *traditions* "taught by us, either by word of mouth or by letter" (2 Thess 2:15), and including God's choice of the community and its sanctification by the Spirit. "God chose you from the beginning to be saved, through sanctification by the Spirit and belief in the truth. To this he called you through our gospel, so that you may obtain the glory of our Lord Jesus Christ" (2 Thess 2:13-14). Because of this call believers "stand firm and hold to the traditions" (2 Thess 2:15).

---

[2]See Roetzel, footnote 17, p. 147, where he indicates that studies show the second thanksgiving in 1 Thess was added later.

The writer speaks of traditions in light of "the coming of the Lord Jesus Christ" (2 Thess 2:1) but sees the parousia as delayed. Although it offers hope to the *community,* members remain confused, resulting in the caution that "no one deceive you in any way (2 Thess 2:3). Furthermore, those brothers and sisters "living in idleness and not in accord with the tradition that you received from us" (2 Thess 3:6), receive stern words from the apostle. "If any one will not work, let [that person] not eat"; also commanding and exhorting these persons "in the Lord Jesus Christ to do their work in quietness and to earn their own living" (2 Thess 3:10.12). The theological interpretation of the parousia clearly affects the life of this community.

Other admonitions and commands to the Thessalonians include keeping away from the idle, and having nothing to do with anyone who "refuses to obey what we say in this letter" (2 Thess 3:6.14). The community assumes responsibility by warning those who go astray (2 Thess 3:15) and by dealing with their impact on the church.

The Pauline writer uses thanksgiving in this letter as the apostle did in 1 Thessalonians.[3] Two thanksgivings in 2 Thess 1:1-12 and 2:3-16 speak of the faith of the church and of God's choice of the community. Furthermore, while this church endures suffering and affliction (2 Thess 1:5-7), it will ultimately be glorified when the Lord comes (2 Thess 1:10). 2 Thessalonians urges Christians to consistently live out their commitment, not to grow "weary in well-doing," and so *build-up* the community (2 Thess 3:13).

The author certainly stands within the Pauline tradition. "He correctly understands the Pauline resistance to religious enthusiasm, the apostle's emphasis on the tension between the "now" and "not yet," and Paul's stress on the implications of the gospel for such human concerns as bread and nurturing relationships."[4] The letter uses Paul's name to address a new situation in the church, but offers little by way of revolutionary ideas.

---

[3]See Roetzel, p. 109.
[4]See Mitton, p. 12.

Colossians and Ephesians

Pauline Christianity develops after the death of Paul, with the letters to the Colossians, Ephesians, Timothy, and Titus, monitoring its progression. In Colossians and Ephesians, Pauline ideas interpret the traditions of Jewish-Hellenistic Christianity. In the Pastorals, we glimpse the legendary Paul addressing a very different situation in the church's life. New controversies burst forth, giving rise to new theological understandings and a different assessment of the church's role. This section focuses on Colossians and Ephesians, offering comments on the relationship and perspective of both letters and then separately examining the details of each letter in regard to its ecclesiology.

The letters to the Colossians and Ephesians contain a number of *similarities*. The same messenger, Tychicus, delivers the letters to both communities. He "will tell you all about my affairs; he is a beloved brother and faithful minister and fellow servant in the Lord" (Col 4:7-8; cf Eph 6:21). "I have sent him to you for this very purpose that you may know how we are, and that he may encourage your hearts" (Eph 6:21-22; cf Col 4:8). Other cross-influences exist as in the following passages, Col 1:25//Eph 3:2; Col 2:19//Eph 4:16; Col 3:9-10//Eph 4:22-24, indicating the origins of Paul's ministry, stressing Christ as head of his body, and identifying Christians' transition to a new existence. One third of the words of Colossians are in Ephesians, although the meanings sometimes differ. In Colossians, for example, the mystery entrusted to Paul in his ministry is the mystery of Christ himself (Col 1:26-27; 2:2; 4:3), while in Ephesians, the mystery refers to God's purpose through Christ to reunite all things within the life of the church.

In both Colossians and Ephesians, *ekklesia* refers to the universal church (Col 1:18.24; Eph 1:22; 3:10.21; 5:23.24. 25.27.29.32). Furthermore, these letters point to the universal influence of Christ, his dominion over principalities and powers (Col 1:15; 2:15; Eph 1:21), and, indeed, Christ's position as head of all things. Cosmic influence predominates and the writers associate this perspective with Christ and the church (Col 1:16-20; Eph 1:10.21-24). These authors develop Paul's concept of the body of Christ by identifying Christ as head of his body, the church. This model of the church remains relational rather than institutional, but the church as people of God is absent. In its place is an emphasis on the heavenly church, the kingdom and the church, and the identification of the church with the risen body of Christ. Furthermore, the "spiritual aspect of the body of Christ emerges very clearly in Ephesians and Colossians—along with the redemptive—historical aspect."[5]

The implications of being church take on significance with both letters containing the complete household codes (Col 3:18-4:1; Eph 5:22-6:9). They take such material from their cultural environment and adapt it for use in the Christian churches. While these two letters contain similarities and common material, each one offers its own perspective as well, and so it is to the individual letters that we now turn.

LETTER TO THE COLOSSIANS

In the name of Paul, the writer of this letter addresses "the saints and faithful in Christ at Colossae" (Col 1:2). The letter itself becomes an interesting blend of Pauline ideas and gnostic influences.[6] Paul himself clearly never visited this community, or nearby Laodicea (Col 2:1; 4:16); Epaphras first preaches the gospel to the church (Col 1:7-8; 4:12). The truth of the gospel bears fruit among them and the gospel "which you heard, ... has been preached to every creature under heaven" (Col 1:23), the mystery hidden for generations. Filled with interesting language, the letter contains many new ideas, particularly in regard to its understanding of Christ and the church.

The *tradition* this community receives is its faith in Christ: "As therefore you received Christ Jesus the Lord, so live in him" (Col 2:6). A considerable amount of the tradition in Colossians relates, directly or indirectly, to baptism. "You were buried with him in baptism, in which you were also raised with him through faith in the working of God, who raised him from the dead" (Col 2:12). The effects of baptism and the

[5]Ridderbos, p. 378.
[6]See Perrin, p. 125.

Christian's union with the Lord, are a recurring point in the letter for God chose to make known "this mystery, which is Christ in you, the hope of glory" (Col 1:27). The language of baptism is reminiscent of earlier letters (Gal 3:28; 1 Cor 12:13), for we "have put on a new nature, which is being received in knowledge after the image of its creator. Here there cannot be Greek or Jew, circumcised or uncircumcised, barbarian, Scythian, slave, free [person], but Christ is all and in all" (Col 3:10-11).

The tradition is clearly faith in Christ, and the Colossians reflect the implications of this belief in their lives. They hear "the word of the truth, the gospel" as does the whole world, and "it is bearing fruit and growing" (Col 1:5-6). The writer prays that they "may be filled with the knowledge of his will in all spiritual wisdom and understanding" (Col 1:9) and because of forgiveness of sins (Col 1:14), strength and endurance will be theirs.

The letter presents a formidable *christological statement*. In the hymn in Col 1:15-20 Christ is "the image of the invisible God, the first-born of all creation, for in him all things were created, in heaven and on earth; visible and invisible, whether thrones or dominions or principalities or authorities—all were created through him and with him" (Col 1:15-16). This exalted image of Christ continues, "he is before all things ... for in him all the fullness of God was pleased to dwell" (Col 1:17-19). Furthermore, reconciliation occurs through him, for he reconciles "to himself all things, whether on earth or in heaven, making peace by the blood of his cross" (Col 1:20). Christ is the creative mediator in this cosmic setting of the hymn.

This flowering of ideas from early writings (1 Cor 8:5; 2:8; Phil 2:10; Rom 8:37-39), underscores the cosmic christology of Colossians. The mystery in Christ (Col 2:3) and the understanding of this mystery reaches new heights, for he is an instrument in creation, of reconciliation, and for the defeat of powers through the cross (Col 1:15-17; 19-20; 2:15). Christians experience this impact since they "come to the fullness of life in him, who is head of all rule and authority" (Col 2:10).

Likewise, the letter to the Colossians explicitly mentions the new relationship of Christ to the church. "He is the head of the body, the church" (Col 1;18; cf 1:24). The community "called in the one body" (Col 3:15), enters into this relationship with Christ. While certain parallels remain with the body image in Corinthians and Romans, Colossians presents new elements, Christ the head predominating within the body, and the church, the body of Christ, becoming the universal church. Ideas of unity prevail, affecting the life of the community. Furthermore, "he has delivered us from the dominion of darkness and transferred us to the kingdom of his beloved Son" (Col 1:13). An exalted christology frames the exhortation, "If then you have been raised with Christ, seek the things that are above, where Christ is, seated at the right hand of God" (Col 3:1) for "your life is hid with Christ in God" (Col 3:3).

Another perspective emerges in Colossians, for Christians "are not admonished to engage in active mission to the world so much as to cultivate the internal peace and loyalty of their community, which is part of the one growing and thriving 'body' throughout the world."[7] In their *community life,* they put on "as God's chosen ones, holy and beloved, compassion, kindness, lowliness, meekness and patience" (Col 3:12). "And above all these put on love, which binds everything together in perfect harmony" (Col 3:14). These characteristics of communal life contrast with the vices they must put to death (Col 3:5-11). Putting away the old nature and embracing the new one, is a reminder of Paul's new creation in Christ.

Colossians also contains the household codes with their patriarchal perspective and focus (Col 3:18-4:1). "Wives be subject to your husbands" begins the section, and then the code deals briefly with the roles of all members of the household. These codes contain spiritual justification for the patriarchal perspective, reflected in statements such as "fitting in the Lord," "this pleases the Lord," "fearing the Lord," "serving the Lord," "knowing that from the Lord you will receive your inheritance as your reward." While Colossians mentions equality, a more traditional ordering of roles also emerges. The church seems to be moving toward a more institutional form in its ministerial relationships as well, for Paul becomes "a minister according to the divine office which was given to me for you, to make the word of God fully known," (Col 1:25),

[7] Meeks, p. 127.

Epaphras is "a faithful minister of Christ on our behalf" (Col 1:7-8), and the letter identifies Tychicus in the same way (Col 4:7).

Nevertheless, the community can "teach and admonish one another in all wisdom"; singing "psalms and hymns and spiritual songs" (Col 3:16). They conduct themselves wisely toward outsiders (Col 4:5) and the church maintains ties with the surrounding communities, particularly, Laodicea and Hieropolis. The writer sends greetings to Nymphas and the church in her house (Col 4:15) and asks that after they read the letter, they send it to the church of Laodiceans (Col 4:16). The Pauline writer gives instructions and the community assumes responsibility for the quality of its life.

Colossae faces *obstacles;* the mood of gnosticism, if not the movement pervades its atmosphere.[8] The community, "estranged and hostile in mind, doing evil deeds" (Col 1:21) prior to its conversion, still contends with influence from its past. "See to it that no one makes a prey of you by philosophy and empty deceit, according to human tradition, according to the elemental spirits of the universe, and not according to Christ" (Col 2:8). Christ "disarmed the principalities and powers" (Col 2:15), and so the writer challenges the community: "If with Christ you died to the elemental spirits of the universe, why do you live as if you still belonged to the world?" (Col 2:20). Heresy begins and the church faces its influence in the various communities. Christ takes on fuller significance in terms of the threats, and church life eventually develops a different character and tone because of these obstacles.

Growth in the community occurs by "holding fast to the Head, from whom the whole body, nourished and knit together through its joints and ligaments, grows with a growth that is from God" (Col 2:19). Maturing in Christ results from ministry, and "for this I toil, striving with all the energy which he mightily inspires within me" (Col 1:29). Inherent powers of growth, rather than the building up imagery of the authentic letters, emerge in this situation.

The letter to the Colossians presents some of Paul's ideas and perspectives. However, its christology portrays Christ as

---

[8] See Perrin, p. 124.

the image of the invisible God. The understanding of church develops with Christ as the head, with the church as the body of Christ, and with the universal church coming to the fore. Likewise, the earlier charismatic communities gradually move towards a more institutional life. The language of the household codes, the emphasis on ministers and office, reflect a more formal tone and more carefully delineated relationships. Thus, Colossians is a transitional letter in terms of the roles and functions within church life.

While the community receives the tradition, the essence of the faith, baptism becomes significant for understanding its life in Christ. Reconciliation takes on a broader view with Christ reconciling to himself all things, not just the world. Suffering on the part of the minister completes "what is lacking in Christ's afflictions for the sake of his body, that is, the church" (Col 1:24). Despite its brevity, the letter to the Colossians is an indispensable source for the development of Pauline Christianity.

THE LETTER TO THE EPHESIANS

Resembling a tract or an epistle more than a letter, Ephesians actually names no recipient, other than "the saints who are also faithful in Christ Jesus"(Eph 1:1). In fact, the writer is not known to the community, for he says "I have heard of your faith" and assumes "that you have heard of the stewardship of God's grace that was given to me for you" (Eph 1:15; 3:2). Written after the fall of Jerusalem and the destruction of the temple, the letter deals with very different issues from those dealt with by the apostle. By the time of Ephesians, the church resolves Paul's primary struggle regarding the Jews and Gentiles. The church is solidly the universal church, and the letter emphasizes the glorification of Christ. This letter is unique in that it lacks an expression of hope in Christ's imminent return.[9]

This magnificently written letter, shares the world of Acts and the Pastorals, with the author probably having a collection

---

[9]See Ziesler, p. 127, who identifies at least a vague expectation in Col 3:4.

of Paul's letters and Colossians available to him. Characterized by balance, maturity of thought, comprehensiveness, and confidence, Ephesians is a profound witness to this later period. Its christology and ecclesiology attain new heights and pursue interesting developments. New images emerge for the church, and Ephesians diverges at times from Pauline theology. Although Ephesians relies heavily on Colossians, it develops its own pattern of thought and its many parallels with the authentic letters offer some interesting comparisons.[10] These parallels include references to the purpose and choice of God, Christian attitudes toward work and immorality, references to patriarchal roles, and the church's commitment to love and unity.

The letter to the Ephesians highlights the Christian *tradition* enumerating aspects of belief. In Christ "we have redemption through his blood, the forgiveness of our trespasses, according to the riches of his grace which he lavished upon us" (Eph 1:7-8). While preserving the gift of justification in Christ, this letter, like Colossians (1:14), adds the dimension of forgiveness of sins, not found in Paul's own letters. Likewise, Christians receive the "word of truth, the gospel of your salvation" (Eph 1:13), believe in Jesus, and are sealed with the Spirit. The writer reminds his audience that Christ is raised from the dead and glorified at the Father's "right hand in the heavenly places" (Eph 1:20; cf 2:6). Paul himself is a minister of the gospel "according to the gift of God's grace" and so preaches "to the Gentiles the unsearchable riches of Christ, and to make all see what is the plan of the mystery hidden for ages in God who created all things" (Eph 3:8-9). The tradition encompasses the elements of the kerygma and also indicates a rich biblical tradition.

The Gentiles hear that they were once "alienated from the commonwealth of Israel, and strangers to the covenant of promise" (Eph 2:12). However, they now form part of the new humanity, reconciled to God "in one body through the cross, thereby bringing the hostility to an end" (Eph 2:16). The letter

---

[10]Perrin, p. 132, notes the following parallels from several sources: Rom 8:28 = Eph 1:11; Rom 8:29 = Eph 1:4-5; 1 Cor 4:12 = Eph 4:28; 1 Cor 6:9-10 = Eph 5:5; 1 Cor 11:3 = Eph 5:23; 1 Cor 12:28 = Eph 4:11; 1 Cor 15:9-10 = Eph 3:8; 2 Cor 1:22 = Eph 1:13; 4:30; Gal 2:20 = Eph 5:2; Gal 4:4 = Eph 1:10.

also speaks of God's purpose, plan, and commandments, and contains allusions to the biblical traditions, including the Genesis creation accounts. This mingling of the biblical and the Christian traditions enriches the church and enhances the quality of the letter. One writer comments: "this letter bristles with traditions."[11] However, these traditions aptly expand to encompass both Christ and the church, and contribute to a developing christology and ecclesiology.

In terms of its *christology,* Ephesians embraces a single motif, "the unity which Christ has brought about: between heaven and earth, Jew and Gentile, man and woman, and above all,... [humankind] and God, a unity made visible in Christ's union with his Church."[12] Christ, so central in the correspondence, is head of the church which is his body (Eph 1:22-23; 4:16), thereby influencing and affecting the quality of Christian life. Absent in Ephesians is the somewhat theoretical christology of Colossians. Rather than a reflection on the nature of Christ's relationship to God, a concentration on its effects seems far more significant. The Pauline writer notes "the fullness of him who fills all in all" (Eph 1:23),[13] but actually spends more time on the reconciliation that actually occurs between Jew and Gentile in the one body of Christ. Through Christ, and by means of Christ, Christian life takes on new meaning and a fuller image of the church develops.

Ephesians presents a highly developed *ecclesiology,* with new imagery and a fuller interpretation of prevailing models. While the body of Christ assumes considerable significance in the authentic letters, such as Corinthians and Romans, Paul does not precisely associate the expression "body of Christ" and the word "church." However, the Pauline interpreters explicitly make this connection. They also present another way of appreciating this model when they identify Christ as the head of his body, the church. The church in Ephesians is the universal church and not the local church as in the early letters. This church embraces Jew and Gentile, for there is "one body

[11] Barth p. 22.

[12] Houlden, pp. 237-238.

[13] See Mitton, pp. 75-79, for a discussion of whether the difficult and ambiguous term "pleroma" refers to Christ or to the church.

and one Spirit, just as you were called to the one hope that belongs to your call, one Lord, one faith, one baptism, one God and Father of us all, who is above all and through all and in all" (Eph 4:4-6). Likewise, this choice of the church in Christ occurs "before the foundation of the world" (Eph 1:4). Ridderbos comments on this pregnant expression and notes that "it is a matter, as always with election, not simply of a decree of God that only later comes to realization, but of the actual appropriation of the church to himself before the foundation of the world."[14] Ephesians also presents the solidarity between the church and creation, for "he has put all things under his feet and has made him the head over all things for the church" (Eph 1:22).

The church is the true Israel, the new temple, built on the "foundation of the apostles and prophets, Christ Jesus himself being the cornerstone in whom the whole structure is joined together and grows into a holy temple in the Lord" (Eph 2:20-21). The household of God (Eph 2:19), the new dwelling place of God in the Spirit (Eph 2:22), the new person (Eph 2:15; 4:22), the mystical person (Eph 2:18), aptly describe the church and resonate with the early New Testament descriptions. However, the writer develops the meaning of church as the bride of Christ beyond Paul's use in Corinthians (2 Cor 11:1-6).

Within the relationship of wives and husbands, the writer identifies significant points that address the relationship between Christ and the church. "For the husband is the head of the wife as Christ is the head of the church, his body" (Eph 5:23). This patriarchal perspective and the body image seem inadequate and so the verse continues: "and he himself is its Savior." By the use of "savior," rather than the head/body relationship alone, the author conveys that all life and vitality in the church come from its head, Christ.[15] Nevertheless, the marriage relationship reflects Christ's love for the church: "He gave himself up for her, that he might sanctify her ... [and] present the church to himself in splendor" (Eph 5:25-27). The qualities of a husband/wife, their nurturing and cherishing of

---

[14]Ridderbos, p. 347.

[15]See Mitton, p. 200.

each other, indicate the quality of the relationship existing between Christ and the church (Eph 5:29). Of their union, the writer exclaims "This is a great mystery, and I take it to mean Christ and the church" (Eph 5:32).

Ephesians deliberately develops parallels between the marriage relationship and Christ and the church. However, the church is only inferred to be the bride of Christ; the explicit connection remains for the book of Revelation. Here the quality of love, its mutuality, tenderness, sacrificial dimensions, and marital union, speak eloquently, despite the strong cultural influences of the household code.

While patriarchy colors the imagery and relationships in Ephesians, the Pauline writer broadens the concept of mutuality in an introductory statement to the section just examined. "Be subject to one another out of reverence for Christ" (Eph 5:21). This command may go unnoticed but its inclusion in the text reveals the ongoing tension between the Christian vision of equality and societal approaches of patriarchy. We read of Jews and Gentiles (Eph 2:11-17), of apostles and prophets (Eph 2:20), and of varied relationships in the household of faith (Eph 6:1-9). Renewal of the individual within the community demands attention (Eph 1:1-21), and unity, true righteousness, holiness, kindness, forgiveness, and love (Eph 4:16.24.32).

People within the church have *gifts for ministry:* "And his gifts were that some should be apostles, some prophets, some evangelists, some pastors and teachers, for the equipment of the saints, for the work of ministry, for building up of the body of Christ" (Eph 4:11-12). The mention of evangelists among the gifts given to the church occurs only in this letter, and the insertion of pastors reflects another perspective on church life. Not only does sharing of gifts occur, but the community grows into Christ, by "speaking the truth in love" (Eph 4:15). Anger may have its place but "do not let the sun go down on your anger" (Eph 4:26). Walking in love (Eph 5:1), non-association with those in darkness (Eph 5:7), joyful and prayerful sharing (Eph 5:19), are qualities that develop individuals and the church.

The letter uses baptismal imagery (Eph 5:26) and applies the *building* terminology to the church (Eph 2:19-22), encouraging building up through ministry and other forms of sharing. These dimensions take on significance because obstacles prevail in the form of "sons of disobedience," "passions of flesh," "every wind of doctrine," cunning, crafty, and deceitful people, who buy into the "unfruitful works of darkness" (Eph 2:2-3; 4:14; 5:11). Obstacles prevail in this period of the church's life.

The letter to the Ephesians presents the abiding truth of the Christian gospel, taking Pauline teaching and presenting it in its universal and eternal aspects.[16] Also notable with this correspondence is a beginning structure within the church, which is the firm foundation for its future development (Eph 2:19-22). Marriage becomes a worthy symbol for Christ and the church. The body images, expanded and focused, present a further perspective in the church's movement towards the more stylized existence of the Pastoral letters. The local congregation, Paul's major concern, gives way to the broader movement and understanding of church. Ephesians views the church from the outside, in contrast to Romans and Corinthians. The concern moves away from the harmony of its inner life to a tangible interest in its external appearance.[17] While so much of Paul can be unearthed in this letter, it clearly represents a later period, a reinterpretation of his teaching, and a changing ecclesial direction. The letter itself acknowledges a maturation "to the measure of the stature of the fullness of Christ" (Eph 4:13). Toward this end, we must "put on the whole armor of God," gird our "loins with truth, and having put on the breastplate of righteousness," equip ourselves with the "gospel of peace" and "the shield of faith" (Eph 6:10-18). The writer seems to anticipate the conflict ahead.

The Pastoral Letters

The letters to Timothy and Titus introduce the reader to a transitional period in the early church, the major transition from the apostolic age to a more functional organization of the Christian communities. While these letters lack the depth and excitement of Paul in the authentic letters, they offer a

---

[16]See Mitton p. 29.
[17]See Ernst, p. 241.

valuable glance at Pauline Christianity at the end of the first century.[18] The author, writing in Paul's name, represents Paul as apostle, herald, and teacher (1 Tim 2:7; 2 Tim 1:11). Instructions for ministry and a faithful presentation of what the apostle would have said in these new circumstances characterize these letters. This section addresses the general perspective of the Pastorals in regard to their content, their theological perspective, and emerging ideas, then looks at each letter separately in order to discover the basic trends in their ecclesiology.

The Pastorals draw on the image of Paul to address the needs of a transitional church. Since the church will be around for a long time, the need for structure begins to emerge. Because of its distance in time from its apostolic roots, it becomes necessary to assure *sound teaching and doctrine.* As a good pastor, shepherding his flock, the Paulinist argues against false teachings, presents criteria for ministers in the church, begins to reflect the separation of various roles, and in doing so, responds to the need for more church structure. These letters present Christianity as decidedly middle-class and witness to the laying on of hands, or ordination (1 Tim 4:14; 5:22; 2 Tim 1:6).

In 1 Timothy, the emphasis is on church order; 2 Timothy contains more material personal to Paul and more scriptural references; Titus contains, like the others, liturgical fragments, domestic codes, but no biblical references, and fewer personal ones.[19] A practicality predominates as opposed to a conceptual understanding of Christ and the church. The letters elicit a response of action rather than answers or dialogue.

Many *types of material* make up these letters, reflecting the interests and concerns of the church, including extracts from church order, domestic codes, liturgical fragments, confessional and homiletic statements, lists of sinners and sins, exhortations and instructions.[20] The Pastorals contain echoes of Paul's

---

[18]For discussion of authorship, dating, and introductions to the Pastorals, see Hultgren, Hanson, *The Pastoral Epistles;* Robert J. Karris, *The Pastoral Epistles,* in addition to the works of Kümmel, Roetzel, and Perrin.

[19]Hanson, *Pastoral Epistles,* pp. 27-28.

[20]See Hanson, *Pastoral Epistles,* pp. 42-46, for examples of types of material.

material and teaching as the following examples attest: 1 Tim 6:12 = Phil 3:12.14; 2 Tim 1:6-8 = Rom 8:12-17; 2 Tim 3:16-17 = Rom 15:4-6; 2 Tim 4:6-8 = Phil 2:16-17.[21] Ideas consistent with Paul's theology include salvation through Christ, God's revelation in Christ, justification without works, and faith as the way to eternal life.[22] However, the differences give us more to consider in terms of church development than do these few similarities.

In these letters, Paul, the patriarch, departs from particular places, handing on teaching and the essence of the faith to new leaders, and then continues on his journey. Emphasis on Paul's apostolic authority gains importance as he passes on the tradition, and the historical and personal details remind us of the apostolic figure, giving credibility to the interpretation of the author. However, the style of the presentation in the Pastorals is staid and deliberate, as opposed to the dynamic, argumentative, and engaging style of Paul. The tone and the moralistic emphasis of these documents tell us that the church is beyond the prophetic and Spirit-filled experiences of the earliest period.

An interesting feature of the Pastorals is the number of references to persons in the church. Of the twenty eight people mentioned, eighteen have a definite Ephesian connection.[23] A distinctive feature is the attention to offices in the church and to ordination. Frequently, the letters reflect society with the descriptions, qualifications, and roles in the church mirroring, in large measure, secular counterparts. The church, concerned with the opinion of contemporary society, even reflects its patriarchal orientation in the Christian households. However, the purpose of the Pastorals is to provide adequate information for church leaders, a handbook of sorts, to enable them to address their pastoral tasks and to pass on the Pauline tradition in a period of heresy.

While the Pastorals draw on Pauline material and pertinent selections from the Jewish tradition and Hellenistic sources, the author is not an original thinker, nor does he offer a

---

[21] See Hanson, *Pastoral Epistles,* pp. 28-31.

[22] See Kümmel, p. 269, which includes these references: 1 Tim 1:15f; 2 Tim 1:9f; Tit 3:15; 1 Tim 1:16.

[23] See Hultgren, pp. 21-25.

particularly creative synthesis. The Paulinist reflects on God and his creation, emphasizing that God created everything good (1 Tim 4:3-4; Tit 1:15). The correct use of creation and the enjoyment of life are values he presents to the church (1 Tim 6:13.17). The author stands well within the Pauline tradition in assessing human sinfulness and identifying vices that reflect our inauthentic existence (2 Tim 3:2-5). However, rather than an emphasis on the power of sin that enslaves, the Pastorals tend to focus on sins committed (1 Tim 5:22.24; 2 Tim 3:6). Salvation in Christ continues to be a gift from God and a present reality for the Christian, with a final realization offering hope, as in Paul's letters (1 Tim 4:16; 2 Tim 1:9; 2:10-11; Tit 3:5). In his christology, the author uses what is available in the form of creeds and liturgical formulas, offering little personal insight. "Christ" and "Lord" are usual titles; "Savior" applies both to God and to Christ, a term Paul uses only once when referring to Christ (Phil 3:20). The Spirit in these letters "does not seem to be integrated into the being of God."[24] The view of suffering is a mere shadow of Paul's theological reflection, with no mention of the cross as the compelling symbol.

A concern in these letters is *the faith*, the sound teaching and doctrine passed on to the churches. While prophecy is still a charism, the emphasis lies elsewhere. Not only tradition, but traditional values, take on great importance, particularly in the household and in regard to women's roles. Some authors would see the Pastorals as response or even reaction to the legendary material represented in the *Acts of Paul and Thecla*.[25] While the theology in the Pastorals represents little new insight, the ecclesiology offers some fascinating developments.

In the Pastorals, the household becomes the social unit of the church and the church's social structure reflects this model.[26] The church is God's family, albeit a patriarchal family, in its organization and ministry. The widely held description of equality in Christ reflected in Galatians 3:26-28, finds little

---

[24]Hanson, *Pastoral Epistles*, p. 41.

[25]See the works of MacDonald, and Osiek.

[26]See Verner, p. 1; the entire book is an interesting study.

resonance in the Pastorals' codes of behavior for the household. Verner notes that the letter's prevailing domestic ideal values prosperity and propriety in the church as they are valued in the larger society. In fact, the household of God bolsters the hierarchical social structure of the church, so that it will be unthreatened by disruptive forces.[27] Quite a change from the earlier Christian house-church which Paul, perhaps wisely, bypassed as a model!

Leadership in the church emerges in these letters in a more official way, with great emphasis on qualifications for the ministry, and with concern for the selection of others to follow the present leaders. While *episkopoi* and *prebyteroi* originate in the secular Greek and Jewish world respectively, they develop their character within the framework of the church. At this stage, roles are not well established and the Pastorals reflect a frequent overlapping of functions. Likewise, none of the early roles are linked primarily to cultic associations but extend to various aspects of teaching, service, and discipline. The unique feature of church order in the Pastorals prepares the church for the second century. In order to understand the development of, and divergence from, Paul's vision of church, we examine each letter independently.

1 TIMOTHY

The letter begins: "Paul an apostle of Christ Jesus by command of God our Savior and of Jesus Christ our hope" (1 Tim 1:1). The use of command instead of call and of savior are uncharacteristic of the apostle Paul. Both these usages indicate sensitivity to the Greek world, its understanding of apostleship, and its view of emperor as a savior. Surprisingly, the author offers no thanksgiving, and so we are quickly introduced to the world of the Pastorals.

The apostle reminds Timothy of his previous urging to "charge certain persons not to teach any different doctrine, nor to occupy themselves with myths and endless genealogies which promote speculation rather than the divine training that

---

[27]See Verner, pp. 146-147, 186.

is in faith" (1 Tim 1:3-4). References to wandering "away into vain discussion" (1 Tim 1:6), behavior "contrary to sound doctrine" (1 Tim 1:10), and departing from the faith to the "doctrines of demons" (1 Tim 4:1), set the context for identifying the *tradition*. In this letter the faith and true doctrine are the gospel entrusted to Paul (1 Tim 1:11.14). Paul indicates that "Christ Jesus came into the world to save sinners" (1 Tim 1:15) and Christians are "to believe in him for eternal life" (1 Tim 1:16).

Rather than focusing on aspects of kerygma, the letter continues with a specific commission: "this charge I commit to you" (1 Tim 1:18), and if you "put these instructions before the [brothers and sisters], you will be a good minister of Christ Jesus, nourished on the words of faith and of the good doctrine which you have followed" (1 Tim 4:6). "Command and teach these things" (1 Tim 4:11); "O Timothy, guard what has been entrusted to you" (1 Tim 6:20). This letter, as the other Pastorals, focuses on the continuity of the apostolic tradition and the soundness of the doctrine. Faith is not so much trusting in God as having *the* faith, which is the content of faith (1 Tim 1:5). Faith becomes a synonym for the Christian religion (1 Tim 1:5. 14; 3:1; 4:9).[28]

The church now lives an ordered existence. The key emphasis on *church order* in 1 Timothy identifies the emergence of a different lifestyle in the Christian community. This letter speaks about leaders in the church, the bishop (1 Tim 3:1-7), deacons (3:8-13), elders or presbyters (5:17-22), and others in the community, men and women (2:8-15), widows (5:3-16), slaves (6:1-2), their responsibilities and the circumstances of their lives. Some interesting features surface.

"If any one aspires to the office of bishop, he desires a noble task" (1 Tim 3:1). The bishop, as we have noted, has probable counterparts in pagan society and is usually associated with finance, but here the writer adds apt teaching to the otherwise moral and family qualifications. The domestic church, with its emphasis on the patriarchal household colors this section, which ends with the query, "For if a man does not know how

---

[28]See Perrin, p. 269.

to manage his own household, how can he care for God's church?" (1 Tim 3:5) The bishop must be thought well of by outsiders, indicating the church's interest in the perception of others. Deacons have qualifications similar to the bishop and should also be tested (1 Tim 3:10). Women in this role, or the wives of deacons as some would read this statement, have comparable demands made on them. These people "must hold the mystery of faith with a clear conscience" (1 Tim 3:9), an indication of their responsibility in preserving the tradition and sound teaching.

"Let the elders who rule well be considered worthy of double honor, especially those who labor in preaching and teaching" (1 Tim 5:17). The elders have spiritual and administrative responsibility in the church, and the presbyter, or elder, originated in Judaism where a certain status accompanies the designation.[29] The significance of this office seems known to the community since it is not specifically mentioned. Ordination, noted in 1 Tim 4:14 and 5:22, designates and equips the person for a specific ministry or office. "The laying on of hands is not here ... to be taken as conveying the grace of office and incorporating one into an unbroken succession that perpetuates itself via ordination."[30]

Traditional roles, often questioned in the early church, get a substantial boost in 1 Timothy. "Women will be saved through bearing children," and should "learn in silence with all submissiveness" (1 Tim 2:15.11). Negative statements endure (1 Tim 2:12-14; 5:11-13), but marriage is a means of sanctification for the woman if she "continues in faith and love and holiness, with modesty" (1 Tim 2:15). The good minister affirms these instructions and solid doctrine (1 Tim 4:16) as the church takes care to preserve order and to maintain consistent values in a changing world.

However, as the letter presents certain roles and responsibilities, another side of the picture begins to emerge and must be taken into account. The freedom and equality of early

---

[29]See Ridderbos, p. 457.
[30]Ridderbos, p. 477.

Christianity is no longer available to women; charism refers to ordination in 1 Timothy 4:14; civic virtues become rather bourgeois (1 Tim 2:1-12); popular philosophy influences the views on wealth (1 Tim 6:6-10). Community life loses some of its sparkle, although Christians "aim at righteousness, godliness, faith, love, steadfastness, gentleness" (1 Tim 6:11). Some of the advice to various groups betrays an anxiety about the effect of their behavior on the reputation of the church.[31] The church is the household of God (1 Tim 3:15), and rigid patriarchal lines of interaction persist, even though respect remains for the ordinary existence of believers. Ministry becomes more focused as particular persons who are ordained for these purposes, oversee, teach, and serve.

In light of persisting contrary doctrine (1 Tim 1:10), leaders, represented by Timothy, must guard what has been entrusted to them (1 Tim 6:20). No arguments ensue with the opposition but rather a concerted effort to pass on the faith and to profess it. The tone of 1 Timothy is typical of the Pastoral letters, indicating the situation and the direction of the church in its third generation. Church order represents a development but also has a dark side, the loss of the emphasis on charisms in the community, already evident in the correspondence.

2 TIMOTHY

This letter presents a more personal reminiscence of Paul, who offers thanksgiving to God when he remembers Timothy in prayer, tells of his longing to see him again, and remembers the faith of Timothy's grandmother, Lois, and his mother Eunice (2 Tim 1:3-5). The apostle speaks of his imprisonment (2 Tim 1:8.16; 2:9) and his holy calling (2 Tim 1:9). "For the gospel I was appointed a preacher and apostle and teacher" (2 Tim 1:11). The latter part of the letter includes Paul's last will and testament (2 Tim 3:10-4:8), containing the details about Paul known to the author and his challenge to the present church. For Paul, the time of his "departure has come. I have fought the good fight, I have finished the race, I have kept the

[31]See Bassler, p. 31.

faith" (2 Tim 4:6-7). Paul greets his friends, tells them of the whereabouts of colleagues, but also speaks ill of particular individuals, like Alexander the coppersmith who opposed his message (2 Tim 4:12-16; cf 1:15-18).

This letter follows the pattern of Paul's writing and draws on the scripture, indicating that "all scripture is inspired by God and profitable for teaching, for reproof, for correction, and for training in righteousness" (2 Tim 3:16). The preservation of apostolic tradition emerges, "guard the truth that has been entrusted to you by the Holy Spirit who dwells in us" (2 Tim 1:14). There is a chain of tradition, "what you have heard from me before many witnesses entrust to faithful men who will be able to teach others also" (2 Tim 2:2). In this period of the church, Christian leaders take care to pass on the essence of the faith to the next generation. In 2 Timothy 4:1-2 the charge is strong: "preach the word, be urgent in season and out of season, convince, rebuke, and exhort, be unfailing in patience and in teaching." Suffering accompanies the ministry (2 Tim 2:10), but the Lord also gives strength (2 Tim 4:17). Rekindling "the gift of God that is within you through the laying on of hands" (2 Tim 1:6) indicates difficult times for the church and also the association of charism and ordination.

The image of church is rather static; "a great house" with vessels of gold and silver, wood and earthenware (2 Tim 2:20). "God's firm foundation stands,"[32] and "the Lord knows who are his" (2 Tim 2:19). The church fears the future and holds little hope that the community has the ability to discern (2 Tim 4:2-6), even though Christians "have died with him" in baptism and will also "live with him" (2 Tim 2:11). The treatment of the last days with the lists of abuses, speaks more to the present situation of the church than to the future (2 Tim 3:1-9). The images of the good soldier, the athlete competing according to the rules, and the hardworking farmer, present useful models for the minister in the church (2 Tim 2:3-6). While roles are not delineated in this letter, a focus on the ordained minister instead of the congregation remains, as well as a harsh branding of persons who think differently and of sinful situations.

---

[32]The foundation can be the church, Christ, the witnessing community, or apostolic teaching. See Hanson, *Pastoral Epistles,* pp. 136-139; Hultgren, p. 126.

Rather than building up the community, the emphasis is on lack of endurance, desertion, opposition. With a sweep of the pen, the Paulinist relegates other views to "stupid, senseless controversies" (2 Tim 2:23), rather than exploring the grounds for the differences. The second letter to Timothy complements the first, identifying the roots of Christian faith and bracing the church for difficult encounters.

TITUS

The somewhat formal beginning of this short letter identifies Paul as "a servant of God," a description never used in the authentic letters and as "an apostle of Jesus Christ, to further the faith of God's elect and their knowledge of the truth" (Tit 1:1). The language of the other Pastorals persists in the use of "command," "entrusted," "sound doctrine," "teaching." This letter also addresses leadership in the church and specifies qualifications of elders (Tit 1:5-6) and bishops (Tit 1:7-11), more for use by the missionary, than for the leader of the congregation.[33] Relationships in the community reflect what is sound and good (Tit 2:1-15). The authority of Titus is intact, "Declare these things; exhort and reprove with all authority. Let no one disregard you" (Tit 2:15). He appoints elders "in every town as I directed you" to "amend what was defective" (Tit 1:5). Reminders about submissiveness of wives to husbands (Tit 2:5), slaves to masters (Tit 2:8), tend to create a passivity in some areas of Christian life. Passion and pleasure sound suspect as sober, upright, and godly lives become the norm (Tit 2:12).

For ministerial leaders the moral criteria resonate with 1 Timothy, with hospitality and teaching also important for the bishop (Tit 1:8-9). Opposition must be silenced and the writer attests that some "teach" for base gain what they have no right to teach" (Tit 1:11). On the other hand, if we examine underlying values in the letter, potential leaders must be able to organize (Tit 1:5-6), teach sound doctrine (Tit 2:1) with confidence (Tit 2:15), sureness (Tit 3:8), and firmness (Tit 1:11),

---

[33]See Dibelius and Conzelmann, p. 154.

choose well (Tit 1:7-9), adapt teaching to various groups (Tit 2:1-10), and care for others (Tit 3:13-14). These competencies are necessary for the organization and development of the local churches. In the letter to Titus the focus is on leaders, whereas Paul would have urged all Christians to assume responsibility for the church.

The Pastoral letters tend to objectify faith in a way foreign to the apostle Paul. Ordination and the focus on the ministry of few, separated from ministry by the community, attest to a later period in church development. Favorite Pauline themes, such as the power of the Risen Lord, and the apostle's vision of church, succumb to the creation of church order and the regulation of Christian lives according to staid virtues, instead of dynamic ones. However, the gospel remains a norm for the church, and elements of belief trickle into the correspondence with reasonable regularity. These letters sober the contemporary reader, and they cannot be dismissed.

The letters to Timothy and Titus attempt to preserve the faith and offer directives for leadership and life. Robert Karris summarizes part of their value: "For a church in transition the author of the Pastorals has provided the roots of Paul's example (2 Tim) and his instructions on church structure and life (1 Tim), the roots of traditional understandings of the church (1 Tim 3:15), the roots of traditional creeds about Jesus (especially 1 Tim 3:16), and the roots of baptismal tradition (1 Tim 6:12-16). A church in transition can be firmly grounded in these roots."[34] The rightful place of the Pastorals as complementary to an earlier ecclesiology and as addressing new needs, insures an appropriate assessment and use of this material.

New Trends in the Pauline Interpreters

The interpreters of Paul present us with different ideas and reflect new trends in the church as it moves into the second century. Some developments are a logical progression of Paul's theology and ecclesiology; others take the community along a

---
[34]Karris, *Pastoral,* p. 104.

new path. All the letters, 2 Thessalonians, Colossians, Ephesians, 1 and 2 Timothy, and Titus, give testimony to Paul's continuing influence in the initial stages of the church's life. In 2 Thessalonians, imitation of Paul and an emphasis on his early insights regarding the parousia and apocalyptic enthusiasm predominate. In Colossians and Ephesians, the interpretation of Paul for a new period reaches its heights in areas of christology and ecclesiology, The Pastorals reveal the legendary Paul handing on the apostolic tradition. While all these letters bear the influence of Paul's thought, the writers, dealing with a living church, develop Pauline Christianity for new situations, while attempting to remain faithful to his spirit.[35]

This section identifies new trends in these letters and the following section offers some evaluative comments. Although our examination of these letters of the interpreters of Paul is less detailed than that for the authentic correspondence, the earlier chapters set the stage for identifying the major areas of development and provide a basis for comparison.

NEW DIRECTIONS

The Pauline interpreters deal with a church solidly established in the Hellenistic world, with Christianity itself more Hellenistic than Jewish. Because the separation of the church from Judaism is a past event for the writers of Ephesians and the Pastorals, and probably for the author of Colossians as well, we can say Church, instead of church. The Paulinists become defenders of the faith and hand on the apostolic tradition. In fact, the origin of the tradition takes on great importance and *the* faith, sound doctrine, and authentic teaching, become the new emphases. For the Pastorals, the past directs the present, while in 2 Thessalonians, the future affects the life of the community, as is the case for the apocalyptic writers. Colossians begins the movement towards the world of the Pastorals with its absence of a sense of urgency and its attention to the present.

---

[35]See Perrin, pp. 134-137, and 268-273, for his assessment of deutero-Pauline Christianity as a movement, and the characteristics of emergent Catholicism.

All the Pauline interpreters face heresy, and their letters are best understood as a response to early gnostic tendencies. In the face of "every wind of doctrine' (Eph 4:14) they invoke the name of Paul while presenting their own understanding of *the faith*. No longer is faith a dynamic belief in the Risen Lord who will come again, but rather the acceptance of revealed truth with tradition providing the essence of the faith. Paul himself often called on tradition for the details of Christian life or for liturgical practice in the churches (1 Cor 7:10; 11:23-26), but the interpreters go further. Now "you received Christ Jesus the Lord, so live in him, rooted and built up in him and established in the faith, just as you were taught" (Col 2:6-7). Ephesians draws on the rich biblical and Christian tradition with its message, in many respects, the culmination of all that preceded it.

In their *christological development* the Pauline interpreters offer new insights. A cosmic christology develops in Colossians and an emphasis on Christ as the image of the invisible God. Christ's preexistence and the universal implications of his influence prevail in these letters. In both Colossians and Ephesians, Christ is the head of his body, the church, specifications never made in the earlier letters. The unity of Jews and Gentiles is a reality because of Christ, and unity at all levels permeates Ephesians, for there is "one Lord, one faith, one baptism, one God and Father of us all" (Eph 4:5-6). While this confession echoes Paul, the interpreters move away from the pluralism experienced in the early church.

The term "savior" applied to Christ and God is a new title, used only once by Paul. Christ's role as reconciler expands from reconciling the world to himself in 2 Corinthians 5:19, to reconciling all things in Colossians 1:20, to reconciling Jew and Gentile in the one body through the cross in Ephesians 2:16. The mystery of Christ in Colossians develops into the mystery of God's purpose to unite all persons in the church in Ephesians. All the Pauline writers speak of forgiveness of sins, individualizing the broader understanding of Paul who regards sin primarily as a power that enslaves.

Ephesians and Colossians offer a broad and deep christology. However, this kind of development is notably absent in the Pastorals, which rely exclusively on the available material.

Paul's interpreters emphasize *ecclesiology* more than christology, and we see new ideas in their letters. The explicit understanding of the church as universal church rather than local community emerges in Colossians and Ephesians. These letters present the specification of Christ as the head of the church, which is his body, and so reorient our thinking about this earlier Pauline model. Christ predominates within the body as it becomes identified with the universal church and expands into a more cosmic reality. The church is founded on the apostles and prophets with Christ as the cornerstone, an idea foreign to Paul. Furthermore, the writers use the marriage relationship to describe the relationship between Christ and the church, indicating a positive view of marriage and family. While a dynamic model of church still remains, a beginning movement to a more structured model of the church is also evident.

The greatest leap in ecclesiology is in the delineation of roles and responsibilities within the church. These letters present moral qualifications for ministers, and a new church order emerges that focuses on bishops, presbyters, and deacons. The emphasis on pastoral offices and the laying on of hands or ordination presents a new view of charism, leadership, and ministry. The primary interest in ministers, with references to pastors and evangelists, characterizes this transitional period in the church. Another new idea is actually an old and prevailing one in society and religion, the restriction of women's roles in this period, as a patriarchal and stratified image takes hold of the church and the household of faith.

Ministers in the church teach, command, charge others, and guard what has been entrusted to them. All the deutero-Pauline letters reflect a more emphatic tone, a more hierarchical tendency, and a more threatening stance towards those who think differently. Opposition receives harsh denouncements as the church establishes its doctrine and its apostolic tradition. The bishop becomes the promulgator of apostolic teaching, defending it against heresy. Offices in the church, although not yet solidly in place, move decidedly in this direction. Power and authority are in the hands of a few leaders, heralding another stage of ecclesial development with a different conception of faith, truth, and authority. Thus, an institutional tendency complements the vision of church as the body of Christ.

Community life within the church takes on the characteristics of a patriarchal society. Household codes advocate submissiveness and passivity, a far different idea from that of the apostle Paul, and subordination marks both the marriage relationship and congregational life. The Pastorals show how a local community unites and organizes itself in a significant way and how responsibility for the community rests with the leadership in the local churches. Relationships change as commands and regulations come to the fore, even among those Paul would consider co-workers. Although the historical Paul exercised strong leadership with his communities, he collaborated with others and fostered responsibility in the communities. Likewise, the apostle's view of conscience, with the conditions of communal responsibility and freedom, recedes into the background.

The trends in the church reflect a new stage of development, revolving around the tradition, christology, ecclesiology, and communal life. The formulations of the faith and solid doctrine take precedence over pluralism as the church faces heresy. Grounding the faith in the apostolic tradition offers little room for debate, dialogue, or argument, and ministers now hand on and defend these truths.

The letters understand Christ's role in its universal and cosmic significance and develop the idea of his preexistence. Christ as head of the church also sets a new direction as a more profound christology slowly begins to take shape.

In terms of ecclesiology, the emphasis is on the universal dimension of the church, and its local leadership moves toward more structure and organization. The church selects ministers, and more specialized ministries give rise to their own leaders.

Community life moves away from the charismatic and relational model of the earlier times to focus on appropriate behavior with patriarchal guidelines for believers. Discernment, equality, and responsibility within the community give way to passivity, submission, and a gradual separation of leaders and followers. The Pauline interpreters set the direction for the second century by offering new ideas and directions. However, they also deemphasize or eliminate key ideas in Paul's vision of church. An evaluation of their contributions seems in order.

EVALUATIVE COMMENTS ON THE INTERPRETERS OF PAUL

The existence of 2 Thessalonians, Colossians, Ephesians, 1 and 2 Timothy, and Titus, attests to the continuing influence of Paul in the early church. However, a rigid line should not be drawn in these letters between the apostle Paul and his interpreters. Likewise, we should avoid the dualistic extremes of authentic or inauthentic interpretations of the message of Jesus or of Paul, of faithfulness or unfaithfulness to the tradition. In terms of our biblical heritage, all the letters under Paul's name can challenge and enlighten the church today. However, we view the later literature as complementary to the authentic letters, since they build on what is already written, and if contradictory in specific areas, test the perspective against the recurring testimony of the biblical tradition. Furthermore, the contemporary church must also weigh its traditions and history in light of these earlier insights in order to reinterpret the scripture for yet another new age.

The theology of these letters meets head-on the challenge of gnostic or other heretical influences, as they admonish all regarding doctrine and behavior. They affirm the goodness of creation and marriage, offering a reasonably wholistic view for the first century. However, alongside the positive perspective, an overreliance on the apostolic tradition and an overconcern with the past, inhibit a more creative approach to opposition and perhaps a more creative application of Paul's original ideas. The letters breathe traditionalism, particularly in terms of teaching, behavior, roles, and relationships. The absence of the charismatic and eschatological elements of the earlier period leads to the flat moralism reflected in these letters.

While the church reacts against heresy, its concern with its reputation among those outside the community and its overcommitment to the patriarchal perspective of society weakens its presentation. The valuing of marriage diminishes when confronted with the witness to patriarchal dominance and the submissive role of women in this relationship. Applying similar restrictions to women's participation in the church is a backward step from Paul, who though experiencing tension between the gospel message and his own background, collaborates with women and affirms them as missionaries, coworkers, apostles, prophets, and leaders in the church. These later writers set their interpretation against a discipleship of equals and more in accordance with the world of their day.

Certain themes in Paul are notably absent in the later Pauline letters. In some instances the earlier letters need no further development, for the underlying teaching prevails, as in the understanding of salvation and justification by faith. Other instances, like the elimination of the ideas of freedom in Christ, leave the Pauline writers with a diminished interpretation of community, conscience, and Christian life. This selective remembrance is a serious concern and creates an aura of suspicion about what is transmitted. While these letters give evidence of the maturing of some of Paul's thought, the reader should also note the compromising of other aspects. We should not lose original insights but rather nurture, develop, and reinterpret them for new times and situations.

These letters do address new situations in enterprising ways. They move towards the special charism of the pastoral office and take the initial steps of creating a new church order. In terms of office, ordination, and hierarchical ministry, they say less than some would hope, but do set a direction for the church. A more organized church is a useful and necessary step in this transitional period. However, the Pauline authors do little to remind the churches of the charisms and the responsibilities of all members of the community. In addressing new needs and presenting new ideas, they neglect to develop Paul's expansive concept of mission and ministry for a new time. In their focus on Christ as the head of the body, they by-pass the dynamic union and commitment of all the members in Christ. Likewise, respectability of leadership persons takes on more significance than true service of the community.

These letters contribute to the realization of the church as both local and universal. They specify Paul's inherent sense of universal church, but the approach to the local churches is a far cry from Paul's own ministry in comparable communities. Again, the patriarchal influences take a strong hold, affecting its leadership, the description of offices in the church, and the now restricted and marginalized roles of women.[36] Certain forms of ministry predominate while the exciting mission of the church and vital communal experiences diminish. The ministry of the bishop or presbyter is not yet defined in superior or cultic terms, but the community begins to lose its sense of being filled with the Spirit. The gift resides in the ministerial office bearer rather than in the ordinary Christian. Käsemann makes a sobering observation of this period: "The Pauline conception of a Church order based on charisma disappeared in the very church the Apostle himself created; and ... this happened because it seemed to that church to be an ideal incapable of being realized."[37] The church in this transitional period loses the original dynamism of the Pauline communities. Likewise, discernment, building up the community in faith, mutual responsibility, and the sense of baptismal commitment fade.

Of the models of the church in Paul, the body of Christ not only remains but develops in a more focused way. The new creation and mystical person underlie some dimensions of the letter's content, while the people of God has little continuing influence. The household and family remain and perhaps grow in significance, but with patriarchal overtones as already noted. The building images become more static, and the writers also use military, athletic, and working descriptions. The emphasis in the church is more on the harmony of external appearances than on inner harmony.[38]

Paul's image in these letters changes to someone who consistently commands and passes on his legacy of the truth. He names people who oppose him as well as other sinners, almost branding them, something he is hesitant to do in his lifetime. In fact, Paul usually does not name opponents, spending most of his time affirming specific individuals in the communities. The historical Paul's respect for others and his realization of their potential for growth expand his vision of church and enable him to utilize everyone for the sake of the gospel. The

---

[36] See Fiorenza, *Memory*, p. 288.

[37] Käsemann, *Essays*, p. 88.

[38] Ernst, p. 241, notes this point in regard to Ephesians.

interpreters tend to bypass this quality, only partially hearing Paul's message to the churches, with the result that they are almost too careful in the development of church life.

The Pauline interpreters broaden our understanding of the early church and provide the source for later developments in the churches, particularly in the Roman Catholic church over the centuries. They prepare their church for the second century in terms of doctrine and structure, directing the universal and the local churches. However, the initial movement of charisms and ministry away from the community, the affirmation of patriarchal influences, the absence of a sense of mission, equality, and freedom in Christ are a great loss. The church seems less dynamic and vital through the eyes of the interpreters, placing the value of these letters as complementary to Paul, and forcing us to recognize their deficiencies as well as their strengths. Perhaps, as we begin to understand their process of interpretation more fully, we will be enlightened to deal more effectively with our transition towards a new period of church life.

8

Paul's Vision of Church and His Challenge for Ecclesial Life

> "May the God of hope fill you with all joy and peace in believing, so that by the power of the Holy Spirit, you may abound in hope." (Rom 15:13)

Paul's letters offer marvelous testimony to the beginnings of the church and a dramatic profile of the apostle in his ministry to the churches. They challenge Christians in every age to ponder the meaning of the church and to rededicate themselves to the ecclesial community. The letters reflect Paul's joys and struggles in ministry and his growth in his understanding of church. However, the value of the correspondence also emerges in the process of interpretation, in the application of ethical principles, and in the pluralism so evident within the early communities. Paul's writings present us with a dynamic portrayal of the local churches, rather than with a static portrait of *the* church. Because of this perspective, his ecclesiology is engaging in its interest and timeless in its significance.

Although the early church reflects dimensions of first-century religion and world view, the apostle radically shifts his perspective in light of God's confounding action in Christ. His awareness of the Spirit's presence leads to exhortations to the community regarding its life and its ministry. His theological framework allows Paul to demonstrate possibilities for Christian existence and to offer hope to the developing communities. Although other writers interpret Paul's message, the authentic correspondence remains a formidable and compelling witness to our Christian origins.

The Grounding of Paul's Vision in Theology and Experience

Paul's vision of church in these early writings emerges from his theological understanding, from his personal experience, and from his ministry. These various components blend together into an understanding that changes in its orientation and develops in its understanding of local and universal church.

HIS THEOLOGICAL PERSPECTIVE

Paul's first instincts as a theologian come from his Pharisaic background and training. They expand with his knowledge of the kerygma and the influence of the Hellenistic world. The conversion experience contains the core of Paul's theological insight, particularly in its perception of the existing relationship between Christ, Christians, and the church. Many influences help to form Paul's theology and his ecclesiology. However, all of these different perspectives need interpretation so that a new Christian synthesis can emerge. Fidelity to the tradition becomes tempered by freedom to adapt the tradition to changing situations.

HIS PERSONAL EXPERIENCE

The apostle's conversion experience is a watershed for his understanding of Christ and the church. However, this experience marks only the beginning of his life and mission in the early church with its own formative influences. Primary among the varied experiences that have a significant impact on Paul is his ministry to the churches.

Ministry provides the context for Paul's theological reflection and for the development of his vision. He relates the gospel to the situation of the churches, where it is enthusiastically accepted, enormously misunderstood, hotly debated, or decisively rejected. The apostle maintains a relationship with these local communites, honing his ecclesial convictions, as they also develop theirs. Christian churches become home to Jew and Gentile, marginalized and oppressed, creative and gifted. Furthermore, Paul reflects on these ministerial experiences and identifies their theological significance, establishing a direct connection between his existential experience and his theological vision.

Moreover, Paul's ministry includes collaboration with others, which builds up the bonds of unity within, and among, the churches. His extensive journeys are occasions for establishing churches, maintaining old ties, supporting community leaders and local churches,—and for a little leather work as well! Paul's ministry engenders a sense of belonging and a deep sense of commitment among his co-workers and within communities.

The apostle's contributions to the early Christian movement rest in his ability to integrate his past with the present situation of the churches. He is courageous in his departure from Judaism and creative in his emphasis on aspects of continuity with the tradition. Likewise, he adapts his gospel to the Hellenistic environment, allowing freedom and flexibility, while also insisting on responsibility and unity. His ability to face obstacles and his consistent urging to build up communities in faith mark this early stage of church life. Paul's ecclesial vision firmly grounds itself in theology and in experience.

The Expansion of Paul's Vision Through Ministry and Models

Paul's ecclesial vision has qualities of idealism and of realism about it. His sense of mission, his awareness of the power of the Lord, his view of the potential of those united in the Spirit, become clearly identified in his models of church which challenge the local communities.

HIS SENSE OF MISSION

Paul's understanding of Christ and his call to be an apostle consolidate his mission in the early church. The first Christians form a missionary movement in the Hellenistic world, taking the proclamation and spread of the gospel as part of their religious commitment. This missionary spirit engenders in the primitive church enthusiasm, urgency, and daring, and this perspective constitutes the identity of the ecclesial community. Paul presses "on toward the goal," always "straining forward to what lies ahead" (Phil 3:13-14).

HIS USE OF MODELS

However, the missionary endeavors have a clear focus and a concrete challenge. To become a Christian means to be church, a people who are the body of Christ, the new creation, and who form the total Christ, the one mystical person. While Paul offers many descriptions of church, only relatively few models critically explain the reality of church in the beginning stages of its life. The models articulate dimensions of Paul's vision while presenting new ideas and possibilities. While they represent different ways of understanding church, all the models center on Christ and the Christian community. Paul's vision expands as he ministers in the churches, and he clarifies and develops it through his use of models.

The Challenge of Paul's Vision for Ecclesial Living

Paul's vision is far from an unrealistic ideal, since he grounds it in his experience and that of the Christian churches. Furthermore, we identify his realistic orientation as Paul exhorts the community in the practicalities of its Christian life and shares a spirituality that insures a concrete commitment to the church.

HIS EMPHASIS ON COMMUNITY

Paul's portrayal of church as a community of believers, called by God, baptized into Christ, and empowered by the Spirit, remains a forceful image. Although believers offer worship to God and service of others, the context for both activities is community. For Paul, community best describes the reality of church, as we see in the relational images and models used in the letters. Furthermore, the Christian community breaks down the prevailing religious and societal barriers by emphasizing equality in Christ for all believers. Within the ecclesial community, women discover alternatives to patriarchal values that facilitate their leadership and ministry in the churches. Likewise, the community empowers its leaders and its members who use their charisms for the good of the body. Responsibility marks this new community, as does freedom and mutual love.

The community of believers is a source of joy for Paul, but they also challenge him to grow and to change, particularly in the difficult encounters of his ministry. Paul is convinced that to be a Christian means to be one with Christ and one with those who believe in him. Community life reflects our faith, and the quality of our ecclesial experience indicates the depth of our commitment.

HIS SENSE OF ECCLESIAL DEDICATION

Paul's spirituality is a spirituality that fosters ecclesial commitment. Rather than simply focusing on the Lord and prayer, he examines the fruits of those encounters, by encouraging a shared vision of church that includes responsible behavior and dedicated service. Everyone bears the responsibility for empowering others with a sense of church. Opportunities for ministry and growth as church constitute a basic perspective for the apostle. Paul challenges Christians to greatness as they live according to the gospel and present every aspect of their lives as spiritual worship. Living as church characterizes the believer's existence; dedication to the church crystallizes faith through service. Both dimensions require an appreciation of the death/life paradox of human existence.

The Interpretation of Paul's Vision by Others

Paul's interpreters continue his influence, adapt his message, and set a direction for the church in the second century. However, the task of interpretation is never complete since different situations and other times demand new understandings of the church.

HIS BIBLICAL INTERPRETERS

The deutero-Pauline writers develop Paul's message and prepare for the emergence of yet another model of church. While their understanding of Christ becomes more expansive and delineated, their understanding of church becomes more focused and hierarchical. The community filled with the Spirit's gifts for its life and ministry is now the church with identifiable leadership and sound doctrine. While these later letters address a new stage in church life, they are best understood as complementary to the earlier correspondence. Unfortunately, in addressing heresy, they overreact, stressing order and doctrine, rather than pursuing gospel values as did the earlier churches. However, Paul can survive his interpreters since his own letters remain as eloquent testimony to his vision of church.

HIS CONTEMPORARY CHALLENGE

The Pauline correspondence offers many approaches to church life and many possibilities for new emphases in the contemporary church. Paul's own insight into the identity of the Christian church emerges from several sources: his diaspora Jewish background, his conversion experience, his ministry in the churches, his contact with church leaders, and his theological reflection. He courageously reinterprets his past in light of his Christian faith and adapts the gospel message to different local churches. Many facets contribute to our own understanding of church, and like Paul, we need to be in touch with all the dimensions. Moreover, we too adapt and reinterpret our tradition for the local churches and for a changing world.

Paul emphasizes radical equality in Christ and collaboration with co-workers of various backgrounds and abilities. He respects the movement of the Spirit in individuals and communities, encouraging discernment, mutual responsibility, and gospel freedom. While his later interpreters identify sound doctrine and pass it on, Paul uses dialogue and persuasion to direct the churches and to insure an authentic understanding of the gospel. When he resorts to confrontation, the situation is serious, but even in Galatia he depends on theological argument to sway the community. In our diverse and sometimes difficult church, Paul challenges us to rethink our views of community life, our perspective on ministry, and our understanding of church leadership and authority. The apostle's letters suggest that all the gifts necessary for the church reside within the churches. His openness to the contributions of all might counter any narrowness in our own attitudes.

Paul's vision of church also results from his ability to deal with crisis and transition and to learn from these experiences. His approach in the letters, and the more restrictive positions of the later interpreters, present a spectrum of responses, and we can assess their effectiveness in light of subsequent history.

Paul's models of church, and the potential models in his letters, suggest alternative images to our hierarchical and institutional emphases. Changing images require sensitivity, creativity, and imagination, as Paul also indicates.

Finally, Paul's emphasis on an ecclesial spirituality that relates to the mission of the church is a perspective that can enhance and broaden any individualistic assessment of holiness. His views on Christian existence resonate well with the emerging laity, a distinction foreign to Paul.

The letters of Paul are a rich source for our appreciation of the difficult but exciting beginnings of the Christian church. However, we can read these letters to confirm what we already know, or we can look to them for aspects of ecclesial life hidden by layers of church history and tradition. Our approach either conceals, or reveals, the message of Paul and the experience of the early Christians. It is my hope that just as Paul's conversion set in motion his work in the church, our conversion to the church and as church will set new directions and inspire a new beginning.

Bibliography

Abbott, Walter, ed. *The Documents of Vatican II.* New York: Guild Press, 1966.

Baird, William. "On Reading Romans in the Church Today." *Interpretation* 34 (1980), pp. 45-58.

Banks, Robert. *Paul's Idea of Community. The Early House Churches in their Historical Setting.* Michigan: Wm. B. Eerdmans Publishing Co., 1980.

Barrett, C.K. *The Second Epistle to the Corinthians.* London: Charles Black, 1973.

Barth, Markus. "Traditions in Ephesians." *New Testament Studies* 30 (1984), pp. 3-25.

Bassler, Jouette M. "The Widows' Tale: A Fresh Look at 1 Tim. 5:3-16." *Journal of Biblical Literature* 103 (1984), pp. 23-41.

Beker, J. Christian. *Paul The Apostle.* Philadelphia: Fortress Press, 1980.

Betz, Hans Dieter. *2 Corinthians 8 and 9: A Commentary on Two Administrative Letters of the Apostle Paul.* Philadelphia: Fortress Press, 1985.

_____, *Galatians: A Commentary on Paul's Letter to the Churches in Galatia.* Philadelphia: Fortress Press, 1979.

Boring, M. Eugene. "The Language of Universal Salvation in Paul." *Journal of Biblical Literature* 150 (1986), pp. 269-292.

Bornkamm, Günther. *Paul.* New York: Harper and Row Publishers, 1969.

Branick, Vincent P. "Apocalyptic Paul?" *Catholic Biblical Quarterly* 47 (1985), pp. 664-675.

Brinsmead, Bernard Hungerford. *Galatians—Dialogical Response to Opponents.* Chico, CA: Scholars Press, 1982.

Brown, Raymond E. *The Churches the Apostles Left Behind.* New York: Paulist Press, 1984.

Brown, Raymond E., Karl P. Donfried, John Reumann. *Peter in the New Testament.* New York, Paulist Press, 1973.

Brown, Raymond E. and John P. Meier. *Antioch and Rome.* New York: Paulist Press, 1983.

Brunt, John C. "Rejected, Ignored, or Misunderstood? The Fate of Paul's Approach to the Problem of Food Offered to Idols in Early Christianity." *New Testament Studies* 31 (1985), pp. 113-124.

Byrne, Brendan. *Reckoning with Romans.* Wilmington, Del.: Michael Glazier, 1986.

Campbell, W. S. "Romans III as a Key to the Structure and Thought of the Letter." *Novum Testamentum* 23 (1981), pp. 22-40.

Cerfaux, Lucien. *The Spiritual Journey of Saint Paul.* New York: Sheed and Ward, 1968.

Conzelmann, Hans. *An Outline of the Theology of the New Testament.* New York: Harper and Row Publishers, 1969.

Collins, John J. *Between Athens and Jerusalem: Jewish Identity in the Hellenistic Diaspora.* New York: Crossroad, 1983.

Cranfield, C.E.B. *A Critical and Exegetical Commentary on the Epistle to the Romans.* vols. I and II. Edinburgh: T. & T. Clark Ltd., 1975 and 1979.

Cullmann, Oscar. *The Early Church.* London: SCM Press, 1956.

Davies, W.D. *Paul and Rabbinic Judaism.* London: SPCK, 1965.

Dibelius, Martin, and Hans Conzelmann. *The Pastoral Epistles.* Philadelphia: Fortress Press, 1972.

Donfried, Karl P. *The Romans Debate.* Minneapolis: Augsburg Press, 1977.

Doohan, Helen. *Leadership in Paul.* Wilmington, Del.: Michael Glazier, 1984.

_____ *Minister of God: Effective and Fulfilled.* New York: Alba House, 1986.

Doohan, Leonard. *The Lay-Centered Church.* Minneapolis: Winston Press, 1984.

_____ *Luke: The Perennial Spirituality.* 2nd ed. Santa Fe: Bear and Co., 1985.

_____ *Matthew: Spirituality for the 80s and 90s.* Santa Fe: Bear and Co., 1985.

_____ *Mark: Visionary of Early Christianity.* Santa Fe: Bear and Co., 1986.

Dulles, Avery. *Models of the Church.* New York: Image Books, 1978.

_____ *A Church to Believe In.* New York: Crossroad, 1982.

Elliot, John H. "Philemon and House Churches." *Bible Today* 22 (1984), pp. 145-150.

Ellis, E. Earle. *Prophecy and Hermeneutic in Early Christianity.* Grand Rapids: Wm. B. Eerdmans Publishing Co., 1978.

Ernst, Josef. "From the Local Community to the Great Church." *Biblical Theology Bulletin* 6 (1976), pp. 237-257.

Filson, Floyd V. "The Significance of the Early House Churches." *Journal of Biblical Literature* 58 (1939), pp. 105-112.

Fiorenza, Elisabeth Schüssler. *In Memory of Her.* New York: Crossroad, 1983

———— *Bread not Stone.* Boston: Beacon Press, 1984.

———— "Emerging Issues in Feminist Biblical Interpretation." *Christian Feminism.* Judith L. Weidman, ed. New York: Harper and Row Publishers, 1984, pp. 33-54.

Fitzmyer, Joseph A. *Pauline Theology: A Brief Sketch.* Englewood Cliffs, NJ.: Prentice-Hall, 1967.

Flanagan, Neal. *Friend Paul: His Letters, Theology and Humanity.* Wilmington, Del.: Michael Glazier, 1986.

Freyne, Sean. *The World of the New Testament.* Wilmington, Del.: Michael Glazier, 1980.

Gager, J. *Kingdom and Community. The Social World of Early Christianity.* Englewood Cliffs, NJ.: Prentice-Hall, 1975.

Gale, Herbert Morrison. *The Use of Analogy in the Letters of Paul.* Philadelphia: The Westminster Press, 1964.

Goguel, M. *The Primitive Church.* London: Allen and Unwin, 1964.

Hanson, A.T. *Studies in Paul's Technique and Theology.* Grand Rapids: Wm. B. Eerdmans Publishing Co., 1974.

———— *The Pastoral Epistles.* The New Century Bible Commentary. Grand Rapids: Wm. B. Eerdmans Publishing Co., 1982.

Harnack, A. von. *The Mission and Expansion of Christianity in the First Three Centuries.* New York: Putnam, 1905.

Harrington, Daniel J. "Sociological Concepts and the Early Church: A Decade of Research." *Theological Studies* 41 (1980), pp. 181-190.

———— "Biblical Hermeneutics in Recent Discussion: New Testament." *Religious Studies Review* 10 (1984), pp. 7-10.

Harrington, Wilfrid. *Jesus and Paul: Signs of Contradiction.* Wilmington, Del.: Michael Glazier, 1987.

Hedrick, Charles W. "Paul's Conversion/Call: A Comparative Analysis of the Three Reports in Acts." *Journal of Biblical Literature* 100 (1981), pp. 415-432.

Hengel, Martin. *Judaism and Hellenism, Vol. 1.* Philadelphia: Fortress Press, 1974.

_____ *Acts and the History of Earliest Christianity.* Philadelphia: Fortress Press, 1980.

_____ *Between Jesus and Paul: Studies in the Earliest History of Christianity.* Philadelphia: Fortress Press, 1983.

Hock, Ronald. "The Workshop as a Social Setting for Paul's Missionary Preaching." *Catholic Biblical Quarterly* 41 (1979), pp. 438-450.

Holmberg, Bengt. *Paul and Power: The Structure of Authority in the Primitive Church as Reflected in the Pauline Epistles.* Philadelphia: Fortress Press, 1980.

Horsley, Richard A. "Consciousness and Freedom Among the Corinthians: 1 Corinthians 8-10." *Catholic Biblical Quarterly* 40 (1978), pp. 574-589.

Houlden, J.L. *Paul's Letters from Prison.* Harmondsworth: Penguin Books, 1970.

Hultgren, Arland J. *I-II Timothy, Titus.* Roger Aus. *II Thessalonians.* Augsburg Commentary on the New Testament. Minneapolis: Augsburg Publishing House, 1984.

Hurd, J.C. *The Origins of First Corinthians.* London: SPCK, 1965.

Jewett, Robert. *A Chronology of Paul's Life.* Philadelphia: Fortress Press, 1979.

Johnson, Luke T. "Rom 3:21-26 and the Faith of Jesus." *Catholic Biblical Quarterly* 44 (1982), pp. 77-90.

Karris, Robert J. "Rom 14:1-15:13 and the Occasion of Romans." *Catholic Biblical Quarterly* 35 (1973), pp. 155-178.

_____ *The Pastoral Epistles.* Wilmington, Del.: Michael Glazier, 1979.

Käsemann, E. "Ministry and Community in the New Testament." *Essays on New Testament Themes.* London: SCM Press, 1964, pp. 63-94.

_____ *New Testament Questions of Today.* Philadelphia: Fortress Press, 1969.

_____ *Perspectives on Paul.* Philadelphia: Fortress Press, 1971.

Kim, Seyoon. *The Origin of Paul's Gospel.* Grand Rapids: Wm. B. Eerdmans Publishing Co., 1981.

Kümmel, Werner George. *Introduction to the New Testament.* London SCM Press, 1965.

Küng, Hans. *The Church.* New York: Sheed and Ward, 1967.

Leaney, A.R.C. *The Jewish and Christian World 200 BC to AD 200.* New York: Cambridge University Press, 1984.

Lohfink, Gerhard. *Jesus and Community: The Social Dimension of Christian Faith.* Philadelphia: Fortress Press, 1984.

Ludemann, Gerd. *Paul, Apostle to the Gentiles Studies in Chronology.* Philadelphia: Fortress Press, 1984.

MacDonald, Dennis Ronald. *The Legend and the Apostle.* Philadelphia: The Westminister Press, 1983.

Malina, Bruce J. "The Apostle Paul and Law: Prolegomena for an Hermeneutic." *Creighton Law Review* 14 (1981, Supplement), pp. 1305-1339.

Martin, Ralph. *Philippians.* London: Oliphants, 1976.

Mearns, C.L. "Early Eschatological Development in Paul: The Evidence of I and II Thess." *New Testament Studies* 27 (1980-81), pp. 137-157.

Meeks, Wayne A. *The First Urban Christians.* New Haven: Yale University Press, 1983.

Meyer, Ben F. *The Early Christians: Their World Mission and Self-Discovery.* Wilmington, Del.: Michael Glazier, 1986.

Minear, Paul S. *Images of the Church in the New Testament.* Philadelphia: The Westminster Press, 1977.

Mitton, C. Leslie. *Ephesians.* London: Oliphants, 1976.

Moltmann, Jürgen. *The Church in the Power of the Spirit.* New York: Harper and Row Publishers, 1977.

Moule, C.F.D. *Essays in New Testament Interpretation.* New York: Cambridge University Press, 1982.

Murphy-O'Connor, Jerome. *Paul and Qumran.* Chicago: The Priory Press, 1968.

_____ "Eucharist and Community in First Corinthians." *Worship* 50 (1976), pp. 370-385; 51 (1977), pp. 56-69.

_____ *1 Corinthians.* Wilmington, Del.: Michael Glazier, 1979.

_____ "Pauline Missions before the Jerusalem Conference." *Revue Biblique* 89 (1982), pp. 71-91.

_____ *St. Paul's Corinth: Texts and Archeology.* Wilmington, Del.: Michael Glazier, 1983.

Osiek, Carolyn. "Jacob's Well: Women's Role in the Pastorals." *Bible Today* 23 (1985), pp. 246-247.

Patte, Daniel. *Paul's Faith and the Power of the Gospels.* Philadelphia: Fortress Press, 1983.

Perkins, Pheme. "Gnostic Christologies and the New Testament." *Catholic Biblical Quarterly* 43 (1981), pp. 590-606.

Perrin, Norman. *The New Testament: An Introduction.* New York: Harcourt Brace Jovanovich, Inc., 1974.

Petersen, Norman R. *Rediscovering Paul: Philemon and the Sociology of Paul's Narrative World.* Philadelphia: Fortress Press, 1985.

Pierce, J.A. "The Twelve as Apostolic Overseers." *Bible Today* 18 (1980) pp. 72-76.

Reese, James M. *1 and 2 Thessalonians.* Wilmington, Del.: Michael Glazier, 1979.

Reumann, J. "The Gospel of the Righteousness of God." *Interpretation* 20 (1966), pp. 432-452.

Ridderbos, Herman. *Paul: An Outline of His Theology.* Grand Rapids: Wm. B. Eerdmans Publishing Co., 1975.

Rigaux, Béda. *The Letters of Paul.* Chicago: Franciscan Herald Press, 1962.

Roetzel, Calvin. *The Letters of Paul: Conversations in Context.* 2nd ed. Atlanta: John Knox Press, 1982.

Russell, D.S. *Between the Testaments.* Philadelphia: Fortress Press, 1972.

Russell, Letty M. "Women and Ministry: Problems or Possibility." Judith L. Weidman, ed. *Christian Feminism.* New York: Harper and Row Publishers, 1984, pp. 75-92.

Sanders, E.P. *Paul and Palestinian Judaism.* Philadephia: Fortress Press, 1977.

_____ *Paul, the Law, and the Jewish People.* Philadelphia: Fortress Press, 1983.

Schnackenburg, Rudolf. *The Church in the New Testament.* New York: Herder and Herder, 1965.

_____ "Community Cooperation in the New Testament." *Concilium* 77 (1972), pp. 9-19.

Schmithals, Walter. *The Office of Apostle in the Early Church.* New York: Abingdon Press, 1969.

Spicq, Ceslaus. *Agape in the New Testament.* Vol. II. St. Louis: B. Herder Book Co., 1965.

Stanley, David M. *Christ's Resurrection in Pauline Soteriology.* Rome: Biblical Institute, 1952.

_____ *The Apostolic Church in the New Testament.* Westminster, Md.: The Newman Press, 1965.

_____ "Authority in the Church: A New Testament Reality." *Catholic Biblical Quarterly* 29 (1967), pp. 555-573.

_____ "Idealism and Realism in Paul." *Way* 21 (1981), pp. 34-46.

Theissen, Gerd. *The Social Setting of Pauline Christianity.* Philadelphia: Fortress Press, 1982.

Thomas, W. Derek. "The Place of Women at Philippi." *Expository Times* 83 (1971-72), pp. 117-120.

Verner, David C. *The Household of God: the Social World of the Pastoral Epistles.* Chico, CA.: Scholars Press, 1983.

Whiteley, D.E.H. *The Theology of St. Paul.* Philadelphia: Fortress Press, 1964.

Wedderburn, A.J. "Keeping up with Recent Studies: VII. Some Recent Pauline Chronologies." *Expository Times* 92 (1981), pp. 103-108.

Weidman, Judith L. ed. *Christian Feminism.* New York: Harper and Row Publishers, 1984.

Westerholm, Stephen. "Letter and Spirit: The Foundation of Pauline *Ethics." New Testament Studies* 30 (1984), pp. 229-248.

Wikenhauser, Alfred. *Pauline Mysticism.* New York: Herder and Herder, 1960.

Wiles, Gordon P. *Paul's Intercessory Prayers.* London: Cambridge University Press, 1974.

Williams, Sam K. "The 'Righteousness of God' in Romans." *Journal of Biblical Literature* 99 (1980), pp. 241-290.

Wilson, R. M. "How Gnostic were the Corinthians?" *New Testament Studies* 19 (1972-73), pp. 65-74.

Worgul, G.S. "People of God, Body of Christ: Pauline Ecclesiological Contrasts." *Biblical Theology Bulletin* 12 (1982), pp. 24-28.

Ziesler, John. *Pauline Christianity.* New York: Oxford University Press, 1983.

*Tentative Pauline Chronology

Date	Pauline Event	Extrabiblical Events	Biblical Reference	Letters
1-10 CE	Birth		Ac 22:3	
26-36		Pontius Pilate, Procurator of Judea		
34-37	Conversion		Gal 1:11-17, Ac 9:1-30; 22:6-21; 26:12-23	
37	1st Visit to Jerusalem		Gal 1:18	
37-41		Gaius (Caligula) Roman Emperor		
41-44		Herod Agrippa 1: King of Palestine		
44		Death of Herod	Ac 12:20-23	
?45-58		Famine under Claudius	Ac 11:28	
?45-46	In Antioch			
46-49	1st Missionary Journey		Ac 13:1-14:28	
?49	Apostolic Council in Jerusalem		Ac 15:2; 6-12	
49		Edict of Claudius expels Jews from Rome	Ac 18:2	
+?50-53	2nd Missionary Journey		Ac 15:30-18:22; Gal 2:1-10	1 Thess
52		Gallio: Proconsul Achaia	Ac 18:12-17	
52-?59		Felix: Proc. Judea	Ac 23:26	
53-58	3rd Missionary Journey		Ac 18:23-21:17	Gal
54-68		Nero: Roman Emperor		1 & 2 Cor Romans
58	Last Visit to Jerusalem		Ac 21:17	
58-59	Caesarean Imprisonment			Phil Phm
59-60?	Journey to Rome		Ac 27:1-28:16	
?60-62		Portius Festus, Proc. of Judea	Ac 24:37	
61-63	In Rome			
?62-64	Death of Paul			

*This Pauline chronology deals with main events and broad categories that identify Paul and his world. The dating is approximate.

+Many scholars place the 2nd missionary journey before the apostolic council in Jerusalem, moving the date of the council to 53.

PALESTINE in HELLENISTIC and ROMAN TIMES

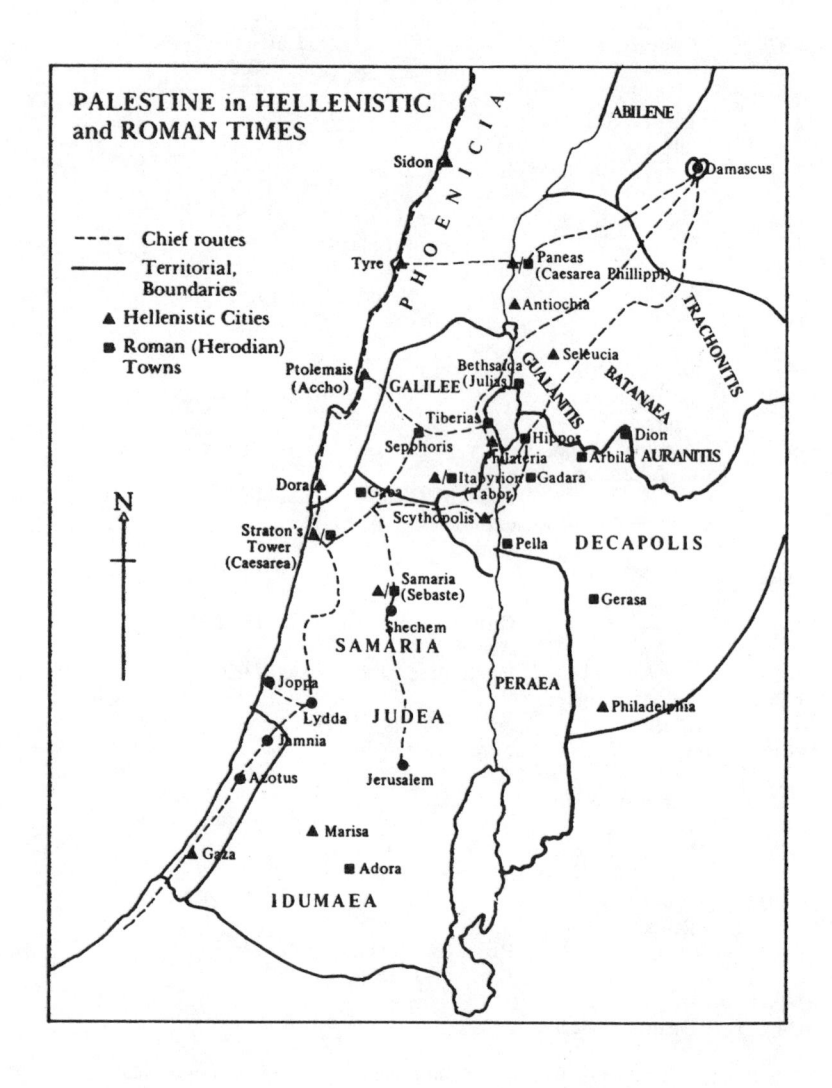

The Jewish Diaspora in the Roman Empire

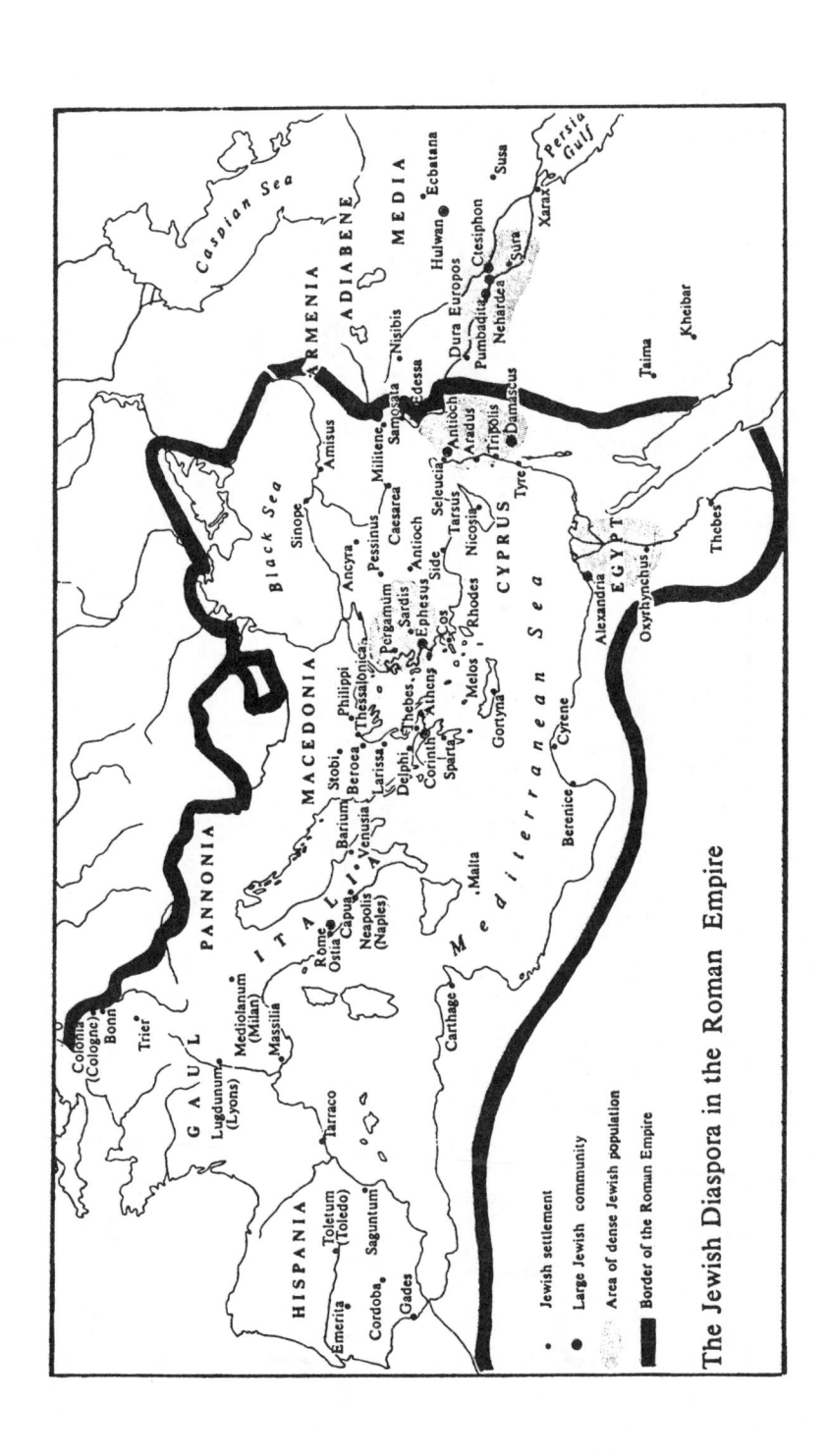

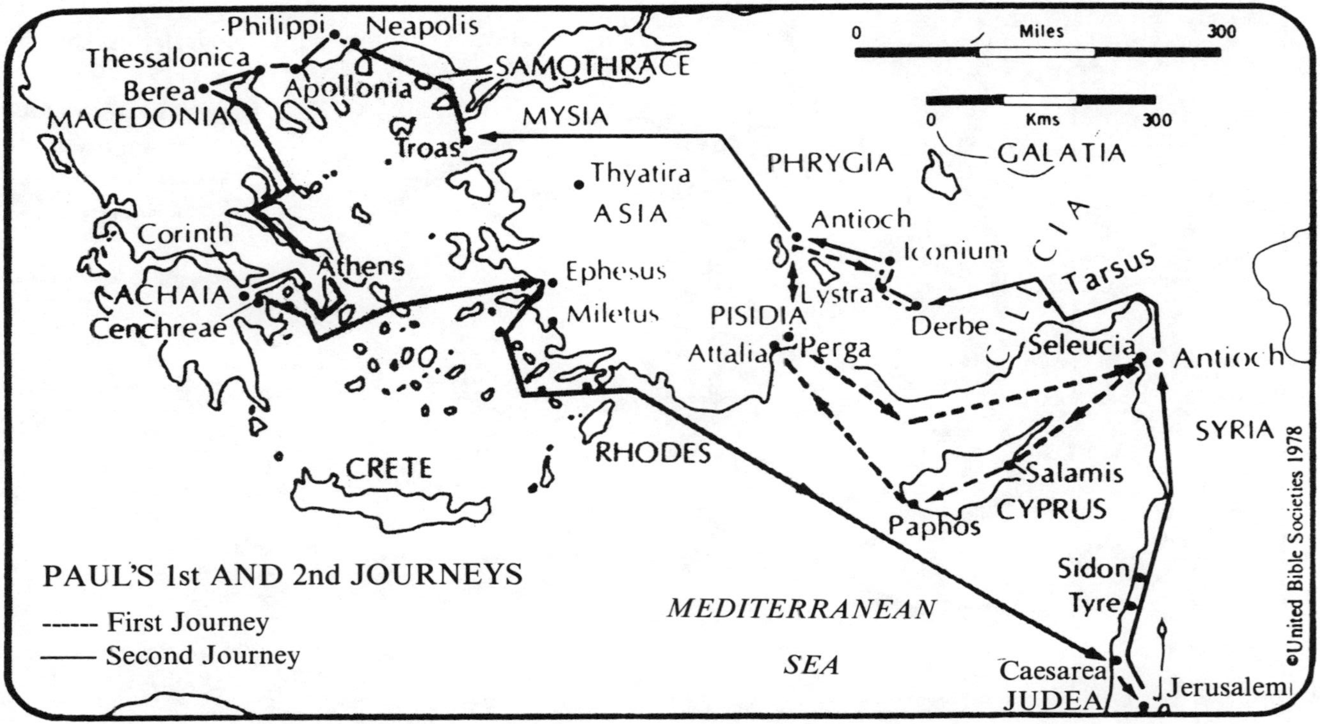

Philippi
Neapolis
Thessalonica
Apollonia
SAMOTHRACE
Berea
MACEDONIA
MYSIA
Troas
Thyatira
ASIA
PHRYGIA
GALATIA
Miles
0
300
Kms
0
300
Antioch
Iconium
CILICIA
Tarsus
Corinth
Athens
ACHAIA
Cenchreae
Ephesus
Miletus
PISIDIA
Lystra
Derbe
Seleucia
Attalia
Perga
Antioch
SYRIA
RHODES
CRETE
Salamis
CYPRUS
Paphos
PAUL'S 1st AND 2nd JOURNEYS
------ First Journey
—— Second Journey
MEDITERRANEAN
SEA
Sidon
Tyre
Caesarea
JUDEA
Jerusalem
©United Bible Societies 1978

PAUL'S THIRD JOURNEY

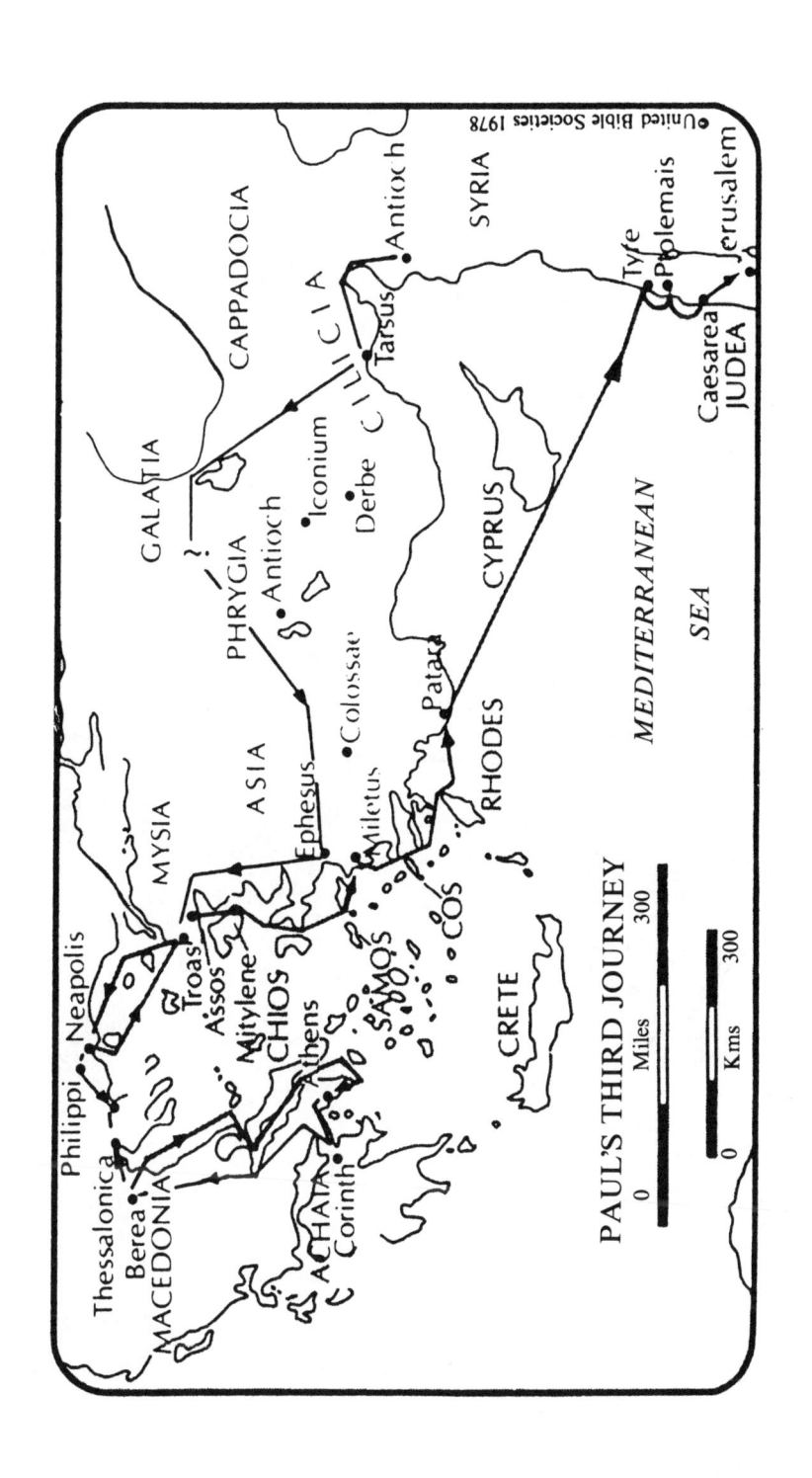

Subject Index

[Significant treatments of important topics are included]

Abraham 25, 44, 45, 78, 91, 107, 108, 145, 146, 147, 155, 161
Acts (of Apostles) 5, 14, 17, 18, 19, 20, 26, 27, 30, 40, 54, 59, 60, 62
Antioch 14, 15, 17, 30, 31, 53, 79, 124, 134
Apocalyptic 2, 14, 42, 43, 45, 51, 56, 57, 67, 74, 195, 218
Apollonius of Tyana 50
Apollos 34, 38, 123, 124, 139, 165
Apostle to Gentiles 2, 18, 19, 58, 68, 92, 101, 192
Aquila 33, 34, 88, 123, 124
Authenticity (authentic letters) 3, 7, 8, 58, 62, 64, 70, 73, 77, 138, 148, 194, 201, 203, 204, 207, 216, 222
Authority 20, 23, 37, 57, 71, 83, 87, 90, 96, 98, 117, 118, 119, 120, 123, 127, 128, 129, 132, 135, 143, 154, 159, 189, 192, 199, 209, 216, 220, 232
-authorities 5, 21, 41, 63, 96, 130, 183, 199

Baptism 20, 50, 55, 60, 104, 113, 114, 115, 117, 156, 160, 177, 185, 198, 199, 202, 205, 215
Bishop 93, 96, 211, 212, 215, 216, 220, 224
Body of Christ 68, 73, 81, 84, 90, 115, 117, 119, 125, 134, 137, 145, 152, 155, 156, 157, 158, 159, 160, 164, 165, 166, 167, 168, 169, 172, 189, 190, 197, 198, 200, 204, 206, 221, 224, 229
Building 140, 144, 146, 165, 206, 224
Build Up 68, 72, 73, 80, 81, 87, 92, 95, 99, 100, 106, 113, 117, 118, 119, 123, 125, 127, 131, 148, 149, 168, 174, 177, 186, 188, 189, 191, 196, 201, 206, 216, 224, 228

Call 3, 4, 11, 18, 19, 20, 21, 22, 23, 26, 35, 37, 44, 45, 61, 68, 90, 103, 106, 108, 116, 119, 133, 142, 145, 146, 147, 170, 171, 172, 173, 188, 189, 193, 211, 229
Cephas (See Peter)
Charism(s) 54, 86, 118, 127, 158, 159, 160, 189, 192, 210, 214, 215, 220, 223, 224, 225, 230
Christianity 2, 9, 16, 36, 43, 46, 47, 67, 145, 202, 208, 218
Christian life 4, 6, 48, 65, 67, 71, 72, 74, 76, 78, 84, 86, 95, 99, 127, 130, 131, 135, 150, 155, 164, 166, 171, 173, 175, 177, 184, 185, 186, 189, 204, 216, 219, 223
Christology 19, 23, 37, 56, 57, 61, 65, 66, 94, 138, 155, 195, 199, 200, 201, 203, 204, 210, 218, 219, 220, 221
Chronology 27
Church—local 4, 15, 34, 40, 68, 70, 71,

72, 73, 76, 79, 81, 96, 100, 101, 113, 118, 120, 121, 123, 129, 133, 134, 141, 142, 143, 144, 148, 160, 166, 167, 191, 204, 217, 221, 223, 225, 226, 228, 231
Church—order 18, 208, 211, 212, 214, 217, 220, 223
Church—universal 4, 133, 134, 167, 193, 197, 200, 202, 204, 220, 223, 227
Claudius 14, 33
Collaboration 34, 73, 80, 87, 92, 96, 100, 117, 121, 122, 123, 124, 125, 130, 168, 192, 228, 231
Community—Jewish 14, 146, 149
Pauline Community (ies) 8, 47, 48, 51, 52, 69, 71, 118, 131, 133, 134, 182, 192, 224
Conflict(s) 26, 35, 40, 51, 54, 55, 59, 72, 79, 80, 84, 92, 119, 128, 155, 207
Confrontation 98, 131, 135, 174, 232
Conscience 68, 84, 153, 182, 213, 221, 223
Controversy 2, 33, 77, 81, 216
Conversion 3, 5, 11, 12, 13, 17, 18, 19, 20, 21, 22, 23, 25, 30, 35, 39, 58, 59, 63, 69, 102, 134, 155, 170, 171, 174, 177, 201, 227, 231, 232
Corporate Personality 161, 165, 166
Co-workers 1, 6, 16, 26, 33, 34, 36, 53, 57, 62, 64, 68, 78, 82, 87, 96, 97, 99, 116, 117, 120, 121, 122, 124, 125, 126, 133, 140, 159, 190, 191, 192, 212, 228, 232
Creation 150, 151, 152, 154, 199, 204, 205, 210
-new creation 25, 90, 104, 137, 145, 149, 150, 152, 153, 154, 155, 163, 164, 165, 166, 167, 168, 169, 177, 178, 200, 224, 229
Cross 56, 61, 64, 83, 95, 105, 109, 110, 116, 153, 182, 184, 185, 187, 199, 203, 210, 219

Damascus 17, 19, 20, 25, 37, 58
Deacon(ess) 34, 62, 93, 96, 125, 212, 213, 220
Dying and rising 50, 114, 171, 184, 185, 186
Delegate 76, 96
Deutero-pauline 7, 194, 195, 220, 231

Dialogue 6, 60, 72, 76, 120, 138, 168, 171, 175, 176, 178, 181, 182, 183, 186, 188, 208, 221, 232
Diaspora 14, 16, 17, 25, 28, 45, 46, 53, 101, 231
Discernment 72, 84, 86, 99, 117, 127, 132, 158, 159, 168, 221, 224
Disciple(ship) 1, 2, 48, 55, 172, 223
Discipline 117, 128, 129, 211
Diversity 3, 4, 15, 36, 38, 40, 52, 55, 57, 58, 59, 70, 80, 82, 84, 101, 119, 122, 130, 131, 155, 156, 157, 158, 159, 160, 167, 178, 192
Doctrine 1, 207, 208, 210, 211, 212, 213, 214, 216, 218, 219, 220, 221, 222, 225, 231, 232

Ecclesial life 40, 72, 117, 121, 131, 168, 172, 174, 182
Ecclesiology 4, 5, 9, 12, 19, 22, 26, 30, 35, 37, 40, 60, 61, 62, 69, 94, 100, 101, 102, 131, 134, 137, 152, 155, 167, 192, 194, 197, 203, 204, 210, 217, 218, 220, 221, 226, 227
Ekklesia 44, 47, 73, 88, 112, 113, 133, 141, 142, 144, 165, 197
Epicureans 50
Episcopoi (see bishop)
Epistles 7, 202
Equality 9, 15, 50, 53, 54, 60, 61, 68, 72, 78, 97, 99, 104, 111, 112, 114, 119, 122, 125, 126, 129, 130, 131, 135, 142, 147, 157, 168, 173, 177, 181, 182, 183, 184, 200, 206, 210, 213, 221, 225, 231
Eschatology 40, 44, 56, 57, 65, 66, 82, 86
Essenes 42, 43, 51
Ethics (ethical principles) 14, 57, 79, 171, 180, 185, 226
Eucharist 115
Evangelization 121, 171, 190, 192
Exhortations 6, 7, 70, 72, 74, 75, 94, 113, 116, 117, 131, 158, 174, 180, 183, 184, 185, 189, 192, 200, 226

Faith 2, 3, 6, 12, 13, 14, 19, 22, 23, 24, 25, 28, 29, 34, 36, 37, 39, 44, 45, 53, 54, 57, 58, 61, 64, 65, 66, 71, 72, 74, 75, 78, 80, 84, 90, 91, 92, 95, 97, 98, 99, 101, 102, 104-112, 114, 116,

250 *Indices*

117, 118, 122, 123, 126, 127, 128, 129, 131, 134, 135, 137, 141, 142, 147, 148, 152, 153, 164, 165, 167-173, 177, 179, 181, 182, 183, 184, 188, 190, 191, 198, 199, 200, 202, 205, 207, 209, 210, 212-220, 223, 224, 228, 230, 231
Family 16, 142, 143, 144, 169, 173, 210, 212, 224
Father 82, 102, 104, 105, 106, 119, 124, 129, 143, 144, 203, 205, 219
Felix 27
Festus 27
Forgiveness 97, 109, 128, 151, 186, 203, 206, 219
Forms of Sharing 72, 73, 75, 79, 85, 90, 94, 97, 206
Freedom 4, 12, 15, 25, 50, 54, 55, 56, 57, 72, 78, 81, 84, 98, 99, 100, 106, 108, 122, 123, 130, 152, 153, 154, 178, 183, 184, 189, 192, 213, 221, 223, 225, 227, 229, 230, 232

Gallio 27
Gentiles 1, 4, 18, 21, 22, 25, 26, 31, 35, 41, 51, 53, 54, 59, 60, 63, 64, 78, 84, 91, 103, 111, 115, 127, 131, 132, 134, 141, 146, 147, 152, 157, 161, 191, 192, 202, 203, 204, 206, 209, 228
Gifts of Spirit (spiritual gifts) 55, 75, 85, 86, 87, 106, 125, 156, 159, 160, 189
Glorification 105, 202
Glory 28, 56, 61, 73, 74, 76, 102, 103, 104, 110, 111, 163, 164, 173, 179, 189, 195, 199
Gnosticism 50, 195, 201
Gospel 4, 5, 6, 8, 9, 18, 20, 21, 23, 26, 28, 29, 30, 31, 32, 35, 36, 37, 39, 54, 55, 61, 62, 64, 68, 71, 72, 73, 76, 77, 78, 79, 81, 82, 83, 86, 89, 92, 93, 94, 95, 96, 97, 99, 100, 108, 112, 119, 124, 126, 127, 128, 129, 132, 133, 134, 135, 141, 145, 146, 160, 165, 168, 170, 181, 188, 191, 192, 195, 196, 198, 199, 202, 207, 212, 214, 217, 222, 224, 227, 228, 229, 230, 231, 232
Growth 4, 21, 28, 32, 34, 54, 57, 59, 68, 71, 72, 74, 75, 87, 92, 94, 95, 98, 126, 130, 131, 138, 139, 140, 144, 148, 154, 159, 165, 169, 171, 173, 174, 183, 185, 187, 188, 189, 192, 193, 201, 224, 226

Hellenism 2, 38, 47, 48, 49, 51, 153
Hermeneutics 3, 12, 65
Hierarchy 36, 122, 130
Holiness 41, 45, 75, 159, 165, 170, 171, 172, 173, 180, 206, 213
Hope(s) 1, 4, 29, 40, 43, 44, 45, 52, 56, 57, 66, 74, 87, 90, 96, 103, 105, 137, 164, 165, 166, 167, 168, 170, 173, 174, 175, 186, 196, 199, 210, 211, 223, 226, 232
House-church(es) 8, 16, 28, 34, 88, 96, 97, 98, 142, 211
Household (of faith) 16, 29, 31, 34, 36, 47, 48, 54, 62, 78, 81, 84, 91, 98, 99, 113, 142, 143, 165, 167, 169, 188, 191, 198, 205, 206, 209, 210, 211, 214, 220, 224
Household codes 200, 202, 206, 212, 213, 221

Image(s) 1, 3, 4, 52, 75, 82, 91, 137, 138, 139, 140, 141, 143, 144, 148, 149, 154, 155, 156, 157, 160, 165, 166, 167, 168, 169, 199, 200, 202, 203, 204, 207, 208, 215, 219, 220, 224, 230, 232
Imitation 64, 119, 141, 171, 185, 195
Israel 1, 17, 21, 22, 25, 40, 41, 42, 44, 45, 46, 66, 69, 77, 90, 103, 132, 145, 146, 147, 149, 166, 167, 205

Jeremiah 18, 59, 149
Jerusalem 5, 14, 15, 17, 21, 26, 27, 30, 32, 33, 41, 43, 59, 60, 61, 62, 63, 71, 77, 79, 88, 132, 14, 147, 202
Jerusalem church 11, 20, 25, 32, 35, 36, 53, 54, 55, 80, 87, 92, 118, 120, 131, 133, 134, 141, 192
Jerusalem conference 30, 53, 60, 132
Jesus' message 2, 3, 66, 191, 195, 222
Jesus movement 15, 26
Jews 4, 14, 18, 21, 24, 25, 28, 45, 47, 53, 59, 64, 89, 90, 91, 106, 111, 114, 127, 132, 141, 147, 152, 157, 166, 192, 199, 202, 204, 206, 219, 228
Journeys (of Paul) 3, 5, 8, 11, 17, 23,

Indices 251

26, 27, 29, 30, 31, 32, 33, 34, 35, 39, 58, 61, 62, 69, 77, 123, 125, 126, 209, 228

Judaism 2, 3, 11, 14, 16, 17, 18, 21, 22, 24, 36, 37, 38, 39, 40, 41, 44, 45, 46, 47, 51, 52, 54, 57, 60, 63, 65, 67, 77, 78, 92, 132, 147, 148, 153, 195, 218, 228

Judgment 45, 56, 79, 86, 103, 109, 128, 129, 182

Junia 34, 125, 126

Justification 6, 18, 21, 22, 24, 45, 61, 64, 66, 78, 90, 146, 152, 180, 200, 203, 209, 223

Kerygma 22, 61, 82, 132, 180, 202, 212
Kingdom of God) 1, 11, 40, 45, 57, 67, 112, 148, 153, 188, 190, 198, 200

Law 5, 9, 15, 17, 18, 21, 24, 25, 29, 42, 45, 53, 59, 61, 63, 67, 77, 78, 90, 91, 108, 111, 132, 150, 151, 152, 154

Leader(s) 5, 16, 17, 25, 26, 33, 34, 36, 52, 54, 63, 72, 79, 87, 92, 99, 100, 117, 120, 121, 122, 123, 131, 132, 134, 135, 142, 154, 159, 209, 211, 212, 215, 216, 217, 220, 221, 223, 228, 231

Leadership 16, 34, 35, 47, 55, 71, 72, 76, 81, 93, 114, 116, 118, 120, 123, 125, 126, 128, 131, 142, 159, 160, 181, 191, 192, 211, 216, 217, 220, 221, 223, 230, 231, 232

Lifestyle 15, 43, 49, 54, 57, 68, 71, 72, 75, 86, 95, 99, 101, 128, 130, 142, 154, 181, 192, 212

Lord's Supper 55, 84, 113, 115, 116, 117, 156

Love 16, 32, 57, 72, 74, 75, 78, 84, 85, 86, 90, 91, 92, 95, 100, 103, 105, 107, 108, 111, 113, 115, 116, 120, 122, 127, 143, 144, 148, 151, 153, 154, 169, 173, 174, 175, 176, 177, 178, 180, 182, 183, 184, 185, 186, 188, 189, 200, 203, 205, 206, 213, 214, 230

Love-patriarchalism 16
Luke 5, 18, 27, 59, 61, 62
Lydia 31

Messiah 19, 40, 44, 57, 66, 104, 109

Ministry 5, 9, 18, 19, 21, 22, 23, 30, 35, 38, 40, 47, 55, 61, 62, 68, 70, 71, 72, 75, 76, 79, 83, 84, 85, 86, 88, 92, 93, 95, 99, 100, 111, 115, 116, 117, 120, 122, 123, 124, 126, 132, 134, 135, 136, 137, 154, 158, 159, 160, 168, 174, 175, 176, 179, 187, 188, 189, 190, 191, 192, 193, 197, 206, 208, 210-217, 220, 221, 223, 224, 226, 227, 228, 230, 231, 232

Mission 1, 2, 3, 4, 13, 14, 16, 17, 18, 20, 21, 22, 23, 25, 26, 27, 29, 30, 31, 32, 33, 34, 35, 36, 37, 40, 41, 42, 44, 45, 46, 53, 59, 60, 62, 63, 67, 68, 71, 79, 96, 107, 111, 112, 115, 121, 122, 123, 124, 125, 126, 133, 134, 141, 142, 147, 156, 166, 170, 174, 179, 191, 192, 200, 223, 224, 225, 227, 228, 229, 232

Models (of church) 3, 4, 9, 35, 48, 54, 55, 75, 84, 93, 96, 102, 108, 117, 119, 133, 136, 137, 138, 139, 143, 144, 145, 146, 147, 148, 149, 152, 153, 154, 155, 156, 159, 160, 162, 164, 165, 166-171, 176, 185, 187, 190, 191, 198, 204, 210, 211, 215, 220, 221, 224, 228, 229, 230, 231, 232

Monotheism 49
Mystery Religions 50
Mystical Person 137, 145, 161, 162, 164, 165, 166, 167, 168, 169, 177, 205, 224, 229

Obstacles 12, 13, 76, 95, 98, 201, 207, 228
Opposition 26, 31, 33, 51, 54, 80, 86, 216, 220, 222
Orthodoxy 17, 117, 126, 127

Parousia 48, 56, 67, 74, 195, 196, 218
Partnership 47, 93, 96, 121, 191
Pastorals 4, 7, 34, 55, 197, 202, 207, 208, 209, 210, 211, 214, 216, 217, 218, 219, 221
Patriarchy 16, 206
People of God 21, 41, 45, 56, 68, 114, 137, 145, 146, 147, 148, 149, 155, 164, 165, 167, 190, 198, 224
Peter 8, 21, 27, 31, 32, 53, 55, 60, 79, 80, 110, 132, 135, 165

252 *Indices*

Pharisee(s) 5, 17, 19, 21, 24, 25, 36, 42, 43, 45, 59, 66, 77, 101, 180
Phoebe 34, 125, 126
Prophet(s) 158, 174, 191, 205, 206, 220, 223
Pluralism 3, 9, 39, 53, 55, 58, 64, 68, 219, 221, 226
Prayer 22, 46, 75, 90, 98, 116, 117, 171, 178, 179, 193, 214, 230
Presbyteroi 211, 212, 213, 220, 224
Priest (hood) 9, 42, 55, 68, 114, 144, 145, 168
Priscilla 33, 34, 88, 123, 124

Reconciliation 22, 57, 84, 85, 104, 152, 186, 199, 202, 204
Redemption 51, 104, 111, 150
Responsibility 4, 14. 20, 44, 45, 48, 65, 68, 72, 73, 76, 78, 80, 81, 86, 98, 100, 115, 117, 118, 121, 122, 123, 125, 128, 130, 131, 139, 145, 149, 150, 154, 155, 156, 157, 158, 159, 160, 165, 168, 171, 172, 178, 182, 183, 184, 188, 190, 191, 193, 196, 201, 212, 213, 217, 220, 221, 223, 228, 232
Resurrection 20, 37, 42, 43, 55, 66, 68, 74, 83, 86, 89, 104, 109, 110, 111, 112, 152, 183, 184, 185, 186, 187
Revelation 13, 19, 20, 22, 23, 24, 36, 42, 45, 61, 64, 77, 99, 108, 113, 170, 175, 176, 209
Risen Lord 5, 18, 19, 24, 61, 66, 110, 119, 149, 154, 168, 217, 219
Ritual(s) 41, 42, 43, 46, 50 51, 53, 56, 65, 68, 113, 114, 115, 116, 117, 144, 147, 157, 160
Roman Citizen (ship) 28, 34
Rome 14, 30, 32, 33, 42, 59

Sadducees 41, 42, 43
Salvation 13, 18, 21, 22, 25, 40, 44, 45, 57, 58, 59, 61, 63, 64, 89, 90, 91, 92, 94, 103, 111, 151, 152, 166, 177, 184, 203, 209, 210, 223
Salvation history 13, 24, 60, 132, 146
Septuagint 41, 44, 46
Service 15, 18, 22, 24, 37, 57, 62, 86, 91, 96, 101, 102, 104, 106, 107, 108, 111, 112, 113, 114, 115, 118, 119, 120, 121, 122, 123, 124, 128, 131, 140, 141, 143, 148, 154, 158, 159, 160, 166, 170, 171, 173, 174, 178, 181, 188, 189, 190, 191, 192, 193, 211, 223, 230
Shared Ministry 121
Sin 59, 65, 67, 110, 150, 151, 152, 154, 161, 185, 199, 203, 208, 210, 219
Social stratification 16, 48
Soteriology 65, 67
Spirit 2, 19, 26, 32, 44, 54, 56, 57, 59, 75, 78, 82, 84, 92, 100, 102, 104, 105, 106, 108, 110, 112, 113, 114, 115, 116, 117, 118, 123, 125-130, 134, 140, 146, 149, 150, 151, 152, 153, 156, 157, 158, 159, 161-168, 173, 175, 176, 178, 179, 181, 184, 185, 187, 189, 190, 191, 192, 193, 195, 201, 203, 205, 215, 224, 226, 228, 229, 230, 231, 232
Spirituality 4, 9, 94, 102, 164, 170, 171, 172, 173, 174-179, 182, 184-190, 192, 193, 229, 230, 232
Stoicism 50
Strategy 21, 27, 28, 35, 53, 71, 79
Structure(s) 2, 16, 36, 39, 54, 55, 68, 102, 117, 118, 135, 143, 154, 205, 207, 208, 221
Structures—church 208, 217
Structures—social 28, 47, 48, 210, 211
Structures—patriarchal 12, 47, 99, 130, 160
Suffering 49, 73, 88, 90, 93, 94, 109, 111, 185, 186, 187, 191, 202, 210, 215
Synagogue(s) 6, 16, 22, 28, 29, 33, 36, 40, 41, 42, 43, 55, 59, 62, 123, 134

Temple 22, 41, 42, 43, 140, 142, 165, 195, 202, 205
Tension(s) 11, 24, 53, 54, 55, 56, 72, 85, 100, 143, 145, 149, 155, 168, 174, 175, 185, 196, 206, 222
Thanksgiving 6, 7, 70, 75, 77, 108, 116, 148, 173, 179, 188, 196, 211, 214
Theology 1, 7, 9, 12, 14, 18, 22, 25, 30, 33, 35, 41, 42, 46, 57, 60, 65, 66, 79, 82, 86, 91, 103, 135, 183, 192, 203, 209, 210, 217, 222, 227, 228
The twelve 11, 59, 61, 62, 110
Torah 41, 42, 43, 46, 66
Tradition(s) 2, 3, 7, 12, 13, 15, 17, 18,

Indices 253

21, 22, 40-46, 52-55, 57, 60, 61, 63, 65, 67, 68, 71, 72, 73, 74, 76, 77, 78, 79, 81, 82, 83, 84, 86, 89, 93, 111, 113, 117, 132, 134, 144, 147, 152, 166, 167, 169, 195, 196, 197, 198, 199, 201, 202 203, 204, 209, 210, 212, 215, 218, 219, 220, 221, 222, 227, 228, 231, 232

Transformation 3, 22, 56, 63, 90, 97, 99, 103, 129, 130, 149, 150, 152, 153, 166, 168, 172, 185, 186

Truth 83, 112, 126, 128, 165, 195, 198, 203, 206, 207, 215, 216, 219, 220, 221, 224

Union 49, 72, 93, 103, 107, 110, 114, 116, 155, 156, 157, 162, 163, 164, 166, 171, 175, 176, 177, 184, 185, 186, 187, 199, 204, 206, 223

Unity 4, 29, 32, 36, 70, 72, 80, 86, 87, 90, 91, 92, 94, 95, 101, 106, 108, 111, 112, 115, 116, 125, 126, 131, 132, 133, 134, 135, 142, 144, 149, 152, 155, 156, 157, 158, 159, 160, 161, 162, 167, 168, 169, 172, 177, 178, 179, 186, 192, 203, 204, 206, 219, 228

Vision 4, 12, 23, 24, 25, 26, 35, 51, 52, 57, 58, 68, 70, 73, 74, 99, 100, 102, 112, 114, 115, 121, 129, 134, 135, 137, 155, 166, 167, 168, 169, 170, 171, 177, 178, 206, 211, 217, 222, 224, 228, 229, 231, 232

Vocation 18, 23, 112, 189

Weakness 64, 88, 102, 106, 109, 111, 150, 187, 191

Witness 1, 20, 36, 39, 54, 58, 99, 106, 152, 153, 193, 203, 215

Women 12, 16, 26, 31, 36, 48, 54, 61, 68, 84, 93, 94, 96, 111, 115, 116, 118, 121, 122, 125, 126, 135, 142, 143, 154, 168, 192, 204, 210, 212, 213, 214, 220, 222, 224, 230

Word 6, 8, 13, 22, 28, 42, 61, 64, 68, 75, 94, 126, 161, 175, 179, 191, 193, 215

Work(s) 5, 8, 13, 25, 27, 28, 31, 32, 33, 34, 37, 38, 45, 50, 59, 62, 68, 75, 76, 83, 86, 90, 94, 105, 106, 116, 120, 121-125, 133, 140, 143, 155, 173, 175, 177, 191, 192, 193, 196, 202, 206, 209, 232

World 1, 6, 9, 11, 12, 24, 26, 29, 34, 41, 43, 45, 49, 50, 53, 54, 56, 57, 58, 90, 104, 107, 114, 130, 145, 150-154, 156, 163, 168, 169, 172, 178, 193, 200, 201, 202, 205, 211, 213, 231

World—Hellenistic/Gentile 2, 5, 6, 13, 14, 17, 25, 28, 37, 39, 46, 47, 51, 52, 53, 55, 58, 69, 81, 138, 150, 165, 211, 218, 227, 229

World—Jewish 2, 5, 165, 211

Worship 14, 16, 29, 41, 42, 44, 55, 86, 89, 91, 102, 113, 114, 116, 117, 131, 141, 148, 168, 179, 190, 230

OLD TESTAMENT

Genesis
1:1-2   149
1:12   151
1:18   151
1:25   151
1:31   151
12:1   44
12:2   145
12:7   44
15:6   45

Exodus
6:2-8   44
6:6-7   145
14:13-
 20:18   44
19:5   145
19:6   145

Leviticus
26:12   145, 147

Deuteronomy
32:42   147

2 Samuel
Ch.7   44

2 Kings
18:30-35 44
19:34   44
20:6   44

Psalms
14:7   45
80:3-7   45

94:14   147
106:47   45

Isaiah
2:1-5   146
42:6   146
42:6-7   145
65:2   147

Hosea
1:9-10   146
1:10   147
2:23   147

Zechariah
2:11   146

NEW TESTAMENT

Matthew
26:26-29 83
28:16-20 20

Mark
14:22-25 83
14:36   66
16:14-18 20

Luke
22:15-20 83
24:36-43 20

Indices

John
6:5-10	83
20:19-23	20
21:15-19	20

Acts
6:1-6	14
8:1-3	17
9:1-2	17
9:1-19	18
9:4-5	19
9:13-14	17
9:26	59
9:26-30	27
11:26	14
11:27-30	27
13:1-14:28	26
13:46	28
15:1-4	27
15:30	26
16:10	61
16:14-16	31
17:17	28
18:6-7	28
18:12-17	27
18:17-18	33
18:18	124
18:18-20	34
18:23-21:17	27
19:22	33, 124
21:15-23:11	27
22:4-5	17
22:4-16	18
24:1-10	27
24:22-27	27
24:27	27
25:1	27
25:9-12	27
26:9-11	17
26:12-18	18
27:1-28:16	27

Romans
1:1	64, 89
1:2	64, 89
1:3	89
1:5	18, 89
1:7	88
1:8	107
1:9	179
1:10	88
1:13	33, 88
1:13-15	89
1:15	64, 89
1:16	64
1:16-17	89, 103, 147
1:17	103, 111
1:18-3:20	150
1:29-31	183
2:1-20	91
2:8	63
2:16	64
Ch. 3	91
3:1	24
3:1-2	91
3:1-3	90
3:1-8	91
3:2-3	24
3:20	151
3:21	152
3:21-26	89, 147
3:22	111
3:24	64, 103, 104
3:24-26	65, 89
3:25	109
3:26	108
3:29	111
Ch. 4	60, 132
4:3	45, 107
4:13	108
4:13-16	151
4:24-25	65
4:25	89
5:1	108
5:2	114
5:3-5	90
5:5	164, 182
5:6	65, 176
5:8	109
5:8-11	184
5:11	104
5:12	150
6:1-7:4	111
6:2	186
6:2-5	91
6:3	109
6:3-4	104
6:4	67
6:5	185
6:5-8	90
6:6	125
6:6-7	109
6:8	109, 185
6:11	185
6:12	125
6:12-13	156
6:14	150, 151
6:16	108
6:23	103
Ch. 7	151
7:4	152
7:7-8	91
7:7-23	91
7:12	24, 151
7:14-25	91
7:16	89
7:24-25	151
Ch. 8	90, 91
8:2-3	152
8:2-4	106
8:3	66, 104, 105
8:3-11	65
8:9	176
8:9-11	161
8:10	152
8:11	105, 140, 163
8:12-17	209
8:15	66, 104
8:15-17	91
8:16	116
8:17	105
8:18	111
8:22	150
8:26	106, 179
8:27	142
8:28	153, 175
8:29	177
8:29-30	103
8:32	109
8:32-34	65
8:34	89
8:35	105, 153
8:37	153
8:37-39	199
8:39	105, 153, 176
Ch. 9	91
Ch. 9-11	89, 91, 132

9:2-3	90	15:10-11	147	2:10	127
9:4-5	91	15:13	105, 164	2:10-14	106
9:6	63	15:15-16	89	2:12	106, 163
9:8	147	15:16	105, 114	2:13	106, 127
9:25	146	15:17	38	2:15-16	127
9:25-26	147	15:18	108	2:16	176
9:27	63	15:20	30, 35	3:1-3	85
9:31	63	15:22-24	88	3:1-20	88
9:31-33	91	15:23	33	3:2	143
10:2	150	15:24	33	3:5	119
10:4	108	15:25	32, 132, 142	3:5-11	139
10:9	89, 107	15:28	33	3:6	30
10:13	104	Ch. 16	88, 92	3:6-9	12
10:14	64	16:1-2	34, 88	3:9	119, 140
10:17	108	16:2	125, 142	3:10	26, 30, 87, 139
10:21	145, 147	16:3	34, 124		
11:1	63, 91	16:3-5	123	3:12-13	140
11:1-2	147	16:5	88	3:16	140
11:11	91	16:6	126	4:3	129
11:11-14	90	16:7	125	4:5	56, 87, 129
11:13	89	16:12	126	4:10	187
11:25	63, 89, 91	16:16	88	4:11-13	33
11:25-26	91	16:17	90	4:14	86
11:29	145	16:19	108	4:14-15	85, 143
11:33	103	16:22	7	4:14-21	86
12:1	90, 113, 156	16:23	33, 34, 133	4:15	82, 119
				4:15-16	64, 171
12:2	152	**1 Corinthians**		4:16	119
12:2-8	158	Ch. 1-4,	86, 108	4:17	81, 85, 87, 124
12:3	140	1:1	33, 126		
12:4	159	1:2	81, 141	Ch. 5	128
12:4-8	90	1:4	76	5:1-2	85
12:6-8	126, 140, 158	1:10	157	5:1-8	86
		1:11	124	5:3-4	86
12:9-10	90	1:12	84, 124	5:4	128
12:11	192	1:12-27	12	5:4-13	88
12:12	179	1:13	157	5:9	32, 81, 85
12:12-15	90	1:14-16	34	5:10-11	150, 183
12:13-18	157	1:16	81	5:11	128
13:1	130	1:16-17	82	5:12	84
13:1-11	90, 183	1:17	64, 82, 86	5:21	66
13:3	183	1:18	56, 109, 110	6:1	142
13:10	151	1:20-22	49	6:1-4	88, 128
13:13	150	1:21-23	64	6:4	133
14:8	175	1:23	109, 184	6:5	24
14:9	89	1:24	103	6:9-10	150, 183
14:13	92, 128	1:25	187	6:11	104, 114
14:15	182	1:26	84, 124	6:15	156
15:1	90	2:1-2	85, 109	6:17	106, 161
15:2	128	2:2	184	6:19	140
15:4-6	209	2:8	105, 199	Ch. 7	84

7:1	85	11:19	127	14:33	81
7:7	158	11:22	86	14:35b	83
7:8	83	11:23	83, 115	14:37	83
7:10	219	11:23-25	83	14:39	158
7:12	83	11:23-26	219	Ch. 15	67
7:17	84, 172	11:24	115	15:3-5	82, 83
7:20	172	11:26	50, 115	15:3-7	21
7:21	84	11:28	127	15:3-8	65
7:24	172	11:29	127	15:4-5	110
7:25	83	11:31-32	84	15:8	19, 119
7:26	57	11:33	86	15:8-9	20
7:29	57, 86	Ch. 12	84, 161	15:8-10	18
7:40	83	Ch. 12-14	86	15:9	27, 133
Ch. 8-10	182	12:1-		15:10	175
8:1	87, 88	14:40	84	15:12	83
8:1-13	84, 86	12:4	106	15:17	110
8:5	199	12:4-6	106	15:21	110
8:6	83	12:4-7	85	15:22	91, 110
8:9	84	12:4-11	102, 140	15:28	104
8:9-13	84	12:5	189	15:45	184, 185
8:12	87	12:6	161	15:45-49	12, 91
9:1	18, 30	12:7	106, 156, 159	15:49	177
9:1-23	84			15:56-57	99
9:8	119	12:8-10	126, 158	16:1-4	84, 87
9:14-18	83	12:12	24, 84, 87	16:5-9	82
9:16	64	12:13	81, 104, 106, 114, 115, 150, 161, 199	16:7	85
9:17	82			16:8-9	32
9:20	25, 28			16:10-11	123
9:21	25			16:12	123, 124
9:23	23, 71	12:14	158	16:13	108, 170
10:15	88, 127	12:14-21	157	16:14	153, 178
10:16	81, 156	12:19	158	16:15	143
10:16-17	115	12:25	84	16:15-18	124
10:17	157	12:26	84, 157	16:16	122, 125
10:20	49	12:27	81, 156	16:17-18	87, 124
10:23	88	12:28	81, 87, 133	16:19	34, 81
10:24	182	12:28-30	126, 158		
10:25	84	13:2	152, 182	**2 Corinthians**	
10:31	173	13:13	182	Ch 1-9	85
10:32	81, 133	Ch. 14	118	1:1	81
Ch. 11	84	14:1	84, 174	1:7	87
Ch. 11-14	115	14:3	87	1:8-11	33
11:1	64, 86, 171	14:5	86	1:11	116
11:2	83	14:12	81, 106	1:13-14	85
11:2-16	84	14:12-15	117	1:15-16	82
11:3-5	84	14:12-23	87	1:19	104
11:5	116	14:20	85, 174	1:24	108
11:16	83	14:23	81	2:1-2	32, 85
11:17	86	14:26	113, 117, 128	2:1-9	85
11:17-34	84			2:3	32
11:18-19	115	14:28	175	2:4	87

2:6-8	128	7:16	173	1:1-2:7	77
2:9	32	8:1	81	1:2	76, 77, 81
2:10	186	8:1-2	31	1:6	77
2:12	85	8:2	67	1:6-7	77, 127
2:12-13	82	8:6	124	1:7	64
2:13	31	8:8	174	1:6-10	79
2:14	176	8:9	104	1:8	12, 78
2:15	56	8:16-23	124	1:9	64
2:17	82, 83	8:18-19	81	1:10-2:10	77
3:3	105	8:19	82	1:11	77
3:5	175	8:19-23	87	1:11-12	12, 20, 64, 119
3:5-6	105	8:23	30	1:11-17	18
3:10	151	8:24	81	1:12	64, 77, 170
3:12	164	9:5	32	1:13	17, 27, 77, 133
3:17	106	9:8	103		
3:17-18	185	9:12	188	1:14	17, 65, 77
3:18	164, 177	9:13	189	1:15	12, 18
4:1-6	18	Ch 10-13	12, 85	1:15-16	102
4:3	64	10:8	87, 119, 140	1:16	19, 20, 64, 77, 79
4:4	49, 64	10:10	27, 59		
4:5	119, 176	10:10-12	119	1:17	20, 30, 59, 77, 132
4:7	85, 187	10:14	64, 83		
4:8	33, 164	10:16	64, 82	1:18	32
4:8-13	88	11:1-6	205	1:18-19	27
4:10-12	111	11:2	144	1:22	77, 141
4:14	67	11:5	20	2:1	27
4:16	67	11:6	85	2:1-10	32
5:1	140	11:7-8	82	2:2	20
5:5	106	11:12	83	2:3	80
5:7	108	11:13	127	2:6-9	79
5:10	186	11:23-28	86	2:7	68
5:11-15	186	11:24	28	2:7-9	21
5:14	65, 84, 176	11:28	81	2:8	53
5:16	18, 108	11:30	187	2:9	80, 132
5:17	67, 104	12:1	175	2:9-10	79
5:17-19	84	12:10	187	2:11	79
5:18	103	12:12	127	2:11-14	31
5:18-20	22	12:13	30	2:11-21	15, 77
5:19	176, 186, 219	12:14	32, 82	2:12	79
5:20	85	12:18	122	2:13	124
5:21	184	12:19	87	2:14	78, 80
6:1	103	12:20-21	150, 183	2:16	78
6:4-5	130	13:1	32	2:21	103
6:8-10	33	13:5	84, 87	Ch. 3	60, 146, 147, 148
6:16	147	13:9	116		
7:2	85	13:10	81, 87, 119, 140	Ch. 3-4	91
7:5	33, 82, 85			3:1-5	77, 79
7:8	32	13:11	173	3:1-4:11	12
7:8-9	85	**Galatians**		3:6	45
7:12	85	1:1	12	3:6-9	78

Indices 259

3:6-14	77	6:14-15	77, 80	5:11	207
3:11	78	6:15	25, 149	5:19	206
3:13	151	6:16	77, 146	5:21	206
3:16	78	6:17	77	5:22-6:9	198
3:16-4:18	79			5:23	197, 205
3:23-29	56	**Ephesians**		5:24	197
3:26	78, 105	1:1	202	5:25	197
3:26-28	79, 150, 210	1:1-21	206	5:25-27	205
3:27	78, 104	1:4	205	5:26	206
3:28	36, 78, 81,	1:7-8	203	5:27	197
	97, 115,	1:10	197	5:29	197, 206
	181, 199	1:13	203	5:32	197, 206
4:1-7	56	1:15	202	6:1-9	206
4:4	66, 104	1:20	203	6:10-18	207
4:6	66, 78, 104,	1:21	197	6:21	197
	105	1:21-24	197	6:21-22	197
4:8	76	1:22	197, 205		
4:8-9	127	1:22-23	204	**Philippians**	
4:12-20	77, 79	1:23	204	1:1	93, 121
4:13	77	2:2-3	207	1:1-2	93
4:13-14	31	2:6	203	1:1-3:1	93
4:14	78	2:11-17	206	1:3-8	94
4:19	143	2:12	203	1:4	116, 179
4:21-31	77	2:14-16	51	1:5	96
4:22-31	12	2:15	205	1:6	57, 173
4:28	44	2:16	203, 219	1:7-8	94
5:1	78, 81, 108,	2:18	205	1:9	127
	154, 170	2:19	205	1:10	127
5:1-6:10	79	2:19-22	206, 207	1:12	93, 94
5:2	76	2:20	206	1:12-26	33
5:2-3	77	2:20-21	205	1:15-17	64
5:3	78	2:22	205	1:15-18	93
5:6	77, 80, 108	3:2	197, 202	1:16	93
5:8	127	3:8-9	203	1:16-17	93
5:11	109	3:10	197	1:18	94
5:12	77	3:21	197	1:19	179
5:13	78, 106,	4:4-6	205	1:19-26	35, 93
	108, 153	4:5-6	219	1:20	156
5:13-15	78	4:11-12	206	1:21	164, 176
5:16	24, 80	4:13	207	1:27	95, 108,
5:19-21	150, 183	4:14	207, 219		170, 181
5:22-23	78	4:15	206	2:2	153
5:25	106, 163	4:16	197, 204,	2:5	94, 104
5:26	80		206	2:6	177
6:1-5	79	4:22	205	2:6-7	104
6:2	151	4:22-24	197	2:6-11	51, 93
6:4	127	4:24	206	2:8	185
6:6	78, 79	4:26	206	2:10	199
6:9	173	4:32	206	2:11	104, 179
6:10	78, 79	5:1	206	2:12	94
6:12	76	5:7	206	2:13	94

260 *Indices*

2:16	94, 95	1:9	199	**1 Thessalonians**	
2:16-17	209	1:13	200	1:1	73, 81
2:17	114	1:14	199, 203	1:1-3	74
2:19-24	96	1:15	197	1:1-11	75
2:20	96	1:15-16	199	1:2	116
2:22	124	1:15-17	199	1:2-3:13	74
2:23	122	1:15-20	51, 199	1:3	7, 103
2:25	95	1:16-20	197	1:4	103
2:26-27	124	1:17-19	199	1:5	64, 74
2:29	122	1:18	197, 199	1:6	75
Ch. 3	94	1:19-20	199	1:6-7	171
3:2	31, 93, 95	1:20	199, 219	1:7	73, 174
3:2-4:3	93	1:21	201	1:8	107
3:4-11	18	1:23	198	2:1-4	74
3:5-6	17	1:24	197, 199, 202	2:2	31, 33, 64, 93
3:6	27, 131	1:25	197, 200	2:4	127
3:7	151	1:26-27	197	2:5-8	74
3:8-11	109	1:27	199	2:7	62
3:9	108	1:29	201	2:8	64, 73, 74
3:12	209	2:1	198	2:9	75
3:13-14	229	2:2	197	2:9-10	74
3:14	103, 209	2:3	199	2:11-12	74
3:15-16	94	2:6	198	2:12	73
3:16-17	94	2:6-7	219	2:14	73, 75, 132, 141
3:17	171	2:8	201		
3:18-19	95	2:10	199	2:17	32, 76, 122
3:19	56	2:12	198	2:17-18	73
3:20	210	2:15	197, 199, 201	2:19-20	76
4:1	94, 95, 170			3:1-7	32
4:2	94	2:19	197, 201	3:2	73, 75, 124
4:2-3	31, 93, 123	2:20	201	3:5-10	76
4:2-9	93	3:1	200	3:6	73, 75
4:4-9	93	3:3	200	3:7	107
4:5	94	3:5-11	200	3:8	170
4:6	116, 179	3:9-10	197	3:10	73, 179
4:8	184	3:10-11	199	3:12-13	173
4:9	93	3:12	200	3:13	67, 74
4:10	94	3:14	200	4:1	76, 172
4:10-16	31	3:16	201	4:1-2	74
4:10-20	93, 95	3:18-4:1	198, 200	4:3	105
4:12	50	4:3	197	4:8	105, 106
4:13	163, 176	4:5	201	4:9	75, 153
4:12-13	94	4:7	201	4:9-11	50
4:15	93, 96	4:7-8	197	4:10	73
4:19	103	4:8	197	4:11-12	75
4:21-23	93	4:12	198	4:13-17	74
		4:15	200, 201	4:13-18	185
Colossians		4:16	198, 201	4:14	74
1:2	198			4:15-17	74, 110
1:5-6	199			4:15-18	74
1:7-8	198, 201				

4:17	67	2:8-15	212	2:11	215
4:18	75	2:11	213	2:19	215
5:2	74	2:12-14	213	2:20	215
5:3	56	2:15	213	2:23	216
5:4-10	115	3:1	212	3:1-9	215
5:5	56	3:1-7	212	3:2-5	210
5:9	180	3:5	213	3:6	210
5:11	76	3:8-13	212	3:10-4:8	214
5:12	120	3:9	213	3:16	215
5:12-13	75, 76, 122, 159	3:10	213	3:16-17	209
		3:15	214, 217	4:1-2	215
5:14	75, 128	3:16	217	4:2-6	215
5:15	74	4:1	212	4:6-7	215
5:16-18	75	4:3-4	210	4:6-8	209
5:18	173	4:6	212	4:12-16	215
5:19-21	75	4:9	212	4:17	215
5:21	127	4:11	212		
5:23-24	103	4:14	208, 213, 214	**Titus**	
5:27	75, 113			1:1	216
		4:16	210, 213	1:5	216
2 Thessalonians		5:3-16	212	1:5-6	216
1:1	195	5:11-13	213	1:7-9	217
1:4	195	5:17	213	1:7-11	216
1:5-7	196	5:17-22	212	1:8-9	216
1:10	67, 196	5:22	208, 210, 213	1:11	216
2:1	196			1:15	210
2:3	196	5:24	210	2:1	216
2:4	195	6:1-2	212	2:1-10	217
2:13-14	195	6:6-10	214	2:1-15	216
2:13-16	196	6:11	214	2:5	216
2:15	195	6:12	209	2:8	216
3:6	196	6:12-16	217	2:12	216
3:10	196	6:13	210	2:15	216
3:12	196	6:17	210	3:5	210
3:13	196	6:20	212, 214	3:8	216
3:14	196			3:13-14	217
3:15	196	**2 Timothy**			
		1:3-5	214	**Philemon**	
1 Timothy		1:6	208, 215	1	99
1:1	211	1:6-8	209	1-2	96
1:3-4	212	1:8	214	6	97, 98
1:5	212	1:9	210, 214	8	97
1:6	212	1:11	208, 214	9	97, 98
1:10	212, 214	1:14	215	10	97
1:11	212	1:15-18	215	11	98
1:14	212	1:16	214	13	97
1:15	212	2:2	215	14	98
1:16	212	2:3-6	215	15	97
1:18	212	2:9	214	16	97
2:1-12	214	2:10	215	18-19	98
2:7	208	2:10-11	210	20	97, 98

		Hebrews		**1 Peter**	
21	98	1:3	51	3:18-19	51
23-24	99				

Notes

Notes

Notes

Notes